ADVANCE PRAISE

"*Changing the Game* offers a fascinating collection of insights and global perspectives from experts in esports and gaming. This is a deeply important book about how one of the fastest-growing industries is shaping our future. A must-read."

—NOLAN BUSHNELL, Founder, Atari, Chuck E. Cheese

"Lucy has vividly articulated her thoughts and views on every aspect of the gaming phenomenon—its evolution from the gamer and game creation to the burgeoning empire of the global gaming cluster. Her rich personal experiences peppered with key gaming personalities bring the gamer lifestyle to her readers. A must-read for anyone curious about the rising gaming and esports sector and those who wish to explore the rich opportunities that this sector offers in game development and design, game tech, esports, and entrepreneurship, among others."

—ALEXANDAR WILLIAMS, Director of Future Economy, Dubai Economy & Tourism

"Gamers and non-gamers should all read Lucy Chow's *Changing the Game*. Lucy includes insightful opinions and anecdotes from over thirty key players and leaders in the gaming industry. With an open-minded approach, Lucy offers a satisfactorily informative discourse on gaming."

—*Readers' Favorite*

CHANGING THE GAME

DISCOVER HOW ESPORTS AND GAMING ARE REDEFINING BUSINESS, CAREERS, EDUCATION, AND THE FUTURE

INDUSTRY INSIGHTS AND PERSPECTIVES FROM 38 GLOBAL EXPERTS

EDITED BY LUCY CHOW

RIVER GROVE
BOOKS

Published by River Grove Books
Austin, TX
www.rivergrovebooks.com

Distributed by River Grove Books

Design and composition by Greenleaf Book Group and Kimberly Lance
Cover design by Greenleaf Book Group and Kimberly Lance
Cover image: ©Alamy Stock Photo/Roman Kosolapov
Author photography by Amreen Hami of Pixels Production Studio

Publisher's Cataloging-in-Publication data is available.

Print ISBN: 978-1-63299-499-8

eBook ISBN: 978-1-63299-500-1

First Edition

To Ray Everett and Max Chow Everett.
Together my North Star.

*"There are times when
a critic truly risks something,
and that is in the discovery
and defense of the new.
The world is often unkind to
new talent, new creations.
The new needs friends."*

—ANTON EGO, *RATATOUILLE*

Contents

PART 3 • WOMEN IN GAMING

PART 4 • REAL WORLD BENEFITS

PART 5 • THE BUSINESS OF ESPORTS

Foreword

Gaming was an integral part of my childhood, and I can still remember eagerly waiting for the latest Atari game to come out. Missile Command. Space Invaders. Baseball. Football. Frogger. Pac-Man. Pong. Centipede. I could go on. But my all-time favorite game was Adventure. I spent hours trying to get through the different color castles, fighting dragons and looking for all kinds of cool objects. When Intellivision hit the market, I wasn't impressed. My Atari was all I needed!

When it came to computers, I got a TRS-80 when these first came out and I was in 6th grade. (Kids, ask your parents. Heck, Millennials, ask your parents.) I didn't know anything about computers, but man did that TRS-80 look cool. I imagined that it was just like the computers that NASA had and astronauts used. The model I had didn't have any external memory. This was way before hard drives were an option, and it didn't even have a floppy disk. My computer had 4kb of internal memory (less than your average email size these days), though I eventually got a cassette drive. That's right, you actually hooked up a cassette tape player to the computer in order to load programs. Because there wasn't really any memory, the only thing the computer did after I turned it on was have a cursor that blinked, awaiting my commands in DOS (again kids, ask your parents).

So I taught myself how to write code in the computer language BASIC. One of my favorite things to do was to make a square out of a few pixels, and then make the square move and change colors. Of course, I couldn't see the colors on the black-and-white monitor, but I eventually figured out how to connect the computer to my color TV.

What a thrill—a colored, moving square. In all seriousness, getting that TRS-80 was a significant event in my young life, because it was an exercise in self-motivation. I had to teach myself how to program and then make the time and effort to write those very simple programs. That desire to learn new skills has served me throughout my life and was a big reason that I was eventually able to become an astronaut.

A few years later, the TRS-80 was out of date, and I got an Apple II computer, ostensibly to help with my schoolwork. There were pluses and minuses to this new computer. The downside was that I had to learn a new operating system (thank you, Steve Jobs). But the plus was that it had a floppy disk! (Kids, I know, the list of questions is getting long.) The best part of my first Apple product was Castle Wolfenstein, a World War II video game. It was cool, addictive, and scary all at once. That computer made it through high school and all the way to the Air Force Academy. My class, 1989, prided itself on being the last class without computers, because beginning with the class of 1990, every cadet was issued a desktop computer. This made my computer popular with my classmates, who wrote plenty of late-night English papers on that machine over the years. I probably could have made some pretty good money renting it out had I been more of an entrepreneur.

As I began my career in the Air Force as a pilot, I got a Turbo-Grafx game system and fell in love with two games—Military Madness and Bonk's Adventure. Sadly, my free time to play video games quickly ground to a halt as my pilot career got busier and busier, I became a father, and then I ended up at NASA as an astronaut. I learned the lesson that we all eventually learn—that there are only 24 hours in the day, and I had to prioritize things, like sleep.

Life as an astronaut is like life in many other modern, tech-heavy industries. We use simulation and training software constantly. One of the most important pieces of software I used as a new astronaut candidate (ASCAN—yes, it sounds like it's spelled) was something called Shutdown Plan. This was a fairly simple piece of software that I could use on my home computer at night after the kids went to sleep. With it, I practiced the intense and complicated procedures that I had to run as a shuttle pilot to keep our rocket engines running, and, as you might guess, shut them down safely once we were in orbit. There were many other programs we used, some were good, some were less good, but all were critical in the formation of young astronauts.

There were, of course, many other software programs that were developed throughout the years at NASA, but two stand out. First was DOUG—Dynamic Onboard Ubiquitous Graphics—not surprisingly developed by a guy named Doug, who was adept at expanding NASA's tortuous acronym vocabulary. It is basically a game engine that shows you the external view of the International Space Station (ISS). You can fly around—up/down/left/right—and rotate in all three axes. You can also add equipment and astronauts to the view, which made this software perfect for planning and training for spacewalks or moving the robotic arm. I used it hundreds of times to prepare for spacewalk training sessions in the NBL (the acronym that stands for giant pool) in Houston, and I even used it while in space to prep for three actual spacewalks. There is a VR Lab in building 9 at the Johnson Space Center, where Doug worked, and they have VR goggles that can put you in the DOUG environment virtually, allowing us to practice spacewalks and even fly around using our spacesuit's jetpack in a VR environment.

The second piece of software that stands out from my time at NASA was RPOP—Rendezvous and Proximity Operations. It was a pretty straightforward piece of software on a laptop onboard the shuttle or in the simulator that gave us guidance and position during rendezvous with the space station, Hubble Space Telescope, or other objects in orbit. The orbiter had a radar that would track the ISS as well as a laser tracking system (TCS, which stands for the laser that helps with rendezvous), and position and closure information from these sensors was fed into the RPOP software. There was also a handheld laser that we could point at the target and then manually enter in data to the program, as a backup to the automated radar or TCS. RPOP would then show us where we were relative to the ISS, where we were going, and what commands we had to give the shuttle to fly the proper trajectory. It was pretty slick and a huge help to us pilots. I wish I'd had something like that when I was flying F-16s!

Today, with the proliferation of computing power everywhere, the importance of software can't be overstated. The 21st century will be more and more automated, and people who understand how to use computing devices to their advantage will be the people who impact the future. I always tell kids if they want a career that pays well and will always be in demand, a) learn how to code, and b) learn how to learn, because whatever you learn today will be obsolete in a few years.

Which is why the timing of this book could not be more perfect. The world is going through a period of accelerating change, and those who are able to change and adapt will be successful, and those who resist this coming change and cling to the past will be left behind. This was true in the beginning of the Industrial Age, in the beginning of the Space Age, and it will continue to be true as we enter an Automated Age. And gaming/esports will be a key part of this new world.

One final note. Gaming is a great way to learn these new skills and learn for the future . . . as long as it's done in moderation. There's nothing better than actually interacting with real humans and looking at them in the eye as you talk to them. As long as you maintain that perspective, gaming can be a great way to have fun and stay ahead of the tech curve. Though, there will never be another Atari Adventure . . .

COLONEL TERRY VIRTS
International space station commander,
space shuttle pilot, test/fighter pilot,
and author of *How to Astronaut*

Preface

How often do you come across a subject or an industry and think, *I need to write a book on this?* If you are like most people, probably never. For me, gaming is one of those industries. It is growing exponentially around the world—and not just the number of players. Gaming and esports have become a multibillion-dollar industry, with investment opportunities, emerging career paths, and innovation popping up around every corner.

I have selected thirty-eight individuals to share their knowledge, expertise, and excitement about this industry with you in the pages ahead. These contributing authors have been generous with their time, each offering some unique knowledge or insight into the evolution and future of esports. They embrace new ideas to disrupt their field and are what I would refer to as game changers. These contributors are writing about an industry that is changing many paths, including the future of work, the skills taught in schools, and even investment opportunities. You will find their bios at the end of each chapter, where you can see the extent of their involvement in this growing industry.

In February 2020, I was invited to an educational conference that was part of the GIRLGAMER Esports Festival. This was not my first esports conference, but each time I attend an esports conference, I wish more people could hear from the speakers and discover how relevant this industry is to career paths for students and even to them. I want everyone to know how games allow deeper connections with our world and create greater cultural understanding. To many of us (and I include myself prior to investigating this sector), gaming is our kids sitting in front of a computer. But what you will soon learn is that is only the tip of the iceberg.

While reading an article titled "After the Virus," published by trend-watching.com,[1] I was not surprised that out of the ten emerging consumer trends that have been accelerated by the COVID-19 pandemic, quite a few are tied to esports and gaming. Whether you are an entrepreneur, corporate executive, parent, or investor, you need to be aware of what people will value and where their priorities will be in the future.

Furthermore, if you have, or plan to have, kids, the gaming arena is one way to ensure they are equipped to capitalize on opportunities in the future. Esports is changing our world in four ways: virtual experience economy, shopstreaming, virtual status symbols, and connecting mentor to mentee.

Virtual experience economy

Whether it's concerts, museum tours, or travel, there will be increasing opportunities for people to get their "experience" fix virtually. This is especially true in the new normal after the COVID-19 pandemic.

Shopstreaming

Shopstreaming is the merging of online shopping and social connections. Livestreaming, particularly in China, is growing rapidly. It's appealing, because it combines shopping with entertainment. This trend is set to go big on a global scale.

Virtual status symbols

Games already allow consumer-players to purchase virtual goods. With trends such as sustainable consumption making a bigger impact on our psyche, virtual goods can replace physical goods as status symbols. And these symbols will not be limited to certain industries and demographics.

Connecting mentor to mentee

There is already a plethora of self-improvement content online. But going forward, there will be new platforms that connect mentors, experts, and teachers with individuals wanting to learn new skills.

To paraphrase Sydney J. Harris, the words *information* and *communication* are often treated as interchangeable, but they are quite distinct. "Information is giving out; communication is getting through."² This book, for example, is filled with information, but I also wanted to have subject matter experts contribute to this book to facilitate true communication to ensure you had the richest experience possible with the content.

A multifaceted industry

Much like other professional sports, esports involves titles, elite players, and large amounts of prize money. It is broadcast, often online, and has a dedicated fan base that numbers in the millions. It has become an explosive multibillion-dollar industry and is finally creeping into the mainstream consciousness. Competitive video gaming has already been announced as a medal event at the 2022 Asian Games, which will take place in Hangzhou, China. Underscoring that esports is indeed an athletic endeavor, the 2024 Summer Olympics, taking place in Paris, will include demonstration esports events.

Being a gamer is just one career path, if we look at the industry as a whole. The ecosystem is actually multifaceted and full of opportunities.

Esports and education

I was fascinated to discover that there is a university in Japan that offers a degree in gaming. In a country where education is still very traditional, this shows once again how mainstream gaming has already become. Esports is being adopted in schools because, at the end of the day, if kids are engaged, they are motivated to learn. Gaming and esports are becoming embedded in school curricula, because critical development traits can be taught using gaming. There is no shortage of examples of schools moving ahead with innovation in this area. Empowering students to create school gaming leagues gives them the opportunity to compete, on par with other varsity sports, and to deepen their engagement and harness their passion toward future career paths.

Women in gaming

I spend much of my time advocating for women and girls, and gaming is full of new opportunities for them. More important, #bossladies are thriving in this industry!

"There are a lot of studies showing that if girls start to take an interest in video games from an early age, they are 30 percent more likely to follow science studies—meaning engineering, mathematics—which are professions that still have more men than women," stated Fernando Pereira, President of Grow uP eSports. Several female gamers have agreed to share their career journeys with us, along with the type of competitions that exist for them today. And there is still so much potential for growth. Video games are a major technological achievement, and classes in and opportunities for STEM-related activities are one way we can ensure more girls enter those fields.

Game world benefits IRL

Numerous benefits of esports can be applied in real life (IRL). The FDA approved the first prescription video game for kids with ADHD mid-2020. To take the stigma away from gaming, it was important that I have experts speak to both the mental and the physical agility required to be a professional gamer. Our psychologist contributors will discuss the positives gained by video games and will showcase the benefits from a scholastic perspective as well as how gaming can help you develop positive life skills. Gaming offers social and cognitive benefits, and ambient games help build and reinforce mindfulness. There is a whole category of developers focused on games for social good—games that raise awareness of poverty, homelessness, or sustainability.

The business of esports

The act of playing a video game and competing in a video game also leads to a passion for creating video games. Simply put, esports is a cultural evolution that has created new industries. Countries are looking at ways to put esports on their national agenda. Sponsors are offering products and services that are not directly related to gaming but that can profit from the enormous platform that esports has already built. Esports is no longer a niche community. Traditional businesses and brands are pivoting to capture the market potential to reach an audience that is rapidly growing each year. Well-known musicians Ariana Grande, Diplo, and Marshmello chose to debut and perform songs in Fortnite to show the innovation, power, and reach of these virtual platforms.

Careers in Esports

With how quickly esports is growing, it's logical that it's becoming an industry that will have many positions opening up for work behind the scenes. In fact, it's a rapidly growing job market, and there is a place for people with myriad backgrounds and specializations. There is even a bar association specifically made up of lawyers practicing in the field of esports! So, now you can still become a lawyer *and* focus on your passion. Artists, musicians, and designers are all collaborating with game developers. The entrepreneurial opportunities in this ecosystem are vast.

The future of esports

The opportunities in this field are global. I alluded earlier to the fact that countries are focused on ways not only to grow their esports infrastructure but also to encourage investment in competitive gaming. Schools are developing curricula that may eventually encourage more entrepreneurs in this space. In short, esports is a gateway to new career paths and unlimited new business opportunities.

I am neither a gamer nor am I deeply embedded in the gaming business. I am an investor, a parent, an entrepreneur, and a school board trustee. I care about the future of work and ensuring our kids are equipped to contribute to a rapidly changing world. My curation and perspective is not from someone inside the industry but as a friend to the new. I have been open to discovering what I can about this industry, and I want to provide the same opportunity to others with this book. I wish to point out that some of the data is no longer accurate, as most chapters were written in 2021. However, this underscores just how rapidly this industry is evolving.

I hope you enjoy taking a deeper look into this sector, that you are as amazed as I am at the diversity of accomplished individuals who are in it, and that you walk away with actionable insights.

LUCY CHOW
Dubai 2022

PART 1

Why Esports Now?

CHAPTER 1

From Stigma to Global Industry

Most of what you'll see here is for gamers, parents, and families of all backgrounds. However, this first paragraph is especially important for the Black and Hispanic community in the United States. According to brookings.edu, in 2017 the median household income for Black families reached $41,511.[1] Unfortunately, the median income for Black Americans is projected to fall to $0 by 2053 (and for Latino Americans by 2070), according to a study from Prosperity Now and the Institute for Policy Studies.[2] This projected crash in median income is a result of negative net wealth, due to a combination of discriminatory housing policies (i.e., redlining), policing/incarceration (which is statistically proven to be racially biased), racial pay gaps, and student loan debt. If you know someone from those two communities, I implore you to share this book with them. It's important they learn how to leverage the video game industry, to help their families avoid the impending financial crisis for urban communities of color.

It's August 2020, and in addition to supporting this book, I'm working on my own esports book and building a lab to combine science, technology, engineering, arts, and math (STEAM) education with esports (like a modern version of the YMCA). I'm also planning a two-day STEAM/

gaming/esports event for next year's Super Bowl, advising several startups in the gaming and esports industry, and launching an online platform for social esports. During the day, I make a six-figure salary as a full-stack web developer for a multinational steel company. All of that is a direct result of my passion for technology, which is fueled by my interest in video games. When I was six, I got Super Mario Bros. 3 for the Nintendo Entertainment System (NES) for Christmas. Fast-forward ten years to the ninth grade, and I started to teach myself how to code, because I had learned you could put video games on the TI-83 Plus graphing calculator.

Another decade later, I had completed my bachelor's degree in information technology and started my own company, all thanks to video games. I know from firsthand experience that the gaming and esports industry can open doors into lucrative STEAM careers. While video games do get a bad reputation (some of it justified), they also add tremendous value to society. I'm excited to share many of the great opportunities in gaming and esports with you as well as how you can make a career out of your passion for gaming. Although, before I dive into that, I want to address the negative perceptions and realities of video games.

The downside to gaming

On March 25 of 2020, the World Health Organization (WHO) officially encouraged people to play video games amid the COVID-19 pandemic. WHO cited active video games, among other activities, as "good for your body, mind, and spirit, especially during the COVID-19 outbreak."[3] Many people in the gaming industry, myself included, publicly criticized WHO's newfound endorsement of video games. Why? Because in May 2019, less than twelve months prior to the announcement, WHO officially classified gaming disorder as an international disease. The terms *disorder* and *disease* are a bit extreme to describe excessive gaming, in my opinion. However, there are several concerns, both for the people who play video games and for the professionals who create them.

It's well documented that, in general, a sedentary lifestyle can contribute to a number of health risks: obesity, type 2 diabetes, some types of cancer, cardiovascular disease, and even early death. Beyond the general sedentary risks, playing an excessive amount of video games can contribute to a range of issues from bad posture to injuries like PlayStation Thumb and Wii Fracture.

While there is a general consensus about how and whether gaming affects the body physically, there is less support for the mental impacts of excessive gaming, even among the medical community. It's no surprise that the Entertainment Software Association (ESA) would object to the WHO's classification of gaming as an addiction or disorder, but even the American Psychiatric Association cautioned the WHO about formally considering excessive gaming as a psychiatric disorder without completing more clinical research. I don't discount that people can become addicted to gaming (too much water and food can be bad for you too), but I do think more attention should be focused on the mental and physical health of the people who produce the games that we enjoy.

As a whole, the gaming industry does a poor job of conveying all of the time, effort, and talent that goes into making these interactive experiences. There is an unsettling consistency in evidence for "crunch culture," in which some companies of AAA games like Tales of the Borderlands and Red Dead Redemption require their teams to work one-hundred-plus-hour weeks.[4] Due to the additional stress, one community manager for a AAA game even reported developing an ulcer and coughing up blood, prompting his doctor to recommend that this gaming professional quit his job.

The gaming industry's no stranger to inequality and mental health problems. In May 2019, one game developer for Mortal Kombat 11 was reportedly diagnosed with PTSD after spending countless hours implementing the game's gore system.[5] This is a real problem that affects real people, so we need to focus on real solutions for them. It's one of the reasons that ignorant prejudice about the gaming industry disturbs me:

It perpetuates divisive stereotypes, which distracts our community from addressing real issues.

I'm blessed that my parents fully support my career in video games, and I'm thrilled they understand (sort of, ha ha) what my business does. But I can remember a time when, instead of actively supporting my interest in video games, they only tolerated it. It's even fair to say that, at times, they were annoyed by it. I can vividly remember them saying, "Turn off that dang Nintendo!" both when I was playing Super Mario Bros. 3 on the NES as an eight-year-old and again when I was playing Halo on the Xbox at age eighteen. And I'll never forget the time that, in the ninth grade of magnet school, my trigonometry teacher permanently deleted the first app I had ever created: a Zelda clone that my twin brother and I were building on our TI-83 Plus graphing calculator. She did that because we had figured out how to turn our calculators into makeshift gaming consoles, and she wasn't willing or able to nurture our newfound interest in software development.

In hindsight, I can now appreciate the context for my parents' former position on video games and my teacher's actions. Frankly, my brother and I were generally being disruptive in class, especially by showing all the other kids how to turn their calculators into gaming devices (and installing PC games on the hidden network drive so we could play them from any computer at school). More importantly, society as a whole had a stigma on video games for decades, unable to bridge the gap between gaming/esports and lucrative STEAM career opportunities. It's no surprise, given all the propaganda and misinformation about the gaming industry, that parents and teachers would view it as a nuisance or bad habit.

Debunking myths

For decades, politicians have been regularly blaming video games for violence in society. However, federal crime statistics show that juvenile crime in the U.S. is at a thirty-year low, and the majority of people who play video games (a social activity) do not commit antisocial acts. MIT researcher Henry Jenkins ironically indicates that, as a healthy outlet for expressing aggression, playing violent video games actually just leads to an increase in playing more violent video games.[6] Video games are also often wrongly criticized for being socially isolating, when they encourage healthy social behaviors like communication and teamwork. In fact, recent studies have shown that virtual reality (VR) gaming can identify and treat conditions like Alzheimer's and dementia.[7] Video games are more than a vital part of our culture; they also provide lucrative STEAM career opportunities for current and future professionals.

Projected growth

Esports and competitive gaming will grow to a $1.1 billion market in 2021. Global viewership for esports in 2021 is also expected to reach 474 million people.[8] Esports demand is even beginning to give traditional sports a run for its money. The 2018 League of Legends World Championship had higher viewership than the 2018 Super Bowl. In fact, by the end of 2021, esports viewership in the U.S. is projected to exceed that for all other sports leagues except the NFL.[9] And that was all before social distancing. In the wake of the COVID-19 pandemic, which practically brought the entire traditional sports industry to a standstill, esports has thrived. There's now more attention on esports than ever before, and as cliché as it sounds, there's never been a better time to start a career in this space.

Back in February of 2020, before the COVID-19 pandemic increased the global demand for video games, esports and social researcher Nico Besombes published extensive research about esports professions. If you look up his research on *Medium*, you'll see that he's identified eighty-eight different career opportunities for aspiring esports professionals.[10] Those span a wide range of functional areas: entertainment, education, administration, business, sales and marketing, communication, information and technology, event organization, media, and performance optimization. Nico's research echoes the "Esports Jobs in 2019" infographic that Hitmarker published in January 2020. Hitmarker's visual report showed that from 2018 to 2019 esports jobs increased 87.03 percent, and 88 percent of those 2019 jobs were paid.[11] This clearly means there are many viable paths to becoming a professional in esports.

Speaking of amazing growth opportunities in esports, I highly recommend keeping a close eye on blockchain and cryptocurrency. I've been a part of that ecosystem for nearly a decade (www.blockleaders. io/marcus-howard), and for years, I've said that the gaming industry is how blockchain/crypto adoption will go mainstream. Blockchain is a great tool to increase transparency and eliminate fraud, while crypto empowers individuals and brands to build thriving communities. With the growing demand for betting in esports, blockchain will be important to help prevent cheating and ensure that minors are prohibited. Digital assets like crypto and NFTs could also give game publishers, teams, and other organizations a new way to add meaningful value to their communities. That said, unfortunately, I've already seen several esports celebrities/teams abuse NFTs to make a quick buck by peddling meaningless digital crap to their loyal fans. It will be interesting to see which groups use this new opportunity responsibly and which ones betray their community's trust in pursuit of short-term gains.

There's been a tremendous focus on esports the last couple of years, especially in light of the shutdown of in-person entertainment like traditional sports. However, if you're just learning about the business of video games, you might not know that the esports market is just a drop in the bucket for the gaming industry. In 2020, the global video game industry reached over $174 billion.[12] That's more than the size of the music and film industries combined. Much as with esports, you can find career opportunities for nearly every business and creative function within interactive entertainment.

Career options

Game Industry Career Guide states there are six distinct functional categories you can choose from if you want to build a career in making video games.[13] The first is game design—game designer, level designer, content designer—where you analyze current games and players so you can design future gameplay experiences. The second is quality assurance (QA)—QA tester, black box tester—where you are responsible for testing current builds of a game to report bugs in the user interface or gameplay experience. Next is the game programming—game programmer, coder, engineer, developer. These people write the code that makes the entire game work. Remember, video games are apps, just like Netflix, Uber, and Instagram. Game programmers are the most technical jobs in the gaming industry but also the most highly paid.

If you're more creatively inclined, you can work in art or animation (animator, modeler, concept artist, UI artist, technical artist), although these are the most difficult jobs to land in the industry. There are also career opportunities in audio engineering (sound designer, composer, audio implementer), but those are also in relatively short supply compared with game programmers. And last but certainly not least is producing (producer, associate producer, production assistant). This role is similar to a project manager or a scrum master, the person who keeps the team organized and aligned on completing the development milestones. While those are the main categories, there are also more traditional categories with jobs in marketing, community management, and operations. As you can see, between the esports market and the larger gaming industry, there are numerous ways you can make a career out of your passion for video games.

MEET MARCUS "ESPORTS" HOWARD

Marcus Howard is CEO of the esports education startup MetArena, and the president of Tampa Association of Gaming, a nonprofit dedicated to growing the gaming industry and STEAM youth programs in the Tampa Bay region. Marcus got Super Mario Bros. 3 on the NES for Christmas when he was six, and he's been playing video games ever since. Video games inspired Marcus's interest in technology, and in the ninth grade, he started coding his own video game on the TI-83 Plus graphing calculator. In 2013, he launched ProjectMQ with his identical twin brother, Malcolm, to solve the largest problem in the global video game industry: game discovery. Five years later, PayPal selected ProjectMQ out of twenty thousand-plus applicants nationwide, as the top digital service of their 2018 business contest.

Today, Marcus consults with universities and businesses around the world, helping them use video games to increase their digital engagement and monetization. In 2019, he co-authored *The Business of Esports* that was published by the University of South Florida. Marcus was a featured speaker on the "Tampa Bay and the Esports Industry" panel at the University of South Florida's 2019 Esports Summit, and on the "Level Two & Beyond: The Future of Esports" panel of Skillshot Media's 2019 Esports Summit at the Georgia World Congress Center.

In 2020, Marcus was 1 of 50 people selected by the Game Awards for the inaugural cohort of "Future Class," a global group of pioneers building a more inclusive future of the video game industry. He's currently building a "Gaming and Esports" digital course, to help gamers understand why the multibillion-dollar gaming industry is how blockchain/crypto adoption will go mainstream. Marcus is also publishing his own book, *Innovate: Gaming & Esports*, that highlights the top thought leaders and innovative companies in the global gaming/esports industry. In his spare time, he scouts indie games (games made by independent game developers) for funding/distribution deals with the world's largest gaming companies.

Marcus is excited about how video games inspire the next generation of innovators to pursue STEAM careers. He is always eager to chat about video games. You can find him on LinkedIn under Marcus "Esports" Howard:

linkedin.com/in/marcus-esports-howard-60785023

CHAPTER 2

Are Gamers Athletes?

Most people outside of esports have a hard time considering professional gamers to be athletes competing in a sport. Even some people who are involved in esports would hesitate to use the terms *athlete* and *sport*. This topic was easier to debate ten years ago, when competitive gaming was still largely underground. But as gaming becomes more popular in mainstream culture and as esports continues to gain more viewers, the argument that esports is a sport has become easier to accept.

Professional gaming is a sport. There's growing research to support its legitimacy,[1] and the U.S. government has already been treating professional gamers as athletes who compete in sports for several years.[2]

I get it. Even if you are a competitive gamer, you may still have some reservations about comparing esports to traditional sports, especially if you've also been competitive in other sports. There are plenty of examples for how esports is very different from traditional sports. However, I'd like to show you some of the similarities so you can see why they are categorized as such.

Are they really like any other athlete?

The U.S. government recognizes gamers as athletes, treating international players who are competing in the U.S. like any other athlete. For example, international players must apply for athlete visas when competing in U.S. esports tournaments.[3]

Don't worry, there's more to this than just getting a visa. Professor Ingo Fröböse has been studying esports at the German Sports University Cologne for over five years now.[4] In fact, Professor Fröböse was one of the first scientists to study individuals who compete in esports. Instead of simply balking at pro gaming and reinforcing the idea that esports is the furthest thing from a "real" sport, Professor Fröböse studied the demands placed on players who compete in esports.

Professor Fröböse found that esports athletes can achieve up to four hundred movements on the keyboard and mouse per minute and that various areas of the brain are being used simultaneously during gameplay. Esports athletes are exposed to physical strains similar to those in other sports, and the necessary hand-eye coordination goes far beyond table tennis, because the player's hands must work asymmetrically. The amount of cortisol produced during an esports session is about the same level as that of a race-car driver. Esports athletes, during a gaming session, have a pulse as high as 160–180 beats per minute, which is akin to fast running. Because of this, esports is just as demanding as many traditional sports.

Aren't athletes supposed to be fit?

Esports athletes are exposed to physical strains similar to those of a traditional athlete. If gamers are enduring high amounts of physical and mental stress while competing, their bodies need to be able to endure it. I wouldn't consider it safe to ask an average citizen to attempt to run a marathon, but Professor Fröböse found that gamers were taking part in similarly high-intensity activities.

So, yes, athletes are supposed to be fit, because fitness provides many advantages for performance during competition. Esports athletes and competitive gamers have a lot to gain if they explore avenues for boosting performance outside of just playing their chosen game, such as being in peak physical condition. As Professor Fröböse pointed out, proper strength and conditioning, along with better nutrition, can not only boost performance but also extend an esports athlete's career.

This is the area I focused on and advocated for with Cyber Athletiks. When it comes to sport-specific training, esports is several decades behind more traditional sports.

Are esports really sports?

Many critics cite a lack of physical exertion as evidence that esports or gaming is not a sport. But in addition to Professor Fröböse's work demonstrating the physical exertion elicited during esports, a 1994 study also showed that basal blood pressure was raised while playing a video game.[5] It's fair to say that playing esports won't condition your body to be able to run a marathon, but the reverse is true as well: Running a marathon won't prepare you for competitive gaming. Esports requires a type of physical exertion specific to esports.

Sports are also often defined by a high level of skill. This objection is easily dismissed by anyone within the gaming and esports community. Esports and gaming require extremely high levels of skill. This is why it's so exciting to watch. Just like other sports, we get to see players who are able to play the game at a skill level most of us could never achieve.

The coverage of esports in mainstream media is often frustrating. After a young gamer has won millions from an esports competition, the interviewer on some morning news show scoffs at the accomplishment and suggests he (the interviewer, who has no training or experience) should start competing in gaming to get in on the money. Right, because it's easy to be the best in the world.

Sports are also characterized by competition between individuals or teams, and esports obviously involves both. Whether it's one-on-one with Street Fighter or five versus five in Counter-Strike: Global Offensive (CS:GO), esports is all about competition.

Finally, sports are entertaining, and they require spectators. I grew up in a house where my family didn't watch or follow sports. I was into gaming and other more niche sports at the time, like skateboarding, and eschewed participation in traditional team-based sports in my youth. I still don't get much out of watching traditional sports, but I understand the appeal. Esports has just as many fans as—and, in the COVID-19 pandemic, potentially more than—traditional sports. It has stadiums and draws huge crowds and is streamed to millions of viewers through services like Twitch. I find esports very entertaining, and with the addition of esports stadiums and casters, it just keeps getting better and more exciting to watch.

Should children be encouraged to be pro gamers?

In my day job as a clinical social worker practicing psychotherapy, I often encounter parents worried about their child's gaming habits or dreams and aspirations of becoming a pro gamer. Perhaps one of the strangest generational gaps is the one between kids who want to grow up to be a pro gamer and their parents, who previously had no clue that esports even existed. When parents come to me worried that their child wants to become a professional gamer, I reply the same way I would if the child expressed a dream of playing any other sport: "Great! Take this opportunity to teach them what being a professional actually means and help them to develop some skills they can use later in life—whether or not they end up successfully pursuing this career path."

Put simply: There is no need to panic. Would you panic if your kid wanted to be an Olympic athlete or a pro hockey player? Probably not. You'd foster that motivation and help them develop some of the necessary skills, all the while knowing that it probably won't ever materialize.

Just like any sport, the elite esports level is reserved for the naturally gifted and the extremely hardworking. That does not mean you should give your kid a hard dose of reality. Having passions and dreams fosters motivation. Esports requires an immense amount of learning, especially in game titles like League of Legends, where the most critical skill is, arguably, learning.

Trying to be a professional at anything is difficult, and trying to be a professional gamer is no different. Assuming your child is already showing potential to be in the top ranks, there are lots of skills they need to start developing and perfecting to be a pro, such as constant learning, discipline in practice, networking, being a team player, communication, organization, performance under pressure, anger management, leadership, independence, and improved physical and mental health. The great thing is, if they're taking things seriously, all of this can be done mostly on their own. And it will be a lot easier and more pleasant if they aren't fighting with their parents every step of the way. If you look at that list again, you will see these skills can be applied to almost any future career. So, even if they change their mind later on, they will have worked on transferrable skills they can use in almost any job.

My esports experience

When I was fifteen, I was obsessed with an esport called Counter-Strike. Esports was still very underground at that time. I became interested in the more competitive scene of Counter-Strike and committed to pursuing the goal of becoming more competitive.

So, I got a part-time dishwashing job, saved up, and bought a computer that allowed me to reach max performance. As I put a team together with some local and online friends, I paid to have a website developed for our team. Then, I started sending monthly handwritten checks (I'm probably older than you think I am) to a company in Toronto so our team could have its own server. From there, we organized team practices and entered amateur leagues.

I'm not sure my mom had any clue what I was doing. What strikes me when I go back to these memories is the entrepreneurial mindset

I and other gamers of my generation had back then and continue to exhibit now. There was no coach guiding me every step of the way. I didn't have my practice schedule all laid out. There was no team already set up that I had to try out for. All of it was created from scratch by me and a few other teenagers. Even more striking, none of it felt like work, because it was something I was passionate about.

Top ten benefits of esports

I often discussed the benefits of esports on the Cyber Athletiks site and have put together a list of what I consider to be the ten biggest benefits of esports:

1. Can improve health
2. Improves hand-eye coordination
3. Teaches critical thinking
4. Teaches problem-solving
5. Increases memory capacity
6. Provides opportunities for scholarships
7. Cultivates team building
8. Creates funding opportunities for schools
9. Creates pathways for industry jobs
10. Cultivates transferrable job skills

Esports in the Olympics?

Esports is becoming more and more legitimate in the mainstream. Texas recently built a $10 million esports stadium, and the 2018 League of Legends World Finals had nearly one hundred million viewers. Even adults who don't game often opt for Twitch instead of cable TV for their entertainment.

With all the recent growth in esports, both gamers and curious nongamers can't help but ask whether esports will ever be in the Olympics. Esports probably won't be an Olympic medal sport anytime soon, but it should be, especially given the number of arguably less "athletic" sports like shooting or archery that are currently included in the Olympic Games.

Esports will, however, soon be in the Olympics as a demonstration sport. Demonstration sports have been around for a long time in the Olympics. Essentially, they are sports held at the same time as the Olympic Games in which competitors are not eligible for medals. Demonstration sports began as a way to showcase a sport or activity that was unique to the host country. Later, they became more of an application or a stepping stone for sports to be considered worthy of inclusion in the Olympics, as was done with badminton, for example, which was a demonstration sport during the 1972 and 1988 Olympic Games. By 1992, badminton had become an official Olympic medal sport. Esports being considered as a demonstration sport for the Olympics could mean that it is being carefully analyzed as a potential Olympic medal sport.

Esports is esports

Although I often make the argument for esports to be considered a sport and for competitive gamers to be considered athletes, I do so to advocate for the legitimacy of it all. Rather than get lost in debate and arguments, I will often just state that "esports is esports and gamers are gamers." It's its own thing, and we should keep it that way.

MEET STUART CAMERON, MSW, RSW

Stuart Cameron is a clinical social worker in private practice providing one-on-one psychotherapy in St. Catharines, Ontario, Canada. He competed in esports in the early 2000s, continues to game, and has loved watching the scene and industry grow to where it's at today. He founded the Cyber Athletiks gaming and esports website, cyberathletiks.com, and its companion YouTube channel, where he advocated for better physical and mental health in gamers and shared his sports performance philosophy specific to esports. He has loved being a part of esports and watching it grow to where it's at today. You can find him on LinkedIn:

linkedin.com/in/stuart-cameron-msw-rsw-22a488132/

CHAPTER 3

The Power of Play

Video games are interactive entertainment. Global gaming software revenue is $150 billion per annum and rising. Unlike linear entertainment, players control the action and decide the outcome of their adventures. They are given agency, which is compelling. Once the misunderstood hobby of teenage boys locked away in their bedrooms, video games are now played by men and women, young and old, on multiple devices and platforms. There are just shy of three billion players worldwide. Games have become mainstream and are socially, culturally, and economically important. And they're good for you too.

Curiously, throughout history, the media has struggled to find good things to say about games, describing them as a trivial distraction or worse. In 1859, *Scientific American* reported, "Chess is a mere amusement of a very inferior character, which robs the mind of valuable time that might be devoted to nobler acquirements."[1] In the 1980s, mainstream media was mostly negative about *The Warlock of Firetop Mountain*, the first in the hugely popular Fighting Fantasy gamebook series authored by Steve Jackson and myself. They were not considered "proper" books because of the descriptive word *gamebook*.

Fighting Fantasy gamebooks are books in which the reader is the hero "playing" through a branching narrative with an added game system. Like video games, they are an interactive experience, not the passive experience of most books. Their readers, children mostly, are empowered through choice. More than twenty million copies of Fighting Fantasy gamebooks have been sold in over thirty languages. Fighting Fantasy got a whole generation of children reading in the 1980s. The books were proven to be great for reluctant readers, and improved literacy, problem-solving, critical thinking, and creativity.

So why the criticism? Thirty years later, 18-rated BAFTA-winning video game Grand Theft Auto V generated $1 billion in revenue in less than a week. But rather than celebrating this and Rockstar North's, the game's Scottish developers, technical and creative achievement as a great British success story, sections of the media went into overdrive, blaming all of society's ills on the game.

Unfortunately, good news about games is seldom reported, and so the perception of the games industry remains poor. The consequence of negative reporting is that most parents and teachers are not aware of the positive attributes of playing games nor of the career opportunities the industry offers. And the investment community usually overlooks the funding opportunities. Of course, an economic argument does not make games a good thing. But there is strong evidence to suggest that game skills enhance life skills and that playing games is actually good for you.

Human beings are playful by nature. We enter the world as babies, interacting with everything around us. We learn intuitively through play and trial and error, both integral skills to playing video games. Games also require problem-solving to succeed. Humans love solving puzzles, which is central to games like Tetris, Candy Crush Saga, and Words with Friends. We love to build and share, and this is the very essence of Minecraft, which can be described as digital LEGO. Whether it's playing activity games like Wii Sports (burning calories at the same time), simulation games like Sim City, or strategy games like Civilization, the experience is likely to be both enjoyable and beneficial. Online multiplayer games have brought a new dimension to video games. Fortnite has become a community platform, a third space where players hang out together and play. The Metaverse is here!

Game-based learning

Think about the cognitive process of what is happening when people play games. It's a case of hands on, minds on. Interactivity puts the player in control of the action. In other words, they learn by doing.

Playing games is fun and entertaining, but the gameplay experience also combines a broad mix of problem-solving, decision-making, intuitive learning, trial and error, logistics, analysis, management, communication, risk-taking, planning, resource management, and computational thinking. Games stimulate the imagination and encourage creativity, curiosity, social skills, concentration, teamwork, community, multitasking, and hand-eye coordination.

Games also give the player continuous assessment and allow failure in a safe environment. Simulation games, for example, are used as a training tool for pilots, surgeons, the armed forces, and other professionals. Game-based learning is a proven success in schools for subjects such as math. Who wouldn't want their children to learn skills while being entertained at the same time?

There are some very successful people who cite games as making a positive contribution to their learning. British technology entrepreneur Demis Hassabis said after selling his artificial intelligence company DeepMind to Google for some $400 million, "I've always viewed my obsession with playing games as training the mind in multiple facets."[2] Mark Zuckerberg's interest in playing games led him to learn to code, which, in turn, resulted in the creation of his multibillion-dollar company, Facebook (now renamed Meta). And there are many more.

Game ratings

Yes, some games do contain violent content. But that is no reason to set public opinion against the entire games industry. Many films contain violent content, but the film industry is not criticized in the same way. And like film, games have age ratings. Some games are 18-rated, for example.

Films and games have ratings for a reason; however, the media tends to focus its reporting on games that are 18-rated, often ignoring their intended audience of adults. Not surprisingly, parents are worried about their children being exposed to these games. Age ratings should not be ignored. Children should not be allowed to play games they are not meant to play. But to put things into perspective, over 90 percent of games are family friendly.

From consumption to creativity

Some parents are understandably worried about the amount of time their children spend playing games. Today's children do spend a lot of time on their screens, whether it's games, the web, social networks, music, messaging, or TV.

Digitally native children are more likely to choose a screen over traditional toys when indoors. But put them outside, and they are more likely to choose a ball over a screen. Responsible parenting requires monitoring of all media, including games, to ensure children have a balanced life indoors and outdoors.

So, let's not think our children will turn into zombies when they are playing games. Chances are, they are learning some useful life skills. We should focus on turning their love of playing games into them learning how to make them. Move them from consumption to creativity. Move them from the passenger seat to the driver's seat of technology. As software engineers, they might even go on to become the next global tech giant. The video games industry is one of few success stories during the

COVID-19 pandemic. Revenues are up, and it's business as usual for developers working remotely from home using cloud-based development platforms. Digital consumption and digital creativity make the industry future-proof. Without a doubt, the video games industry ticks all the right boxes for the post-pandemic digital economy—creative, knowledge-based, high tech, high skills, high salaries, digital, export focused, IP-creating, and regional. Games are going to eat the world. You can put your money on it!

MEET IAN LIVINGSTONE

Ian Livingstone is one of the founding fathers of the U.K. games industry and founding partner of Hiro Capital. He also cofounded iconic games company Games Workshop in 1975 with Steve Jackson, launching Dungeons & Dragons in Europe and later Warhammer, White Dwarf, Citadel Miniatures, and the Games Workshop retail chain.

He co-authored *The Warlock of Firetop Mountain* in 1982, the first interactive gamebook in the Fighting Fantasy series, which has sold twenty million copies worldwide. He has written fifteen books, including international bestseller *Deathtrap Dungeon*. Part book, part game, the Fighting Fantasy gamebooks were the first books to have a branching narrative with a games system attached.

Livingstone moved into video games in the 1990s and helped launch the character Lara Croft that is featured in Tomb Raider, Hitman, Deus Ex, and many other blockbuster titles. He later served as chairman of Playdemic, developers of the mega-hit mobile game Golf Clash, and was an investor in Mediatonic, developers of the global hit video game Fall Guys.

He is currently chairman of Sumo Group plc, developers of Sackboy: A Big Adventure. Most importantly, Livingstone is a huge games player and collector. He considers himself very lucky to have enjoyed a forty-five-year career in the games industry and says he will never retire, as technology and social behavior constantly evolves the industry, bringing with it new experiences and opportunities. Games, he says, have become the third space, the Metaverse, where people come to meet, play, and hang out together. You can find him on Twitter at Ian Livingstone CBE:

@ian_livingstone

CHAPTER 4

The Workplace of the Future

When I tell people I'm an esports immigration lawyer, I get reactions that range from "What in the world is esports?" to "How does immigration law have anything to do with esports?" Mostly, people just want to know how I ended up in such a niche profession, one that excites and challenges me on a daily basis.

Why esports?

To start, esports is the professional, competitive play of video games. Video games in and of themselves are fun and exciting—who wouldn't want to work in this industry!

Esports has come a long way from its humble beginnings. Twenty years ago, esports tournaments were held in living rooms, garages, and basements. Ten years ago, esports made it onto network television in South Korea, and competitions evolved into organized grassroots events. Today, esports is a global phenomenon with major fan bases throughout Europe, China, Brazil, South Korea, and North America. Esports competitions sell out iconic venues like Madison Square Garden and the Mercedes-Benz Arena in Berlin, representing a multibillion-dollar industry that encompasses digital media, merchandising, and, of course, sports entertainment.

How esports found me

The reason I love the esports community the most is its international nature. As a Korean American, I grew up with an innate sense that borders were meant to be crossed. I traveled between Korea and America throughout my childhood, and that combined with living in the vibrantly diverse community of Los Angeles contributed to my love for discovering new countries and cultures.

My undergraduate studies at UCLA focused on international relations, Asian American society, and Japanese language and culture. After college, I had the opportunity to live and work in Japan through the Japan Exchange and Teaching Program, an international exchange initiative administered by Japan's Ministry of Foreign Affairs. I was on my way toward pursuing a career as a U.S. diplomat, which I believed would satisfy my desire to explore the world.

However, that's not at all where life would take me. My father, who up until that moment in life had never asked anything of me, made a very earnest request: "Please go to law school." He undeniably knew me better than I knew myself. As much as I yearned for the glamour and adventure of living abroad and moving from country to country, I'd never been the type to unreservedly follow directions or accept authority without challenge—I was a natural-born leader, and I liked to learn things the hard way, my way. In his seasoned wisdom, my father recognized that my headstrong character was incompatible with the life of a government bureaucrat. And so, I headed to law school with the notion that if I didn't enjoy law, I would still be young enough to switch gears and pursue a career in international diplomacy if I still wanted to.

Back in 2010 when I started law school, the United States was still reeling from an economic crisis now known as the Great Recession. With unprecedented rates of unemployment, even for skilled professionals like lawyers, the anxiety of coming out of graduate school with student loans and no job to pay them was real. I began to survey law students and young lawyers ahead of me to get advice on how to guarantee myself employment after graduation.

The results were unanimous—get work experience and get it now. Show potential employers that you already know how to do the job and contribute from day one. I took that advice to heart, contacted the school, and requested that my status be changed from full-time to part-time student. I then applied to a dozen or more legal internships and said *yes* to the first one that would have me—an immigration law firm.

Within weeks, I had unequivocally fallen in love with the job. I continued to work full time at immigration law firms and finished law school by taking night classes.

Immigration law gave me the opportunity to explore new cultures and languages, meet people from all over the world, and not only learn their stories but also play a critical part in their journey to the United States. My work focused on facilitating the migration of talented doctors, scientists, engineers, chefs, artists, and other highly skilled professionals. As the startup world started to boom in Silicon Valley and Silicon Beach in Southern California, the need for legal counsel that was responsive to the unique needs of the fast-paced startup world grew. Because existing law firms were not meeting that demand, I decided to start my own law firm and do things my way.

Others thought I was destined for failure. At the time, I had been a licensed attorney for less than three years, had just had a baby, and had significant financial obligations, including a mortgage and student loans with no savings. Nevertheless, I was driven by the need to provide for my son, a deep-rooted desire to succeed, and confidence in my skill and ability despite my age.

As a young professional, I leveraged a quality that older, more experienced attorneys did not have—a native understanding of the internet, social media, and my generation's demand for wholesome experiences and desire for community. I wove digital nativity into the foundation of my law practice, and word soon got out that if you wanted a delightful, modern immigration experience—I was the one to work with. This led the esports community to find me, because the speed and communication style of traditional law firms was starting to affect the bottom lines of some of the top teams in the industry.

Esports is fast

The esports world is fast. Blink, and you might miss news of the latest player trade or a major streamer's departure from their organization. With the average age of esports players hovering around 21.2 years[1] and getting younger, thanks to popular titles like Fortnite and Clash Royale, many of my clients had never left home before entering the esports space, let alone read a contract or interacted with a lawyer. As a result, communicating critical information to an adult does not come naturally or easily to my clients.

Much of immigration law depends on the attorney's ability to quickly glean key information from documents and what is shared from a client, with most law firms and modern businesses relying on email or phone to do most of their business. Gen Z, however, has adopted texting and instant messaging as its primary mode of communication. Where most law firms require clients to communicate with attorneys on the firm's terms, we engage with our clients on *their* Slack channels and Discord servers. With most of the traditional gatekeepers to attorney access eliminated, our clients enjoy open and direct lines of communication with us—whether through text, WhatsApp, or Twitter, our clients can expect that we not only use the same tools but also speak the same language.

Esports has its own language

"Wish my coach would smurf in soloQ."

"If you don't look, you won't know if they're inting or popping off."

"No flame for garbage KDA. I main tank in OW and never played CSGO."

Have no idea what that means? Not to worry—most people outside the esports community wouldn't know that these individuals were commenting on the performance of specific players. Learning the language of esports requires a passion and love for the games; esports takes video games beyond a hobby or phase and ingrains video games into your very lifestyle by influencing the clothes you wear, the beverages you drink, and the content you consume.

While I grew up playing video games like Sonic the Hedgehog, Super Mario Brothers, and The Sims, gaming fell to the wayside for me as my interests turned to music, boys, and fashion. Well, guess what? Today, esports *is* music, boys, and fashion. Companies like Riot and Epic are taking gaming to new heights through cutting-edge music collaborations and in-game concerts.

Esports players are the new teen heartthrobs, admired for their inhuman reflexes and godlike skill in the game. Brands like Ateyo are not only setting fashion trends in the esports space; they are innovating best-in-class technical apparel specifically for pro gamers. Every day, the esports industry is iterating and developing more color and depth. Because esports as a business is still in its nascency, young professionals working in esports today have the privilege and opportunity to make history by shaping an entire industry from the ground up.

However, I didn't always feel this way about video games and esports.

Esports is not just for kids

My husband works in the video game industry and has always been an avid gamer. Early on in our relationship, I felt that his obsession with video games was a poor use of his time, time that could have been better spent with me! I resented his attention to video games for nearly a decade, before I finally realized that video games were more than a silly pastime for him, as they were for me. For my husband, gaming was a gratifying way to relieve stress. It was an effortless way to stay connected to his friends who lived on another continent. Playing with them was a creative outlet and important source of community, and, of course, his livelihood. I hadn't given video games the respect they deserved, because I had been too close-minded about my own experience.

Now, as a wife, mother, lawyer, and business owner, demand for my time and attention from all kinds of angles abound. Video games and esports have become a way for me to stay balanced. With a high-stakes job and a family to grow, it is easy for me to put all of my "adult" responsibilities first, leaving little to no time for recreation, joy, creativity, or laughter. Now that esports is part of my day job, there is fun and excitement built into every email, research project, invoice, and speaking engagement.

While I'm in my thirties and pretty young by most definitions, most in the esports community would consider me a "boomer" or senior citizen. Working in the esports community allows me to stay connected with Gen Z and beyond, giving me a lifeline into the latest technologies and trends. Working with youth also provides daily inspiration from their creativity, tenacity, and hunger for a better world. Boomers and young people alike have so much to gain from the esports space. Whether you have been a lifelong gamer and are eager to work in the esports space, or even if you have never picked up a controller before—esports is a community and lifestyle I highly recommend. GLHF.

MEET GENIE DOI

Genie Doi is a legal unicorn, a rare breed of immigration lawyer whose practice is laser-focused on the esports industry. Genie has earned the unicorn moniker due to her highly specialized practice at the intersection of immigration law and esports. She is one of a very few practicing lawyers bringing her legal chops to the table to help international gamers compete legally and continue to make a living by competing internationally. You can follow her on Twitter and LinkedIn by visiting:

twitter.com/PureGenieUS
linkedin.com/in/genie-doi-7973b361

PART 2

Esports
and
Education

CHAPTER 5

A Game Changer in the Field of Education

While it started as a popular digital platform for interaction and entertainment, esports has now gone beyond that. Today, esports offers huge, organized live event competitions with a massive supplier industry around the live competitions and online tournament platforms. Esports has created various jobs in the industry, from professional players to coaches, event managers, and financial analysts. Some of these roles are assumed by professionals who have expertise in these areas but who are not specialized in esports. This industry is increasingly receiving recognition, as sport entertainment and competitive gaming have rapidly become institutionalized with the establishment of national and international governing bodies. Esports even features many of the trappings of traditional sports, including professional players, teams, uniforms, coaches, managers, agents, leagues, competitions, events, player transfers, commentators, and college scholarships.[1]

Digital services, such as Netflix and Spotify, have changed the way we consume culture and entertainment. In a few years, esports has developed from a minor side hobby for young gamers in small groups to a global, multifaceted ecosystem of professional clubs, sports organizations, sponsors, businesses, fans, and people of all ages who enjoy gaming. But there are many challenges in the esports industry as instruction of the skills specific to the industry remains fragmented, speculative, and a largely untapped resource. The rapid growth in esports has led to a supply shortage of qualified talents to innovate within the industry, and the knowledge gaps present barriers to entry for new brands entering the esports space. Some say that over 50 percent of esports practitioners believe the industry lacks technical, operational, and management talent.[2] Professional esports education is a vehicle to sustain the future development of the esports industry.

New jobs

The total number of jobs in the esports industry grew by 87 percent year over year to reach 11,000 in 2019, according to a job industry report released by the U.K.-based recruitment platform Hitmarker, which is one of the global leaders in esports recruitment.[3] The growth was primarily driven in a proliferation of senior-level esports positions, which increased in 2019 by 194 percent to 3,443 available jobs. The majority (56 percent) of roles were generated in the U.S., followed by remote working positions in the U.S. (15 percent) and the U.K. (6 percent). At one point, the esports recruitment company predicted that esports job listings would increase by an additional 104 percent through 2020, with over 22,500 positions expected to be posted. According to Andrew Flowers, former economist at Indeed, job postings for esports-related roles rose 343 percent between December 2015 and December 2019, and we've seen numbers continue to increase.[4] Business development roles are projected to become the fastest-growing sector within esports, with Singapore set to displace either Canada or Germany as one of the five leading countries in esports recruitment.

Esports revenue is predicted to grow even more each year. Imagine how many more jobs will be created from esports. This in-demand industry and future employment boom makes implementing esports into education immensely important. Students who are interested in esports have a higher tendency to be academic achievers and interested in high-paying STEM fields valued by employers.[5] This sort of beneficial factor should help parents feel comfortable letting their children enroll in an esports academy or taking esports courses in school or outside of school.

Esports in schools

Despite this, it's essential to focus on esports education to equip children from an early age, if they wish to pursue their passion or career in esports. When schools and parents provide students with esports education, they are not only giving students the future opportunities to pursue a career but also sharpening the essential soft and hard skills that are transferable in any industry. The study of esports can give students the necessary academic and technical skills to succeed in future STEM and non-STEM learning opportunities and careers.

Can you imagine a traditional sports team in soccer or basketball without a coach? The same level of significance for coaching applies in esports as well. Esports education that is currently offered in schools worldwide includes classes in event operation, analysis, marketing, streamers, programming, and business development.

As this expands, educators and parents might have some dismissive views on having esports in their schools. The old paradigm has been to keep children from playing too many games. However, there is much to be gained from combining the world of esports with that of education. Esports can be used to assess students' interests and skills. It also makes education fun for children.

Most students like to play games. When we restrict game play, it will only cause tension between adults, educators, and kids. However, if we embrace (and care about) their interest in esports, we show support that will then result in greater engagement in school, and we show that we understand and support their interests. Giving students early exposure means gearing them for future opportunities. If we can evaluate and spark their interest, we can help them succeed in life. While we see many huge teams of esports out there, it's not necessary to have vast teams in schools. The fundamental part of having esports in school is building and growing the team regardless of how small or big it is. The curriculum should be coherent and focus on the bigger picture, student interest, and success. There are discussions on whether elementary students should play games or enroll in esports courses. Although it might be concerning to parents, elementary students can and should play age-appropriate games.

With a carefully designed program, parents shouldn't worry about their children playing esports at school. To address the skepticism, there is a need to educate parents that esports is not a threat, but rather an opportunity to learn and practice critical and analytical thinking. By playing games or becoming involved in team activities, students learn to work as part of a team and how to strive to reach goals with their teammates. Students can also learn about leadership and how to run or manage a team or esports events.

When starting an esports program, you will need to do some assessments to help students grow. For example, you may want to start with a more general esports introduction. Later, programs can be customized to suit students' needs and interests. Some schools or academies could provide training programs focusing on developing better playing and enhanced technical, strategical, and behavioral skills in esports through a series of hands-on curriculum and fun activities. Of course, the programs should be formalized and customized to the school's environment.

By adding esports to the school's curriculum, students will learn important soft skills such as critical thinking, decision-making, communication, and analysis. Video and computer games can help students learn in many ways by expanding memory capacity, addressing attention disorders, and helping students to be more tech savvy.

Esports in higher education

When we speak about education in esports, most market activity happens at the higher education level. This happens as part of formal vocational engagement through business and event management modules, but also as undergraduate courses with a concentration in esports. Esports is also present in student societies, nonprofit league events, and educational integrators. The varying degree with which these elements are emphasized also reveals the regional differences that explain the development of esports within the education segment.[6]

Western Europe and North America are the two most mature and developed esports education markets. As of 2020, they accounted for approximately 60 percent of the global base of dedicated esports computing hardware. Despite rapid projected growth from the Asia-Pacific region, these two markets will receive a COVID-19-related boost, as higher education seeks out new incentives for student engagement and courses that will attract and retain students.[7]

At the university level, there are schools worldwide that offer certificates, associate degrees, and bachelor's degrees in esports management. There are also quite a few universities that give out scholarships to students who excel in esports to help them pursue their passion. These scholarships strengthen esports' position in the education industry. In the U.S. there are four-year-degree programs in esports, and in the U.K. slightly different esports programs take three years.

A few additional reasons the U.S. and the U.K. have more universities for esports education and more leagues or agencies are their stable economies and internet connections. As we know, esports requires a reliable internet connection, and gaming equipment can be expensive, which is often cost prohibitive. On top of that, many game developers are located in the U.S. and the U.K., whereas in Asia, there are more developing countries that are still working to create a more stable internet connection.

Building communities

Due to today's technology, innovation, and consumer behavior, gaming trends vary in each country. In Southeast Asia, for example, mobile games are a huge hit, mostly because they are more affordable. Meanwhile, in Germany, gamers tend to stick to their PC games. Japan has had huge success in console games. That said, game developers and publishers must consider the country they want to enter or expand so they can focus on developing their games according to the market's preference.

Esports is not just about playing games. It is also about building communities that help people thrive. When you consider implementing esports into the school's or university's curriculum, you must acknowledge that the esports ecosystem is different in each country. Due to cultural differences and demographic factors, each country has its own way of adapting, developing, and managing esports implementation.

There also is a need for the government to get involved to promote esports into the school's or university's program and fast-track it. Private- and public-sector collaboration will most likely push esports to school and university programs faster. The esports management curriculum developed by ibMedia Group focuses on future and current job availabilities across the esports and gaming industry as well as opportunities outside of these industries.

Esports is an education game changer. With the rise of scholastic esports, educators now have a unique opportunity to validate their students' interests, support their social-emotional learning, and connect them with future workforce aspirations.

MEET FRANK SLIWKA

Having been within the games, esports, and digital entertainment industry since 1997 and recognized with the German Game Developer

Award, the European Games Award, and Asia's Sports Industry Award in 2017 and 2018, Frank Sliwka has a verifiable history of commitment to growth, expansion, and profit-and-loss optimization in the games, esports, and media competitive industries in mature and emerging markets across the Asia-Pacific region, the U.S., and Europe. Frank has over twenty-four years of corporate leadership and entrepreneurship in the media, gaming, and exhibition and conference industries. He is adept at achieving maximum operational output with minimal resource expenditure and consistently exceeds performance goals.

Through strategy and years of expertise in exhibitions and conferences (B2B, B2C), Frank established Game Developers Conference (GDC) Europe as one of the most important game industry conferences in the world, and Games Convention Asia (GCA) as one of the main industry events in Asia.

In 2000, he started to work in the esports sector and created the first world-leading business platform for esports, International Esports Conference (ESCONF), in 2004. At the end of 2004, Frank founded the German Esports Association (ESB) where he was then elected as chairman. In 2008, he was elected as vice president of the International Esports Federation (IESF).

Today, Frank is the chief operating officer of Epulze and the founder of Esports Holidays. Before that, he worked with companies like ESL, Electronic Arts, Gamescom, United Business Media (UBM), Crytek, and Malaysia Digital Economy Corporation (MDEC).

Being part of an international network of senior executive-level relationships through active participation on boards and industry associations, Frank enjoys his position as global game industry expert and someone who shapes industries. He is focused on developing overall corporate growth strategies and partnerships in the areas of media, publishing, sponsorship, and entertainment. Frank Sliwka can be found on LinkedIn:

linkedin.com/in/franksliwka/

CHAPTER 6

The Learn with League Initiative

Esports are often touted for their economic and cultural value, but far less has been made of the opportunity they present for advancing child and young adult educational and emotional development. Like traditional sports, esports can provide a powerful landscape for teaching critical development traits, such as perseverance, resiliency, and teamwork. The surrounding cultural momentum, player enthusiasm, and inherent collaboration make these games natural learning spaces while creating a meaningful path to holistic development for young gamers, including health, wellness, regulation, and better online behavior. Key to unlocking this opportunity, however, is the respect, guidance, and support of caregivers paired with dedicated programs that directly support a young person's learning journey.

The Learn with League initiative, a program by video game developer Riot Games, leverages the game and esport League of Legends toward a larger purpose: helping bring validation to young people's passion for esports and setting them up with the lifelong skills to thrive.

The power of video games

Understanding the role of esports in education relies on understanding how multiplayer games have captivated us globally. While improvements in technology and design have helped, at their heart video games are simply fun, challenging, and immersive experiences. They provide a sense of mastery and accomplishment while taking us on fantastic adventures. Multiplayer games are highly social, and the surrounding communities afford a deep sense of belonging, while playing online can further transcend cultural and physical barriers, uniting us through shared goals.

As with traditional sports, competitive gaming taps into our more primal needs, bringing us together not just to play but also to support our chosen teams. The spectacle of a full-scale esports competition can easily rival the experience and crowd of any major sporting tournament. The required technology has also become common in homes, schools, and community centers—not to mention the ability to enjoy many games now on our phones. For free-to-play games, there is no further cost to play with others, and watching their tournaments online is typically free.

The cultural gap

Esports has enjoyed a meteoric rise to its place as a cultural institution. Yet there remains a stubborn and lingering stigma of gamers as addicted loners, with many dismissing or underestimating the importance of games and esports in society.[1] [2] This cultural gap has led to a contradiction wherein we support and celebrate traditional sport in education but not so for esports.[3] Therefore, for young people passionate about esports, we fail to meet them where their hearts and minds are and miss the opportunity to recognize them and support their development. We also fail to appreciate the role online games can play in equipping a young person with the skills they need to flourish.

Perhaps most disturbing, sensing a lack of support or dismissal from parents or that support depends on the "right" activity, a child may start to question their own worth and may even suppress their personality to meet expectations out of a sense of shame. A 2015 internal Riot Games study conducted among 4,557 high school students in Australia and New Zealand revealed feelings of isolation and shame when talking about video games with their parents or teachers. While 95.2 percent said their friends recognized and celebrated their gaming achievements, only 6.3 percent felt similar recognition from their parents, and only 2.2 percent came from their teachers.

This gap causes feelings of disempowerment and disconnection, which affect a young person's natural expression, personality, health, and holistic development. Under these conditions, children may find it harder to attune to and regulate their thoughts and feelings. They may also develop an ongoing worry that they will not receive support from their caregivers, which can even cause them to avoid developmentally appropriate risks in other aspects of life.[4] In short, they fail to thrive.

All sporting experiences, including esports, can be enhanced with the support of others—be they parents, teachers, coaches, or peers. When we fail to provide this support, our children stop sharing their stories or celebrating their experiences with us. This lack of solidarity erodes an environment of trust and deprives the child of a safe space for learning. It also deprives them of vulnerable and safe conversation, which is needed for healthy psychosocial development. If we are going to close the cultural gap between esports and education, we must create a path for unconditional support and help parents and teachers meet students where they are.

With this in mind, in 2016, while working for Riot Games, we asked ourselves, *What if we not only chose to meet young people around their experiences in League of Legends but also took responsibility to empower caregivers in this journey?* We set out to tackle that question through an experimental learning initiative called Learn with League, using the free online game League of Legends.

What is League of Legends?

Released in 2009 by Riot Games, League of Legends (or LoL) is one of the most popular online games of all time. Played on a digital field, or battle arena, teams of five must defend their base and work together to advance across a map. The first team to conquer the opposing base wins. Players can choose from 150 different characters, each unique in their abilities, backstory, and visual presentation. The result is a unique experience every game.

Today, LoL has a thriving esports scene, with professional leagues around the world. Throughout the year, fans gather to watch the most highly skilled players compete, with the pinnacle being the world championships hosted by Riot Games each fall. In 2019, "Worlds" was broadcast globally in over fifteen languages, averaging 21.8 million viewers per minute worldwide.

The early genesis of Learn with League

In 2016 at Riot Games, there were two strong narratives: *Be the most player-focused games company in the world* and *Support LoL as a generational sport.* As a company, we began to think about what this meant not just for the individual player but also for the broader playing community. At the same time, we were becoming aware of the need to foster a culture of sportsmanship around the game.

Though we had had some success with prior sportsmanship initiatives, we were still struggling to generate sustained change due to the challenges of online play. Digital spaces lack the same rich presence and nonverbal communication enjoyed when you are face-to-face. Online games are often played among relative strangers and, in our case, in a competitive situation. Thus, without any type of intervention, gaming spaces are prone to gaps in trust and empathy and, in time, can invite antagonism. We knew we needed to do more to overcome these challenges and to inspire a greater sense of teamwork and personal accountability toward upholding the spirit of the game.

A parallel opportunity was emerging to equip the next generation with the skills for sportsmanship, health and self-regulation, and ultimately deep individual character growth when playing LoL. Doing so would, in turn, support efforts to improve in-game behavior on a societal level. So, we set the ambitious goal to leverage the wide-scale appeal of League of Legends and its availability as a free-to-play game to help equip the next generation with these important life skills. And from this, Learn with League was born.

Unlocking esports' educational potential

Esports can teach many important life skills, including perseverance, respect, empathy, communication, and resilience, as well as how to manage stress, be a teammate, and be mindful of others' needs and cultures. Not only do young people require these lessons to be successful in modern society; if they do not participate in more traditional sporting activities, they may miss them altogether. Furthermore, the social immaturity of children makes them especially susceptible to absorbing and repeating the bad habits of online interaction without our intervention, which is where education comes in. Without some sort of schooling, the cycle of problematic behavior will continue as the next generation comes online.

Given that esports was already culturally established yet largely absent from schools, we needed to understand this gap. Working with parents, educators, and caregivers, we learned there was an opportunity to help them connect with their children in esports and to demonstrate the profound potential impact esports can have on young people's development, health, and well-being. We also saw a need to address the misinformation or stigma surrounding video games and to alleviate the fear that to support their children's interest in gaming, they must become gaming experts. A parent need not be a professional football player, for example, to connect with their child. They just need to be authentically present by sharing their child's experiences, asking questions, and celebrating their child's accomplishments.

Learn with League methodology

Based on these findings, we saw an opportunity to create educational esports resources for the home and classroom, built on a collaborative approach that brings the learner and caregiver together. Learn with League is a completely free, comprehensive educational framework that supports young people's participation in esports and video games at home, in school, and within their local community. Learn with League was founded on the belief that every child deserves to feel supported not just in their passions but also through a sense of belonging, importance, and a unique ability to contribute.

Centered on play, Learn with League specifically aims to nurture the following abilities in children:

- Personal management, including identity, health, wellness, and emotional regulation
- Positive and productive interactions, including aspects of sportsmanship such as a team-oriented mindset, respect, discipline, responsibility, resilience, and a positive attitude
- Mastery and high performance

For facilitators, Learn with League seeks to close the gap between the theoretical and the applied, equipping teachers with the tools and resources to unlock esports as a teaching medium and helping parents to feel empowered to support their child's development. Learn with League also recognizes that carers may not be experts or even gamers themselves, and it seeks to build bridges with young people to allow for better outcomes.

The actionable extracurricular resources and workshops in this initiative align closely with national core curricular objectives such as active-learning activities, discussion questions, and relevant learning objectives delivered through esports. The legitimacy of esports as a teaching ecosystem was important. Playing League of Legends was not just fun but also a vehicle through which we could teach developmental lessons similar to traditional sports with more focus on the digital. To this end, we engaged experts around the world in health, education, esports, child development, and more to ensure that our approach was sound and in the best interest of the child and caregiver.

By participating in the various programs within the Learn with League initiative, young people, with the support of a caregiver, build strategies for looking after their mental health and personal growth, preventing and responding to negative behavior, and demonstrating appropriate online behavior. At the same time, teachers, parents, and caregivers develop strategies for leveraging video games and esports in the classroom and home as well as gain a deeper understanding of their value and importance to young people.

Learn with League was piloted in Australia and New Zealand in 2016. Since its inception, over three hundred schools have participated in the initiative, hundreds of thousands of people have viewed the resources, and many partnerships have formed, all with the goal to provide greater support and opportunity for young players.

Where we go next

As of this writing, Learn with League is being translated into languages beyond English, and the methodology is being adapted to other Riot Games titles. Learn with League invites other gaming companies to use this methodology with their games to support player learning and development. This highlights a powerful opportunity for companies to give back to communities and players. Learn with League also will invite other educational institutions to introduce esports into their extracurricular offerings.

Gaming *is* a meaningful life pursuit. As esports becomes more widely accepted in the home, school, and local community, young people who choose to play online games will be cherished and celebrated. Supporting this pursuit of gaming affirms that young people are accepted for who they are and, with our mentorship and guidance, can unleash their full potential in the world.

To learn more, you can read the Learn with League Report at https://oce.learnwithleague.com/wp-content/uploads/2020/02/Learn-with-League-Report.pdf, which provides an extensive overview of the initiative, its educational methodology, and its programs.

MEET KIMBERLY VOLL & IVAN DAVIES

Kimberly Voll

Dr. Kimberly Voll is a game developer, programmer, cognitive scientist, and interactive-media researcher who has been playing video games since the 1970s. She has long referred to games as "engines of culture" for their ability to transcend differences and bring people closer together through a shared experience. During her time at Riot Games, she witnessed the incredible scale and popularity of esports, which continues to influence her work on gaming in society. In addition to making games, she also supports game development more broadly, focusing on the unique opportunity developers have to create more inclusive spaces and help the next generation succeed in our digital world. You can find her online at:

linkedin.com/in/kimberly-voll-phd-a005aa14
twitter.com/zanytomato

Ivan Davies

Ivan specializes in traditional and digital community-based experiences. He works with organizations, governments, and institutions to build communities that thrive. At Riot Games he was accountable for one of the largest communities in Australia and New Zealand. In this role, he founded and co-authored the Learn with League initiative.

When working as a teacher, he pioneered the design, implementation, and post-implementation analysis of the Assessment for Learning framework to improve student performance. This formative assessment framework became integrated into the U.K. education sector and has since been widely adopted by several education authorities throughout the world, including North America and Australia.

To improve opportunities for all children to play, learn, and develop through cricket, in 2005 he codesigned and delivered Chance to Shine, the first joint community and school event in the U.K. Since then, over five million children have participated in this initiative.

Ivan also has experience working with communities, teams, and professional athletes across multiple sports, including football, cricket, rugby, and esports. In his spare time he acts as an advisor and board member for several not-for-profit organizations, participates in a range of local community initiatives, and enjoys spending time with the whānau.

You can find him online at:
linkedin.com/in/ivan-davies-279698a
twitter.com/IvanSynabe

CHAPTER 7

The Need for More Esports Programs in Schools

Esports is currently still in its acceptance stage by learning institutions around the world. While esports teams have formed in several universities and high schools across the U.S., more schools need to include them. Gaming and esports are paving the way to future careers, and parents, educators, and administrators should be aware of the positive impacts gaming has on our youth. The slower schools are to adopt gaming in recreational activities and in the classroom, the further they will fall behind.

There are several factors that make having an esports team in schools important. According to ViewSonic, not every child is interested in traditional sports.[1] Some kids lack the interest or the drive to succeed in something like basketball or hockey. Those kids who you see as "unathletic" may actually shine at games like Super Smash Bros. or Fortnite. This is great for childhood development, because it helps to build team spirit and encourages cooperation and teamwork. Learning these skills in esports is no different from regular sports.

Gaming has also been seen to help foster inclusion at a young age by allowing kids to meet different people who share similar interests.[2] Using gaming to help kids learn about acceptance allows them to learn about others through something they love.

Esports recreational programs allow children to develop their gaming skills at a young age. These kids are then able to find opportunities for scholarships that allow them to play at university levels if these universities have esports programs. Gamers should have more scholarship opportunities since they exhibit the same characteristics as those involved in traditional sports. Competitive gamers practice hard and learn how to work together in teams. They also learn how to navigate the gaming industry, which is a huge market today.

Esports programs in public schools and universities would help children develop for the future. Not only will they be learning great life skills, solid communication skills, and strategic planning, they'll also be having fun playing games.

Esports provides youth with leadership opportunities

Developing leadership skills is arguably one goal of education, and esports teams provide their members with an opportunity to build and showcase those skills. A student at Shenandoah University was recognized as a student leader[3] at the National Association of Collegiate Esports[4] awards. This award is given to students that exhibit great leadership inside the classroom and in esports competitions. Those who have earned this award typically conduct themselves well in the classroom and in matches.

Team-based video games allow students to use leadership skills when planning and executing strategies, which will be critical in their professional careers. Just like being the captain of a football team or the branch manager at a major company, leaders on esports teams have an obligation to lead their squad into victory.

The amount of work that goes into formulating strategies in esports can make an average person's head spin. Team leaders need to study every mechanic of the game to develop a thorough plan. These deep dives allow them not only to understand the rules of the game and effective tactics but also to see potential exploits and tricks their opponent may not see coming. Leaders of esports teams also need to keep up to date on the latest updates to the game's software. Updates tend to come during every new season to a competitive game and often include major changes. Some of these changes can greatly affect an already existing strategy.

Not only are these leaders responsible for scoring wins; they also need to keep team morale up. Without rallying a team, they'll no longer have the will to participate in matches, especially if the team is on a losing streak. Team captains are responsible for leading their team through tough times and getting them to focus on scoring big wins. These responsibilities are similar to those of any sports team leader, and the skills learned through gaming leadership can be used later in the students' professional and personal lives.

Scholarships and job opportunities through esports

If leadership and important soft skills are not enough to convince you that having esports teams in public schools and universities is important, then perhaps revenue-earning opportunities will. Scholarship opportunities and jobs have seen spikes in growth as esports' popularity explodes.

Attending classes at universities is becoming increasingly expensive. To provide financial assistance for students, various new scholarships are emerging. Gamers and esports competitors can now earn a scholarship for gaming.

The North America Scholastic Esports Federation (NASEF) has partnered with the National Association of Collegiate Esports (NACE) to provide students with opportunities through esports. Over $16 million in esports scholarships already exist from NACE member universities, with more coming from NASEF, and more than 180 registered NACE universities offer esports programs.[5]

But esports still struggles to make its way to a varsity level across the country. Traditional sports offer a wider range of scholarships, with sports like baseball offering roughly three hundred division 1 (D1) scholarships. Esports funding should be comparable to traditional sports, because esports should be seen on the same level. The esports market is just as big, if not bigger, than traditional sports. Competitive gamers should receive the same scholarship opportunities as those in traditional sports, because they exhibit similar characteristics to those on sports teams.

The esports job market has been growing. Gamers can now pursue their passion in a full-time role. Gaming and esports companies offer careers in several different concentrations that include game development, marketing, writing, and video production. The esports and gaming jobs platform Hitmarker has reported that esports jobs grew roughly 87 percent in 2019.[6]

Full Sail University has made a great effort to provide educational opportunities in gaming, offering specialized classes. These classes better equip students who are passionate about gaming with the skills they need to get the job they want—in any field, including gaming.

Game Designing reported there were sixty-three colleges with varsity esports programs in 2018.[7] While it is great to see colleges embracing the power of esports and gaming, there is still much more to be done. If we want our kids to be better equipped for the future, we should start pushing for more gaming education and recreational programs now.

Gaming is now considered mainstream

Today, gaming is a multibillion-dollar industry and is enjoyed by people all over the world. If we look back to the 1980s, during the age of Pac-Man and Donkey Kong, gaming was seen as something you did with a few friends at your house or at a bar. Now, it involves huge tournaments that are sponsored by major corporations and broadcast worldwide to millions of viewers. Spectators now fill stadiums to watch esports competitions like the Overwatch League (OWL) and Call of Duty League (CDL). The 2019 League of Legends World Championship (Worlds) had over one hundred million viewers. The industry has certainly come a long way.

Gaming has a major influence on our lives now. Mobile gaming allows people to play as they are heading to work or relaxing at home. Single-player adventure and role-playing games have had millions of dollars poured into them to create vast and immersive cinematic worlds.

Newzoo has reported that the number of people who are active gamers around the world will reach 2.81 billion in 2021.[8] While the gaming audience is still predominately male, the number of female gamers is on the rise. In 2020, the Entertainment Software Association reported that roughly 41 percent of gamers in the U.S. are female.[9]

Gaming is no longer seen as something only for geeks. Studios with enormous budgets, extensive spending on advertising, startups emerging to better serve gamers, and arenas packed to capacity for esports events show us that gaming is now mainstream.

The United States Esports Association

The United States Esports Association (USEA) is a nonprofit promoting the development of recreational esports throughout the United States according to its value pillars of education, recreation, and diversity and inclusion.[10] Through integrated recreational programming, member players are developed along the core aspects of recreational play: sportsmanship, teamwork, personal fulfillment, integrity, respect, loyalty to one's peers, and the pursuit of excellence.

In addition to programming engaging players, the USEA provides educational literature, workshops, and webinars for member parents to learn about everything from what esports is to why recreational esports is a uniquely enriching experience, as well as what opportunities gamers have within the world of esports beyond recreational play.

By partnering with like-minded organizations and influential community figures, the USEA furthers the immense accessibility to recreational community that esports uniquely provides, and brings esports programming to everyone, regardless of race, gender, ability, or socioeconomic background. It is through working with like-minded partners and building robust recreational programming that the USEA allows anyone anywhere to experience community through esports.

MEET MIGUEL GIL

Miguel is the founder of the USEA, a nonprofit organization with a core mission of fostering the growth of recreational and amateur esports in the U.S. Miguel also serves as a member of the advisory board for the Gamers Outreach Foundation and is a member of the Digital, Technology and Innovation Commission for the Global Esports Federation.

Prior to leading the USEA, Miguel spent thirteen-plus years at Microsoft Xbox, where he was mostly involved with the Xbox hardware team in a variety of roles with a focus on portfolio management, strategic planning, business development, and financial analysis. He has a passion for the consumer electronics industry and served as a board member of the Consumer Technology Association Accessories Division between 2012 and 2019. Miguel earned a BS in engineering from University Fermin Toro and later received his MBA from Stetson University. His personal passions include family, tennis, golf, F1 racing, and trying to become better at racing games.

You can find him online at:
https://www.miguelgil.digital

CHAPTER 8

Creating a High School Esports League

Video games are an integral part of newer generations, and that's true for me as well. Esports has existed since the late 1980s and is something that takes a competitive game and turns it into a competitive sport. For these reasons and many more, it has been my goal to implement an esports team in the American School of Dubai (ASD).

The Middle East and North Africa (MENA) region has had an increase in video game sales ever since they became popular in the early twenty-first century. Esports tournaments have popped up throughout the U.A.E. and other parts of MENA during the same period. The first major tournament there was in 2015, and the sport lay dormant for a few more years until two very large and very successful tournaments occurred in 2019, the Insomnia Gaming Festival and GIRLGAMER Esports Festival.

I want to expand esports to schools in the MENA region and hold similar tournaments to the likes of the Collegiate Overwatch Tournament in North America. There, a large prize pool and Activision Blizzard, the makers of Overwatch, actually help host the tournament. Esports in schools is growing every day, and I want to expand it to Dubai, where video games are an important part of many kids' lives.

If ASD can lead by example and create an esports team first, not only will it bring attention to the school but it could also become a sport added to the Middle East South Asia Conference (MESAC). This is an athletic and academic conference consisting of six top international schools in the Middle East and India. Currently, MESAC hosts competitions in basketball, baseball, academic games, wrestling, golf, and the like. Adding an esports component would be a great opportunity for students to bond, create friendships, and become leaders by participating and creating their own esports teams. It helps students build a skill that can get them scholarships to many universities in the U.S. and create a culture where esports are treated the same as traditional sports.

Branching out

For the first time, because of COVID-19, there is a possibility to branch the league out further than we could have imagined. Because we can't gather in one area, the league for the first year (or the first several years) will be played online, meaning that schools not located in Dubai can participate. This can help give the league more attention from new sources throughout the Middle East and elsewhere.

The concept of introducing esports to ASD is not a recent idea. I have been advocating for this for a few years. I first proposed the Esports Club in February of 2020. The mission statement was "The Esports Club is here to build strong teamwork, perseverance, respect, and compassion as a competitor, teammate, and as a student in ASD. We focus on the mutual respect of fellow players as well as paving the way for esports innovation in schools across the MENA region. We want club members to participate in tournaments across the U.A.E. and be able to learn and have fun from doing so. We hope to see you there."

The club's goal is to create a good environment for students and to focus on the United Nations' sustainable development goals 5 and

9. Goal 5 speaks to gender equality, which is something I want in the league. Goal 9 pertains to industry, innovation, and infrastructure. The league is focused on innovation within the gaming space in the MENA region. Besides this, we had four main goals of our own:

1. To pave the way for schools in the MENA region to understand the importance of the esports industry and the jobs that come from it

2. To allow students to participate in tournaments and grow bonds between their teammates as well as with other teams

3. To build a strong community of people who can support each other when they leave Dubai

4. To possibly form teams in university and beyond, and to build relationships

This league will be built on trust and teamwork, and our goal is to make people feel like a part of something rather than a person in the vast ocean that is Dubai. We hope to form lasting relationships outside of school and to create possible job and university opportunities because of this club. We are looking to create something different, something that truly sets people apart.

While we've moved the idea from a club to a team and now potentially a league, our goals remain the same:

• Have fun

• Develop leadership skills

• Make friends

• Enjoy the competition

These are the foundations of a great league. Currently, we have three schools, including ASD, working on esports teams, and other MESAC schools that are thinking about setting esports teams up.

Recently, the director general of The Knowledge and Human Development Authority (KHDA) paid a visit to ASD. KHDA is responsible for the growth and quality of private education in Dubai. When I pitched my thoughts about an esports league to Dr. Abdulla Al Karam, he was extremely supportive and asked me to send him a proposal.

We need the KHDA's support to help expand the idea of a league. From here, the KHDA's role in setting up the league is focused on endorsing the league and the schools that participate in it. They will also take on the role of pushing the idea of a league to other schools throughout Dubai. This is the role I want KHDA to play, which I mentioned in my proposal.

I want to work with the KHDA to set up an esports league so we could get government backing to make it not just an idea but a reality. As part of the government, the KHDA is well known for how important they are when it comes to schools in Dubai and the power that they hold. This power is important for the league to be recognized at a higher level than it otherwise would be.

The support of the KHDA is key. This expansion could create something bigger than just a league. Our hope is that it will gather sponsors and be seen throughout the MENA region and beyond. We want to take the rapidly growing video game space in the U.A.E. and build something competitive out of it, something larger than itself and the other leagues throughout the world.

An esports league in Dubai can capitalize on the gaming market and bring more attention to the region. If the league becomes an in-person event over the next few years, it could even be an event in which people pay to see it in person, similar to leagues in the U.S. (Overwatch, R6S, etc.).

I want to expand Dubai's gaming space and the future of esports by bringing it to its largest group of consumers—teenagers—by having the top gamers participate in a high school league. Hopefully, with the support of the KHDA, this vision can be realized.

MEET MAX CHOW EVERETT

Max Chow Everett is Canadian but has lived in Dubai for most of his life. Truly a third-culture kid, he currently attends the American School of Dubai (ASD).

Max founded ASD's first esports club, a growing group with 40 members, because it has been a passion of his to see video games receive the mainstream audience and attention they deserve. He coordinates bi-yearly competitions and manages all teams, practice, and tournaments. It is an added bonus he is able to support students who are good players!

Minecraft was one of the first games Max played, and partly because of that, he has developed an interest in architecture and urban planning. He will most likely pursue a degree in business as he is interested in finance, politics, and advocacy. Perhaps he has a future as an entrepreneur, urban planner, or a politician!

He likes to be challenged and actively participates in regional and global business and debate competitions. His varsity team placed first in Academic Games, and his team also placed second in the DEWA Business Cup Challenge 2021, earning them a coveted internship opportunity.

Max is also a proud Eagle Scout and was elected to be Senior Patrol Leader in 2021 for Troop 813. Fewer than 4 percent of scouts earn this coveted rank of Eagle. You can connect with Max at:

mchoweverett.23@asdubai.org
mchoweverett@gmail.com
https://www.linkedin.com/in/max-chow-everett-963735231/

PART 3

Women in Gaming

CHAPTER 9

My Journey as a Professional Gamer

My parents bought our first PC in 1983, when I was six. The computer was in our kitchen, and my brother and I would play Gorillas together, and I learned programming in QBasic. We eventually got our own computers, and for my sixteenth birthday, in 1999, a friend of my dad who worked at IBM in Norway gave me a hub when he visited us. It was a device to connect multiple computers together.

I invited all my friends who had a PC back then to join me in my parents' garage, and we connected all our machines together. It was my first LAN party. Most of the time, as we were playing, I was just figuring out how to fix my PC, because it was always broken. It was usually either the ethernet card or the graphics card.

This sounds so cliché, but we were the ones who were bullied in school, and meeting up to improve our computers and our play was a great way to become friends and build an alliance against the bullies. It was a wonderful hobby to share with people who were brilliant, passionate, peaceful, and warmhearted. Most of us were in chess club at school, and the game was a fantastic way to get to know and trust each other. But the chess club meetings usually ended up with us programming, thinking, and creating together. Some of my early classmates excluding me resulted in me finding my best lifelong friends.

Just before I turned sixteen, I looked around the internet for bigger LAN parties. In Bremen, there was the Creative Computer Network Bremen (CCNB). In a youth center, there were regular LAN parties where table soccer and Counter-Strike were played. I helped to set up the LAN party, played many rounds of Counter-Strike, and made new friends there.

After I had participated in every CCNB LAN for a long time, there was no stopping me. I logged in at LANparty.de, where I also found the CCNB and searched for more local LAN parties. In 2002, I found innovaLAN and their "Summit" in Osnabrück. One day, I just drove to the Stadthalle, in Osnabrück, and asked the first person I found in the parking lot if I could help. They gave me a yellow vest and let me bring in cars so the LAN guests could quickly unload their PCs and sleeping things. Marco Grimm, of innovaLAN, eventually asked me to help set up all his LANs and run tournaments. Of course, I did this for some time at the Summit, NorthCon, MultiMadness, and Activation. It was fun.

Through the LANs, I also got to know the World Cyber Games (WCG). There were points on LANs through which you could qualify for the WCG, and I started to collect these points. During one of the parties, a player was missing from the DkH team for the Unreal Tournament. We collected points as a team, and I also collected points in one-on-one mode.

In the meantime, I lived in Bielefeld, in a student flat at the university with five roommates, where I got to know a player of the clan respawnkiller. We played a lot together with DkH and rK, a team with KiLLu and daddy. They were very talented and qualified for many UT tournaments. From them and from my trainer, Asja Baric, at DkH, I learned some tricks like how to keep map control and how to time items better.

In 2003, I began to do some freelance work for the Electronic Sports League (ESL). I helped promote games and hardware at LAN parties for ESL's customers. At some point, I had collected enough World Wide Championship of LAN Gaming points to participate in the German Qualifier of the World Cyber Games at CeBIT, in Hanover. Some players traveled to the event even from Switzerland, such as sono from mousesports.

I was very excited for my first match on stage in front of an audience, and I wanted to overcome the nervousness to be able to prove my real abilities to the audience. The stage fright was even more overwhelming than in the one-on-one matches at the LAN parties.

Against my first opponent, I won only with difficulty, at least it felt that way. I changed my weapons timidly and got stuck on the rocket launcher, because I could not think well with all the excitement. My aim saved me in the first match; otherwise, I would have been right out.

After that first match, I froze. My hands were shaking, and my pulse was racing. I made the decision to leave fear out of the game. *You did not get this far*, I thought, *not to try it now*. During a break I confided in a few friends who had more tournament experience but who were relatively indifferent to the tournament. Everyone said, "Oh, you'll be fine . . . and if not, then next time." I was walking around, drinking sips of water, angry with myself that I could not swallow my fear.

I was still shaking from stage fright, but the more I thought about it, the more that first win gave me a silver lining. I kept the first success in my heart and bit my way through the preliminary round. The audience applauded me louder and louder as I progressed. At some point, a friend came up to me and said, "They clap because a woman is winning. They think it's cool!" That was the first time I noticed there were no other women in the tournament.

In the grand finale, my luck and talent had reached their limits. I lost to mouz|sono and shook his hand. It was an honor to meet him and to be able to exchange some thoughts on the game with him. At the award ceremony, when I heard the commentators calling me the German Vice Champion in Unreal Tournament 2004 and the first woman ever to take part in the World Cyber Games, I was so excited and felt deeply honored.

This moment probably made me even more curious about the esports world, which resulted in me and some other people from all over Germany starting eMAG, Germany's first online esports and gaming community website with news and forums. I ran eMAG as editor in chief from 2003 until 2005.

Between January and July 2004, I began an internship at GIGA TV, which was part of NBC Europe. I was a commentator for Unreal Tournament 2004, and I wrote articles about computers, games, and all kinds of electronic gadgets for the TV format GIGA Help. In September 2004, in my role as editor in chief at eMAG and as a professional UT2004 player and commentator, I was invited by the WCG to do the live commentary for the finals in San Francisco, live on GIGA TV.

Also in 2004, I was in the running for a position with ESL, but since I had already enrolled at the University of Bonn, I decided to tell them that I could no longer take a full-time job. One day after the interview, they called and offered to hire me as a working student for the PR department. As a PR manager, I handled all press-related tasks on weekdays and traveled the world on weekends.

Since photography was my hobby, I also started taking sportive photos of all our events and started a picture database. In 2006, McCann-Erickson New York was doing a campaign for Intel. They hired me as the photographer for the campaign, and it ended up on billboards all over the world. When I got the call from McCann, I was in Leipzig at the Games Convention, and I had to rush to a store to buy a bigger camera for the campaign.

I squeezed all my courses at university into two or three days, so I could be at the ESL office twenty hours each week. I remember writing lots of papers for my courses on planes and in cars. When I graduated in

2009, I got promoted at ESL and became the vice director of community management.

That same year, I founded the NGO eSports Yearbook with my good friend Tobias M. Scholz, who I had founded eMAG with. At eSports Yearbook, I scout for and empower the world's most talented esports scholars. Their research is made available within the industry and at universities through our book every year. Having managed these relationships between scholars and universities for more than a decade, Tobias and I have connections with the most renowned scientists in the field who work either in academia or in the industry.

In 2013, I was invited by the University of Bonn to hold a keynote on jobs in esports. I met lots of friends from school once again, and I had never stopped enjoying and supporting the trips to Stratford-upon-Avon, which the Department of English, American, and Celtic Studies was organizing each year. Professor Uwe Baumann, who was responsible for these study trips and who remembered me from different courses I was enrolled in, asked me about my job at ESL and asked if I wanted to write a PhD thesis in the esports field. I immediately knew that I would not turn down this offer. From then on, I was busy every day trying to find a research topic.

I had more than 280 pages of a thesis when I realized that many smart people had already discussed my topic extensively. I had now spent many years researching, and I had learned a lot, but unfortunately, I had to put this dissertation (on esports, games, and learning) on ice, as it would not have provided the world with groundbreakingly new insights. I found a new topic for my thesis around the end of 2016: I wanted to do my research on multiplayer online battle arena (MOBA) games and their impact on our culture. I also wanted to define the MOBA genre.

In December 2018, I held a lecture at Bonn University on esports in popular culture in the module "Anglophone Literature and Popular Culture" in the MA degree program for English literature and cultures, engaging students in a discussion about the stereotypes, the history, and the marketing aspects of esports. In the winter of 2019, I handed in my PhD thesis. It was accepted! On June 4th, my disputation took place, and I passed cum laude.

In 2020, I became a board member of the Esports Research Network (ERN). The ERN helps researchers around the globe to connect. Today, I am still working at ESL, but they are now called ESLGaming GmbH.

The future is bright for esports, especially since it is an incredible brand and marketing opportunity for nonendemic companies, such as Red Bull, Mercedes, and Warsteiner. Companies like ESLGaming reach more fans than those in other entertainment sectors. Since ESL-Gaming can run all its tournaments online, it is relatively unaffected by the current pandemic. We have had an even bigger viewership after COVID-19 began to plague our planet. Esports entertains everyone, everywhere, and it is now seen as the cultural medium that it is. I think that is because it really is without borders, connecting us worldwide and interculturally.

MEET JULIA HILTSCHER

Julia has been a fixture in the global esports scene since her surprising victories as a professional player at the World Cyber Games. For more than seventeen years she has been designing tournaments at the most important esports company in the world, ESLGaming, in Europe and around the world. She has initiated and managed the eSports Yearbook and has joined ERN's board of directors. You can find her online at:

linkedin.com/in/juliachristophers
twitter.com/JuliaHiltscher

CHAPTER 10

Female Firsts in the Middle East

The big "beige box" my brothers used to sit in front of always fascinated me. I was obviously too young to understand what the heck those machines did, but the way my parents spoke about the computer definitely meant it wasn't something common for everyone to have. Computers were a luxury back then, but little did I know they would become a huge part of my life. I first got into gaming when I started spending hours watching my brothers play video games, and if I'm being honest, I had no idea what they were doing or what the game was even about. I was only four years old.

A year later we moved to Texas, and computers seemed more advanced. By then we had a computer and a laptop in the house, and I would sit next to my brother every day after school and watch him play RuneScape. In 2003, my brother finally offered to make me an account. I was extremely excited, and for the next few days, I focused on what I would specialize my character on in the game.

I was a bit sad when I saw my brother making my avatar male. I sometimes saw the pretty female characters, and when I asked him why I couldn't have been female in the game, he explained to my seven-year-old self that people would be mean to me online. He told me there weren't many females playing the game and that it would make me feel singled out. I never understood why people would be rude to a female gamer, but I continued playing the game as a male character for the next six to seven years.

I also did not understand why my brother felt the need to protect me until I became a bit older and faced the bullying a gamer receives once they know she is female. I would often get told "Go back to the kitchen!" or "Go put some makeup on!" even while being extremely good at the game, only because of the simple fact that I was a girl. I finally understood, and I thanked my brother. His choice to make my character male had taught me not to go into games caring about my gender but, instead, to focus on the task at hand, which was to learn and become good at the game.

I moved back to the U.A.E. when I was in high school, and every day after football practice, I would go to the gaming cafes here in Dubai with a group of my friends. The cafes tended to be extremely male dominated, and I always remembered to carry a hoodie to try to mask the fact that I was female. It was uncommon for girls to go to these places, but I did not have a computer at home, and it was just so much fun playing with my friends.

I started playing League of Legends in 2014 and instantly fell in love with the game. It was always changing and challenging. I tried to make a female team by searching for others on Facebook at the time, but I couldn't really find a reach, or the few I did manage to find did not want to be known as female gamers.

Even after my friends stopped playing and after I graduated high school and went on to college to study public relations and journalism, I would still go to the gaming cafes to play. I felt extremely uncomfortable, because I was a girl alone, walking into a place filled with dozens of guys. I remember situations where some guys would try to take pictures of me or forcefully try to speak to me or make weird noises passing by. I ignored it all and just minded my own business. After a couple of years of going there almost daily, weekend League of Legends tournaments had begun, and I was getting asked by some of the familiar faces there to join. I started playing with them, and I loved the competitive nature of it. After gaining their trust, I started going to many other tournaments around the country. Although we might have only won a few, it was the experience that mattered to me.

By the time I had graduated university and gotten a job, I had saved up enough to get a custom-made PC so I could balance time between a full-time job and gaming. I would wake up at 6:00 a.m. to get in a game before work most days. Mainly I did it to put myself in a good mood before going to the place I dreaded the most: work. My job had become extremely depressing, to the point where I was completely unmotivated. Nothing interested me anymore. I eventually even stopped gaming for a while.

As a recent graduate, I had a horrible boss. I promised myself I'd just gain some experience there before I looked for something I truly loved. Sadly, after some grueling months, I was sitting at my desk at work writing a book with my boss and decided to quit. And just like that I handed in my resignation and decided to pursue streaming games full time.

My sister was one of the first reporters to cover esports here in the Middle East. She told me about a press conference she had been invited to relating to a huge GIRLGAMER festival happening in Dubai. I was so excited and wanted to join her, but, unfortunately, I had to work. So, I asked her to share everything she knew about it with me. The festival was the opportunity of a lifetime! I had never been more excited about an event before. So, I tried to find out all that I could about this festival. I couldn't believe there was something related to esports in the Middle East and that it was also all about female empowerment! Soon after, I got in touch with Paul Roy from Galaxy Racer Esports (the local organizer of the festival), and he wanted to discuss the involvement of women from the region. We were going to put together the first all-female Middle Eastern esports team.

After a huge press conference, we started the registration process. We chose the best players from the country and had them all start practicing. This reminded me about my mission to make an all-female team in 2014 and made me realize how times had changed. The GIRLGAMER Dubai Festival Worlds Edition would host the best female teams from six different regions that were coming here to compete. I was in shock when I learned there had been a female scene in esports that I had never even heard about. It made me realize how far behind the Middle East was in terms of esports as a whole, but I was happy that at least organizations like Galaxy Racer were taking that into account and trying to make a difference.

I've worked hard to be really good at esports and hope to be one of the leading names when it comes to female gamers in the region and to always be known as someone who made it possible for female gamers to pursue esports as a career here in the Middle East. I hope the next generation of gamers gets these opportunities much earlier in their lives than I did and that their families support it. Although my family supported me fully, I got in at a much later age than what is ideal for an athlete.

The GIRLGAMER festival was a huge eye opener for me and made me realize this is what I want to pursue as a career. I became the first Pakistani female (as well as the first female in the U.A.E.) to receive a professional esports athlete contract. And I was honored to become the captain of the first Middle Eastern all-female esports team. As of now, Galaxy Racer Esports has hired me for two positions: part-time player and part-time PR representative for the organization.

Dreams do come true, if you chase them. I went from writing a book for my boss to writing a chapter of my own today!

MEET MADIHA NAZ

Madiha Naz, better known for her gamer name "Madi," is the first Pakistani female to pursue esports professionally. She is the team captain for the first all-female MENA League of Legends team at a global leading esports organization, Galaxy Racer Esports. Madi has a bachelor of communications and is a huge PR enthusiast. When she is not working, you will find Madi out on an adventure or reading a book. Follow her online at:

instagram.com/madixolol
twitter.com/MadiXOlol
twitch.tv/madiha_lol
linkedin.com/in/madiha-naz-588342173

CHAPTER 11

GIRLGAMER:
Creating Opportunity for Women in Esports

We're often asked why we'd create such an event as the GIRLGAMER Esports Festival that seemingly perpetuates and promotes gender segregation rather than unity. The mission is pretty straightforward: We want to create equal opportunities by creating a space for a traditionally marginalized subset of gamers: women.

Today's gender-equality issues are mostly discussed in relation to the workplace, where women often have fewer career opportunities and are still paid less than men. It's our team's belief that the best way to tackle that hard battle is to start with educating a younger generation about how opportunities should be equal for everyone, regardless of their gender or race. Every change starts with education, and what better way to target kids and young adults than using their most popular medium as the platform to deliver the message?

Traditionally, video games have been largely developed by men, which also led to the games themselves predominantly reflecting male thinking. Female gaming characters have often been represented either by princesses in distress or by sexualized avatars. This limitation itself reveals how games have been marketed over the past decade. And although things have started to get better, there is still much that needs to be improved before equality is within reach.

We argue that women should have the same competing opportunities as men. They can be equally skilled when given the same conditions to develop in a nonhostile environment. It is a misconception that women already have the same opportunities just because most existing tournaments don't expressly forbid them to participate. The usual excuse for low numbers of competing women is that they aren't skillful enough to join the main competition, so they are placed in a special category—if they are included at all. But to understand how these opportunities are not being given, we have to analyze all the levels, from grassroots to pro, while also taking into consideration existing issues within modern society.

At the grassroots level, women face entry barriers that they have to overcome mentally, such as online bullying, sexual harassment, and toxic behavior much worse than what men have to face. This step alone demotivates a majority of potential women gamers from investing their time into developing their skills and pursuing competition. Something that was supposed to be fun—playing games—instead harms the mental health of the players.

On a semiprofessional level, women also face integration issues. Despite being just as skilled as their male counterparts, many women players are rejected from teams solely because of their gender. Most teams of male gamers do not want to risk having a woman on the team, because it may create instability or might make communication uncomfortable for the rest of the team. Female gamers are then forced to find other women to form female-only teams with. The lack of integration opportunities for female gamers makes it much harder for women to progress to a professional level.

Very few women gamers, in fact, are lucky enough to even be given the chance to compete professionally. And the truth is no one wants to be the face of a gender and take on the psychological burden of being constantly questioned about how it is to be a woman in a man's league. They just want to be a player, equal to all others and compared on the basis of their skills. There have also been multiple cases of women being admitted into professional male teams solely for marketing purposes while having their competitive abilities largely neglected.

Regarding societal issues, the reality is we are still living in a chauvinistic world, where men's egos struggle with being beaten by women, and that includes in video games. But esports is an activity where men and women can compete side by side and against each other on the same level. That's what we truly wish to accomplish someday.

The **GIRLGAMER** Esports Festival exists because there is a need to create a safe environment for women to engage in an activity that they love. Increasing the female representation in esports is also important for the industry as a whole, and we believe it can be accomplished by creating this kind of event to give women more competing opportunities to showcase their talent. We are helping to forge role models that younger girls can look up to and aspire to become.

Defining all these goals is easy, but striving toward them is never a linear path, and we're still learning. Gender equality in esports doesn't necessarily mean a fifty-fifty balance. It just means that both genders have the same opportunities and are treated as equals in all levels.

Since the creation of the **GIRLGAMER** Festival in 2017, we've observed many more women joining the competition. More professional esports organizations started assembling female teams, and some even began to include women in the ranks of their flagship teams. Some game developers have also started to promote women leagues more actively while giving proper importance to in-game female character representation.

Getting girls to engage with video games at a young age is also very helpful for closing the gender gap in the most affected work environments. This early engagement with video games can also cause them to be more interested in careers in science, technology, engineering, and math (STEM). One study has already concluded that young girls who develop an early interest in gaming are three times more likely to pursue a career in STEM.[1]

GIRLGAMER has evolved from being a yearly held festival into a global phenomenon. In 2019, this festival happened all around the world, welcoming participants in Australia, Singapore, South Korea, Spain, and Brazil. Support continues to increase from brands that are starting to understand how important this mission is and now want to be a part of it. Since our first collaboration with Sephora in Portugal in 2018, which was the world's first women-oriented brand to do an esports brand activation, we've now worked with other incredible brands, such as Benefit Cosmetics in 2019 and 2020, Carefree in 2020, and L'Occitane in 2020, introducing them to the world of video games and helping them to create amazing experiences for their customers—many of whom are actually passionate about video games!

Another important milestone has been our dedicated contribution to the creation of the first-ever Arab female team, playing under the fastest-growing esports, gaming, and lifestyle organization, Galaxy Racer, who took part in our League of Legends competition in Dubai in 2020. This team is bound to break stereotypes in the Middle East. Now, more than ever, girls are owning their power.

GIRLGAMER will continue pushing toward equality, because we believe there is still a ways to go until the day when the need for such a festival ceases to exist. Ultimately, each of us should strive to make the world a more inclusive and better place. We're doing our part. What about you?

MEET FERNANDO PEREIRA

Fernando's involvement with esports dates back eighteen years, as a founding member of Grow uP eSports (2002), a multinational organization currently with over two thousand members, supporting competing teams and managing professional streamers. He currently represents Macao as a full member of the International Esports Federation (IESF).

As an entrepreneur passionate about technology innovation and finding new creative ways to engage with digital communities, he worked in areas surrounding the gaming industry, such as virtual worlds and virtual reality, before completely diving into the world of live entertainment, using esports as a platform to deliver engaging experiences for a vibrant audience and for brands that want to communicate with the new digital consumer.

With a deep understanding of the industry, built by playing competitively across the years and by participating actively in several tournaments around the world, he created the **GIRLGAMER** Esports Festival in 2017, a festival that emphasizes gender equality, to create more opportunities for young girls to enjoy gaming in a safe environment.

In just three years **GIRLGAMER** expanded globally, having been hosted across four continents, in nine countries, growing to become the world's leading event focused on diversity and inclusion. After being nominated among other prominent events like BlizzCon and Dream-Hack, **GIRLGAMER** won the "Best Esports Festival" award by Everfest and XLIVE in 2018. The last edition was held in Dubai in February 2020, establishing itself as the U.A.E.'s largest esports and entertainment festival held to date.

His efforts led to the first foray of several well-established female-oriented consumer brands into esports, such as Sephora (2018), Benefit Cosmetics (2019), Johnson & Johnson (2020), and L'Occitane (2020).

Besides the world of esports, you'll likely find Fernando launching new business concepts from creative and technological ideas in the years to come. Find him online at:

linkedin.com/in/fernandoxpereira
twitter.com/imissapixel

CHAPTER 12

Girl Scouts and Gaming

In the summer of 2014, Women in Games International (WIGI), Game Mentor Online, and the Entertainment Software Association (ESA) launched the Girl Scouts of Greater Los Angeles (GSGLA) video game design patch. All badges or patches earned in Girl Scouts are meant to show a girl's achievement and are most meaningful when a girl can clearly articulate what she has accomplished. Patches are fun ways to document a council or local area event. They are always worn on the back of the uniform.

All patch programs include content from the National Leadership Journeys to provide girls with meaningful experiences on their path to leadership. When a patch is proposed, it's about exploring new things, discovering new skills, building skills for leadership, and having fun! The patch is awarded to Girl Scout members who learn how to design video games. It also requires them to program the games, rather than just design them.

The Boy Scouts of America (BSA) had added a belt loop for game design, but the BSA program did not involve technology. (Their programs must be able to be completed at a nature camp.) Not to be left behind, we pursued the project with the Girl Scouts. There are a few key differences between the Boy Scouts and Girl Scouts when it comes to their respective gaming achievements. For one, the Girl Scouts merit award is a patch, rather than a badge, which means that it isn't nationally recognized yet. Sheri Rubin, President and CEO of Design, Direct, Deliver and a lead volunteer for the GSGLA patch program, stated, "Fostering interest in technology and video game development in females of all ages . . . is the main inspiration for working towards a national badge."

WIGI's mission is to cultivate resources to advance economic equality and diversity in the global games industry. The organization serves professionals in games development, hardware, publishing, media, education, and esports, based on a fundamental belief that increased equality and camaraderie among genders can make global impacts for superior products, more consumer enjoyment, and a stronger gaming industry. WIGI advocates for issues crucial to the success of women and men in the games industry, including a better work-life balance, healthy working conditions, and increased opportunities for success.

Here is how we created a STEM-aligned video game patch focused on getting young girls excited about technology and science. The essentials we needed were a curriculum, access to the equipment and resources, funding, and volunteers.

Curriculum

Patches are generally four-hour programs completed in a day and are often run by councils or with partner companies or organizations. We designed a program guided by this, and it also included two hours of hands-on computer time. In addition, we wanted an individual to be able to complete the patch requirements at home or in a troop of thirty at an offsite location. Furthermore, it could not require a download. Everything had to be accessible on public library computers. The GSGLA patch was created to always include an online and digital interactive experience. STEM alignment from the beginning was key, especially as it pertains to girls. As of this writing, out of 10.8 million STEM-related jobs, only 26.7 percent are held by women. The U.S. government suggests that "strong gender stereotypes discourage women from pursuing STEM education and STEM jobs."[1] This patch is one way we can show girls that STEM can be a path for them as well.

Access

The GSGLA was a natural partner from day one. It had an eager network of girls in middle school, and also had the facilities to hold the patch session. The original goal was for WIGI and the GSGLA council to expand the program to other metropolitan areas. To accomplish this, WIGI will host training for additional video-game-industry professionals (most likely at large industry events like the Electronic Entertainment Expo [E3] and the Game Developers Conference [GDC]). Public awareness will help get the word out about this wonderful initiative. GSGLA kicked off the program at Girltopia, which brought media attention. The program was advertised in all GSGLA STEAM patch publications. There were six regions in total. Each regional area of GSGLA would host one session at their facility.

Funding

Finding sponsors to help fund curriculum creation, volunteer training, and other associated costs was important. This is where we were immensely grateful to the ESA. Fostering greater workforce diversity has become a priority for today's leading technology companies. The International Game Developers Association (IDGA) reports that women make up 24 percent of the industry's workforce—a number that has doubled since 2009.[2]

Data collected by the Higher Education Video Game Alliance (HEVGA) suggests these numbers will continue to grow. According to HEVGA's Our State of Play report, approximately 30 percent of students enrolled in college and university video game design programs in 2014–15 were women—nearly twice the number of women enrolled in other computer science and STEM programs.[3] Video game design programs also have significantly higher retention rates, averaging a rate of more than 88 percent.[4]

The ESA Foundation also provides grants to organizations that leverage video games to create positive social impact for American youth. The ESA Foundation provided grant support to the GSGLA, as the initiatives aim to help young girls develop critical thinking and problem-solving skills, bolster their creativity, and introduce them to game design as a career path, aligned with the diversity mission. Specifically, the funding covered our booth and promotion at Girltopia as well as the purchase of thirty laptops and mice!

Volunteers

Volunteers were needed to facilitate and lead the patch workshops. Video game professionals in the Los Angeles area were trained to guide girls through the patch programs. We had partnerships with local studios such as Sony Santa Monica and DICE LA. WIGI and GSCLA worked together to accommodate patch workshop requests from troops in the greater Los Angeles area.

To expand, WIGI hosted training for additional video game industry professionals at large industry events like E3 and GDC. Importantly, we had female speakers talk to the girls about their careers in game development to show them that gaming isn't just for guys. Without strong gender role models, it can be hard for girls to see themselves in STEM careers. Like the saying goes, if you can't see it, you can't be it.

We were able to complete fourteen sessions (in two years), which is approximately 420 Girl Scouts. The patch sessions could accommodate thirty scouts at a time, and every session was at full capacity. From what was reported to me, all surveys completed afterward gave the patch program rave reviews.

We hosted three of these sessions at game studios for the girls so they could have the opportunity to see what a development studio was like.

Shannon Studstill at Sony Santa Monica Studio (God of War's studio) hosted a few, and EA DICE down the street from them also hosted.

All of the people I worked with at GSGLA moved on to other cool opportunities. The new GSGLA STEAM team didn't know of our plans to expand from a patch in LA into multiple cities (Austin, the Bay Area, New York, and Chicago). Unfortunately, after hitting multiple walls to keep the program going, we had to let it go. I'm so thankful for the experience, however, as well as the lessons learned. My dearest takeaway has to be the friendships with the other women I worked with in WIGI to create the patch. There are so many groups out there for underrepresented voices in the gaming space, and every person or group I've worked with in my fourteen years shows real dedication to making a difference in their communities.

MEET AMY ALLISON

Amy Allison is a fourteen-year veteran of the gaming industry with experience in publishing, marketing, and advocacy. Her career in gaming began in video production services, where she made trailers for video games. She also ran the internal video department for a large publisher and later moved to a Hollywood trailer house to start a successful gaming vertical. Years later, she expanded into the VR gaming ecosystem as a business leader. She is currently the director of marketing for Skydance Interactive, a top-selling VR game at a development studio in Los Angeles, California. For twelve years with WIGI, she has created programs for companies and individuals to help increase and retain the number of women in the gaming industry. She has now transitioned from executive board to the advisory board for WIGI. Follow her online at:

linkedin.com/in/amyangrynirdsallison

CHAPTER 13

Esports in Pakistan

Can you imagine our delight when *the* Lucy Chow asked us to contribute an article on esports in Pakistan for her book? Asad Ehmed, chief strategy officer and resident gaming expert, and I did a virtual high-five! And to be honest, I may or may not have done a small twirl!

So, why are we so excited to be contributing this piece? First, we get to talk about esports, which is one of our favorite topics. Second, we get to share insights and knowledge about esports in Pakistan. Third, we get to talk about some of the amazing talent Pakistan has to offer. And, finally, we get to present our future plans for this space and pitch in front of all of you esports enthusiasts to partner with us and really grow this sector.

But before we get to that, let's take a step back and take a lay of the land and look at both the positives and the negatives.

The Pakistani government has launched substantive programs for digital competence and freelancing. Resultantly, Pakistan ranked third in revenue generated in the global freelancing market,[1] and the number of Pakistani freelancers skyrocketed from 4 percent in Q3 2018 to 42 percent in Q2 2019, cementing the country's position as number four in the top freelance countries ranking for 2019.[2]

Support for the tech sector has also resulted in a steady increase in tech exports. In the fiscal year 2020, Pakistan reported a 12 percent increase from $995 million to $1.11 billion in Pakistan's information technology (IT) and IT-enabled services export remittances.[3]

Unfortunately, in comparison, the country's economic share from the gaming industry is far too little, and there is substantial work to be done for the esports and larger gaming industry by the government before we can see such massive results in this space.

However, the good news is that, even without the government's intervention, with total winnings surpassing $4.28 million by 256 players, Pakistan ranks twenty-seventh out of 145 countries listed on esportsearnings.com and is ahead of Singapore at thirty-one, Turkey at thirty-three, India at sixty-two, and the U.A.E. at sixty-eight.[4] However, with 29 percent of the country's 212.2 million people[5] falling between the ages of fifteen to twenty-nine (roughly 61.5 million),[6] we should obviously have a lot more esports players and professional gamers.

The irony is that Pakistan produces twenty thousand IT graduates every year,[7] so, technically, there is no shortage of raw talent. But there is a shortage of skills-development opportunities, grooming, exposure, apprenticeship options, and access to finance, and there are cultural constraints and multiple other barriers that must be overcome.

All these reasons became the basis for Epiphany, a social enterprise working toward catalyzing impact, women, and microentrepreneurship in Pakistan since 2017 to enter this arena and start focusing on gaming and esports, smack in the middle of COVID-19.

Another reason for us to dive in is the economics. You already know this, but just to put it into perspective: The esports industry was worth $950.3 million in 2020 and is expected to surpass $1.6 billion by 2024,[8] making it one of the most lucrative industries across the globe.

At an individual level, Arsalan "Ash," a celebrity Tekken player from Pakistan and Red Bull Athlete, personifies the rags-to-riches fairytale in real life. Ash played for the first time at the international level at the 2018 King of Fighters Gulf Cooperation Council tournament in Oman, nailing wins in both King of Fighters XIV and Tekken 7. He took the world by storm when he started winning one competition after another, bagging three top esports awards, including the Player of the Year award for 2019.[9] Not only has he been able to become financially independent, but he also brought Pakistan into the limelight.

Since then, several Pakistanis have gone on to win internationally. With over \$3.6 million in winnings at Dota 2 competitions, Sumail Hassan ranks number eleven among the top players of the game.[10] He is also the youngest video gamer to exceed \$1 million in earnings in esports.[11]

At Epiphany, we believe there are hundreds of Ashs and Sumails out there, and we want to nurture this talent, especially in young women. As Pakistanis, we have grown up playing video and arcade games; every Pakistani in their late thirties and forties remembers inserting coins into arcade machines to play Pac-Man or playing Tetris on a Game Boy.

Still, when it comes to international tournaments, it was only in 2019 that PUBG (the publisher of PlayerUnknown's Battlegrounds) officially came to Pakistan, and the first authorized in-app tournament by the name of PUBG Mobile Pakistan Challenge was launched.[12] Unfortunately, however, government authorities do not fully grasp the potential of esports for Pakistan, and this year, we saw the Pakistan Telecommunication Authority (PTA) banning PUBG on July 1, 2020.[13] The ban was lifted after the Islamabad High Court directed the PTA to do so a few weeks later.[14] A lot of work still needs to be done before concrete steps are taken from the government's side to nurture this industry.

The challenge also remains on the financing side. Establishing an esports team, training them, and having them participate internationally are huge financial endeavors, and so far, limited players have risen to this challenge. By and large, individual gamers are to be credited for keeping this industry alive and buzzing.

With the recent interest by influencers and content creators in esports and gaming, the number of tournaments is growing as well. Other efforts to support this industry include Mountain Dew's annual esports event, Dew Arena, since 2018; Global Game Jam events in Pakistan since 2016; and some sponsored tournaments by esports enthusiasts. But consistent and sustained efforts are still required if we truly want to see Pakistan progress in this arena. This is, again, a major reason for Epiphany to enter this space: There is a lot of work to be done, and we should have started yesterday!

It is also frustrating, at times, that brands in Pakistan, both local and international with a presence in the country, are shying away from supporting this industry. We just need to glance across the border to see all this activity taking place in China and India and look where they are today.

Esports presents enormous untapped potential for brands to engage with different target audiences in large numbers. For instance, we have seen brands such as L'Oreal, Nike, and Gucci forming partnerships to promote esports. In fact, sponsorship accounted for 61 percent of the total esports revenue streams in 2020.

To sum up our vision, we want to attract more talent from Pakistan and other emerging economies in this space so these countries can experience great economic growth. On the other hand, we believe that esports and gaming present unequal opportunities to be inclusive and affect people from diverse backgrounds with diverse skill sets.

Now, let us recap Epiphany's journey to date. We started conducting gaming and esports-focused webinars from June 2020 and have, so far, hosted more than twenty-five sessions on various topics, including investment in the industry, programming as a career, indie game development, and the past, present, and future of esports. The good news is all of the content is available on Epiphany's YouTube channel (www.youtube.com/epiphanypakistan).

We also have a quarterly series called "Wonder Women in the Gaming World." Our first Wonder Women session featured women from Pakistan in different roles (QA, design, development, creative writing, etc.). Our next Wonder Women session featured women founders and leaders from the U.S., Brazil, and Canada. The next Wonder Women session in December 2020 showcased incredible female talent from Asia and the Middle East. We then held two Wonder Women sessions in March to celebrate International Women's Day featuring women in esports from Pakistan, U.A.E., Turkey, Zambia, Nigeria, Germany, U.K., U.S., Canada. The objectives of "Wonder Women in the Gaming World" are to highlight female role models who are making their mark in this industry, to attract more female talent to gaming, and to find solutions to the challenges faced by women in games.

Another initiative that we are undertaking is a series of game jams. Through game jams, we are aiming to enable people from all walks of life to create games. The first game jam was hosted in November 2020. There were sixty hours of nonstop fun, where developers, nondevelopers, and game designers, as well as novices, artists, writers, and anyone with a creative streak, were able to join in. A set of exciting workshops and seminars were also offered. Individuals and teams from all over Pakistan came together on the last weekend of November to create a theme-based game. The idea was to enable people to create their own games and realize how easy and fun that can be, to encourage them to interact with and learn from each other, and, of course, to draw more people into the industry. In the future, we would like to host women-focused game jams, as well as those centered on sustainable development goals.

Then, one more initiative, Celebrity Game Jam, is an interactive forty-five-minute online event showcasing successful faces from different professions—acting, music, media, entertainment, sports, banking, entrepreneurship, and venture capital. Celebrity Game Jams are meant to be fun interview sessions, where invited guests play a preselected game. While they are playing the game, the host asks them spontaneous questions (mostly related to the guests' experiences, including entrepreneurship) according to the evolving situation in the game.

A key objective behind Celebrity Game Jams is to encourage more people to explore careers as pro gamers. Through these Celebrity Game

Jams, we will also be highlighting dynamic women as much as possible. The first Celebrity Game Jam was with a super talented Pakistani woman who is a theater artist, comedian, content creator, improviser, actor, educator, and traveler.

MEET ASAD EHMED AND SAMAR HASAN

Asad Ehmed

Asad Ehmed is a serial entrepreneur, micro venture capitalist, startup architect, and consultant with extensive wide-ranging corporate and entrepreneurial experience in the Middle East and Asia. He is currently acting as chief strategy officer at Epiphany, helping to position the organization as a game changer in social, creative, and women entrepreneurship in Pakistan.

Asad possesses strong know-how in technology, games, entertainment, fashion, and retail businesses, as well as in-depth knowledge of economic mechanisms of ecosystems. With extensive industry knowledge rooted in the Middle East and North Africa (MENA) and Asia regions, he assists businesses in conceptualizing, implementing, and optimizing monetization-related processes. During his entrepreneurial journey, he cofounded successful tech and entertainment companies, including a tech venture studio, a gaming/entertainment company, and a VR technology studio. He was also a partner at a premium PR and event management company in the U.A.E., Lebanon, and Hong Kong.

Asad's experience in the gaming industry spanning Pakistan, Saudi Arabia, Jordan, and Ukraine, coupled with his passion to see the industry flourish in his home country, led him to co-create Epiphany Games in 2020 with his colleague Samar Hasan.

He remains focused on steadily growing the network of like-minded organizations and individuals to help push forward gaming and esports in Pakistan. Presently, he is conceptualizing future interventions to make this field socially acceptable in Pakistan while designing esports programs. Follow him online at:

linkedin.com/in/asadehmed
twitter.com/AsadEhmed
instagram.com/asad.ehmed

Samar Hasan

Samar is a seasoned professional and serial entrepreneur with over fifteen years of experience in nonprofit, corporate, social, and creative entrepreneurship sectors. A skilled communications specialist, Samar has been a passionate advocate of gender equality, financial inclusion, and economic empowerment of marginalized communities in Pakistan. She has been fortunate to have been part of life-changing projects: She helped launch a liberal arts and sciences university, a vocational and technical education center, a technology and entrepreneurship higher education institution, and a financial inclusion organization. She also led a nationwide PR and outreach campaign to provide one million trainings in digital skills and freelancing across the country.

Samar launched Epiphany in 2017 as an impact enterprise, catalyzing social, creative, and women-led businesses in Pakistan, where she designs entrepreneurship and skills-development curricula and provides strategic oversight, capacity-building support, and investment-related advice to microenterprises, startups, and small and medium enterprises. Samar has a panache for identifying market gaps, crafting innovative programs, and implementing them. One such experiment in the recent past is Epiphany Angels, a network of like-minded angel investors vested in spurring entrepreneurship in her country.

Epiphany Games is another vertical that Samar is co-heading with her colleague Asad Ehmed. Inspired by the tremendous economic opportunity available in the gaming and esports industry, they are on a mission to equip as many young people to enter this field as possible.

Samar is currently designing gaming and esports interventions for 2022 and beyond. Reach out to her at:

samar@epiphany.com.pk
linkedin.com/in/samarhasanofficial
twitter.com/SamarHOfficial

PART 4

Real
World
Benefits

CHAPTER 14

Forging Paths in Africa

A frica is an emerging gaming and esports market. There is no established esports blueprint or business model to follow here. If Africa follows the established esports models on other continents, it will need to factor in indigenous culture, sustainability, and scalability.

Every esports activation or engagement can be based on four stages of sustainability and scalability:

1. Awareness

2. Acceptance

3. Recognition

4. Expansion and evolution

The first stage is creating the needed awareness at all levels, from the home via parents to the governmental level, of the benefits of esports and its potential for socioeconomic development. After establishing awareness, the general acceptance of esports by all as a tool for development by government, brands, school systems, and parents is the next crucial step. The next stage is when brands and multinational corporations recognize the significance of esports and begin to invest huge financial resources to create the needed blueprint for national development.

Finally is the convergence of technology, entertainment, artificial intelligence, augmented reality, virtual reality, the internet of things (IoT),
education, and future applications of related technologies to support the
expansion and evolution of esports.

The reality of esports in Africa differs from that of other continents
in terms of hardware, software, people, internet penetration, culture,
and belief systems. While gaming on personal computers is prevalent in
other parts of the world, Africa is a console-dominant region with a passionate desire for simulated football or soccer games. The natural love
for these sports extends to a digital entertainment experience. Sporting
games are the most popular and favorite on the continent, as they dovetail into the exploits of African football players playing in the big football
leagues and exploits of nationals at international football tournaments.

Console dominance

In Africa, console gaming is king due to family and finance. Entertainment in Africa is family oriented, and therefore, a console at home is
a reward for the kids who behave well. For the most part, a console
is part of the family entertainment system in the living room, even
though it was purchased with the little boy in the house in mind. It
must be understood that most family homes in Africa have just one
television that serves a dual role: TV watching and as a display for the
family entertainment system.

The battle between console systems and PCs has been won basically
on their affordability. A console is cheaper, easier, and quicker to set
up, compared to a personal computer. Moreover, at the age when the
PC was introduced into Africa, it was an expensive machine designated
for office use or a professional environment rather than homes. With
this distinction, it's easy to see how consoles came to dominate personal
computers in the African gaming and esports space. The accessibility of

PC gaming has a long way to go on the continent and hinges on when it becomes more affordable.

Although PC use for gaming is slowly on the rise in Africa, the total cost of hardware setup is still generally too expensive for a single individual, so its spread has mostly been limited to the wealthy. But with current budget-friendly laptops being manufactured, more and more young and passionate young Africans are beginning to appreciate the PC-gaming landscape.

However, Africa does have a community of passionate gamers who have spent thousands of dollars assembling their own gaming gear. These are the exception: the working-class, tech-savvy individuals who work within the game developments space. They typically are in entertainment or have related careers in technology.

Mobile penetration reality

4G internet and affordable smartphones on the African markets have propelled the mobile esports space. There has been a tremendous increase and growth in communities that engage in mobile games, such as PlayerUnknown's Battle Grounds and Call of Duty Mobile. It is certain that mobile esports will take a lead on the continent soon, due to the availability of hardware, cellular data usage, and the lack of restrictions on location and ability to play from anywhere in the world.

Esports education

Esports in Africa should not only consist of tournaments and big prize pools. It also should focus on the principle of problem-solving, which is part of every electronic game. The principle of learning and acquiring knowledge via play is one that comes to kids first and that can be sustained with esports education programs tailored for kids to learn and explore. Esports also offers a wide spectrum of skill sets for future employment, and with that comes knowledge transfer.

Culture and tourism

Africa should leverage its diverse culture and tourism potentials to drive esports. This can be achieved by incorporating esports activation within the tourism and hospitality spaces. Festivals and celebrations on the continent can be used to promote esports development for the youth in its communities. These celebrations draw people from all walks of life and can also have an esports component in which citizens and guests can compete. As an added bonus, hospitality facilities like hotels can have esports as part of their calendar of activities for tourists who patronize their facility.

Football

The beautiful game of football, or soccer, is passionately loved by all Africans, young and old. Children across the continent are seen playing on dusky fields, training along city sidewalks, aspiring to become the next top football legend from Africa. That same passion can be seen in the youth who express their enthusiasm and energy by playing games.

Leveraging football will boost the growth of esports on the African continent, but most importantly, it will also open new opportunities for the entire football ecosystem to bridge with the youth who love the digital experience. This will provide alternative exposure of the sport to a younger audience that has a strong affection for esports and esports teams rather than traditional sports teams.

Partnerships to develop African esports

The African esports community is fast growing, and it needs both public and private partnerships to develop the industry. Africa needs businesses and individuals to explore the needed partnerships in Africa via tournaments, education, technology, community building, entertainment, tourism, and sportsmanship while engaging brands in technology and the emerging markets of Africa.

Population growth

According to the United Nations statistics, "there were 1.2 billion youth aged 15–24 years globally as of 2015, accounting for one out of every six people worldwide. This is predicted to increase to one out of every four people, which means there would be 1.3 billion youth by 2030."[1]

The above statement is true and presents both challenges and opportunities. The entire esports and gaming ecosystems present an avenue for tremendous alternative employment. They allow the creation of jobs and a better livelihood for young people while still allowing them to enjoy what they love to do with their peers.

The video game and esports industries in Africa are still nascent, but they have a growing following with over 70 percent of Africans under thirty-five years of age. This presents a great opportunity for Africa to work with the technology needed in the esports market.

Collaboration among African countries

For Africa to compete globally and sustain and scale up its esports space, the various countries need to collaborate effectively across the entire continent. We must create initiatives that bridge the gap and formalize a partnership to encourage the growth of esports in Africa.

Africa Esports Championship

The Africa Esports Championship is one of such initiatives to champion the African agenda: esports for Africa by Africans. The initiative is the first of its kind and has a reach of thirty African countries. With twenty active members in esports countries supporting this initiative, the African Esports League (AEL) Season 1 was held in Kenya, and due to the COVID-19 pandemic, the 2020 season was held online. This collaboration is bringing together a range of like-minded, self-driven entrepreneurs in esports in both private businesses and national federations.

It's important to understand the critical essence of this initiative and what it does for the African gamer. For us, it is our own esports "World Cup," where talent and professionals in Africa are recognized and given their own platform to excel in their chosen esports careers.

Africa games showcase

The AEL also recognizes indigenous African games and gaming studios. We believe in creating a greater awareness and support for locally made games and that showcasing them to our younger audience also opens up the space and presents opportunities within the game development sector.

About Ghana Esports Association

The Ghana Esports Association is an organization that acts as a bridge between government, industry, and community, coordinating efforts to create an environment that encourages amateur and professional esports in Ghana, from grassroots initiatives to full professional-level competition in esports and related technologies. The Ghana Esports Association is a membership body of esports in Ghana and a member of the International Esports Federation (IESF).

eSportsGhana is creating pathways for amateur and professional esports players, building a structure with the government, industry, and community in mind. eSportsGhana is also offering a centralized infrastructure for Ghana's digital gaming ecosystem, as well as supporting semiprofessional and professional teams, plus community-led projects and alternative education via esports- and videogame-related technologies.

A number of organizations are collaborating to form the foundation of eSportsGhana, bringing on board their various expertise and years of knowledge in their own efforts to make Ghana an esports nation.

Engagement

Esports is engaging with younger audiences, in particular. Esports is also a beneficial alternative solution to the negative and socially destructive tendencies of youthful exuberance. Esports requires quick thinking and direct participation from each player. There is also a strong sense of community in this sector. In addition, esports is creating thousands of new jobs across the world. This, in turn, is creating a fresh demand for people with specific skills forging career paths, which Africa needs.

MEET EBENEZER KWESI HAYFORD

Ebenezer Kwesi Hayford is developing esports collaborations with stakeholders in Ghana and internationally with the Ghana Esports Association, which focuses on grassroots participation and content creation.

Ebenezer has been instrumental in organizing esports events and helping professional gaming communities develop in Africa. He is also the founding member of the Africa Esports Championship. His dream to connect Africa with a championship tournament is currently ongoing, with twenty countries already on board and committed to the project. He is also a proud member of Africa Esports Championship and WeSCO.

Kiddie Esports is one of Ebenezer's initiatives to help kids develop a growing interest in esports and to build correct pathways via education, empowerment, and exposure.

Follow him online at:
linkedin.com/in/thekwesihayford
instagram.com/qkwecy
twitter.com/Kwecy

CHAPTER 15

Creating Social and Emotional Bridges

O ver the last few decades, video games have grown to be the largest global media industry with a reported net worth of over $174 billion.[1] Today, 75 percent of households in the United States have at least one person who plays video games.[2] The popularity of play among adolescents is particularly notable, with more than eight in ten teenagers (84 percent) reporting they have a game console at home or access to one, and 90 percent reporting they play video games on a computer, game console, or phone.[3]

As a form of technology, video games not only are entertaining but also provide the opportunity to communicate and interact, bridging the gap between unmediated play (such as board games or traditional sports) and mediated play (i.e., games played through a screened device). Video games allow individuals to connect from across the globe in shared, playful spaces that are accessible nearly anytime, anyplace.[4] The popularization of esports has also added a new dimension to the world of video games: playing games as a profession.[5]

The growth in scope and popularity of the video game industry has created increased debates about the potential negative impact of their use, such as increased aggression, addiction, and antisocial behavior.

While these topics are important to discuss (and have been at length),[6] [7] the focus on the potential negative impact of video game play has led to a diminished understanding about the potential benefits games may have as highly engaging and accessible digital tools.

Social and emotional benefits of video game play

The idea that people who play video games are basement-dwelling, socially isolated teenage boys is one that has been evident since the popularization of arcades.[8] This stereotype has been portrayed in television, movies, and countless internet memes, despite the fact that there is little scientific basis to these attributes among game-playing populations.[9] [10] Not only do females constitute about half of the game-playing population, but the average player is also in their midthirties.[11] Speaking specifically to the more social aspects of the stereotype, research has found that gamers do not report different levels of social support or general sociability than their offline counterparts.[12] [13] Researchers have also noted that online games do not cause any long-term negative effects on players' social abilities.[14] A similar lack of support for the other dimensions of the stereotype (e.g., lower life satisfaction, higher rates of loneliness, and obesity) has also been noted.[15] [16] Over the last few years, researchers have started to move beyond simply demonstrating the lack of validity of this stereotype and have started to explore the potential social and emotional benefits of video game play.

In particular, the social benefits of online gameplay have been well documented. This is, at least partially, due to the social nature of games themselves, with over 60 percent of gamers reporting they play games with others, either online or in person. Furthermore, about half of the most frequent players of online games (49 percent) report they "feel video games help them connect with friends."[17] While games may seem to be antisocial activities from the outside looking in (i.e., a player sitting alone at their computer wearing a headset), players are often connected to a space populated by hundreds or thousands of other players. Many of these games (particularly online) are also designed to encourage and facilitate social interaction among players through in-game challenges that often require a group to complete these challenges.[18] [19] While it may be possible to complete these challenges alone, doing so with a group of others makes the in-game tasks easier (and more enjoyable).

The social and emotional benefits of video games go beyond simple collaborative gameplay. Pena and Hancock found that emotional communication predominates in-game conversation, more so than task-oriented conversations.[20] Knowing this, it is not surprising that coplayers are often described as close, trusted, and valued friends, [21] [22] with up to 75 percent of online players reporting making "good friends" within their gaming communities.[23]

The mediated context of games plays an important role in helping to develop and support these friendships. Players have a level of anonymity (i.e., "you don't know me") and invisibility (i.e., "you can't see me") when playing online. Combined, these features create what is often referred to as the *online disinhibition effect*,[24] because they provide a sense of freedom to socially engage and experiment online without fear of real-world repercussions (e.g., being socially ostracized at school or work). These features have also been linked to increased self-disclosure and social closeness in a way that is not found in traditional face-to-face social contexts.[25]

Despite the wealth of positive social outcomes discussed above, there are still many dissenters who argue that relationships formed in online games are "weaker" and "less valuable" than more traditional social relationships in terms of both the quality of the friendship and the context in which they develop.[26] This contention largely stems from the reduced ability to send and receive nonverbal cues. In traditional face-to-face communication, we convey a wealth of information through nonverbal cues, such as facial expressions, gestures, and eye contact. Because these cues provide valuable social information that players cannot communicate through text or in-game avatars, the relationships formed in games are assumed to be more impersonal and less intimate than those supported by nonverbal communication.[27] [28] However, researchers have come to discover that the absence of these cues may actually be more beneficial than harmful in online communication. For example, a lack of nonverbal cues helps to support the online disinhibition effect,[29] which can stimulate open and intimate conversations by removing the fear of immediate social repercussions.[30] [31] Therefore, while a lack of nonverbal cues is traditionally thought to limit the quality of communication, without them, online games can provide a space that fosters increased intimacy between players than is traditionally found in offline communication.[32] [33] That said, some researchers have also noted that gaming spaces can accommodate—and have—for a lack of traditional nonverbal cues by offering emojis and other in-game gesture commands.[34]

Researchers have also noted links between gameplay and skill development, such as visuospatial skills,[35] [36] increased attention,[37] flexible thinking,[38] and creativity.[39] Online gameplay has also been linked to increased perspective taking,[40] leadership skills,[41] and reduced stress.[42] The positive effects of well-being may also be much broader, with recent work from Kowert demonstrating how video game play can contribute to various outcomes related to life satisfaction, including a growth mindset, mindfulness, and resilience.[43]

Online games are particularly effective tools for social and emotional skill development because of their provision of the communicative flexibility provided not only by the online disinhibition effect[44] but also by the playful nature of games themselves. The shared tasks of the game (e.g., fighting an enemy) are at the forefront and can guide most of the conversation while also mediating the pace. The pressure of having something to say and knowing when to say it is relieved by the game providing a perpetual cycle of conversation topics while also mediating the pace based on in-game actions.

For example, if someone asks a question, players have the ability to take time to carefully craft their answer, because any number of in-game tasks (i.e., fighting an enemy, traveling to a town, looking for a clue) could delay an immediate response. This, in and of itself, provides a range of social accommodations not found in face-to-face communication,[45] such as a reduced pressure to maintain and direct social communication[46] and send and receive nonverbal cues. These are abilities that some players may struggle with (e.g., those who are shy or socially anxious) and can overcome in an online gaming context. This can then lead to greater social success and the potential transfer of these skills into more offline, real-life contexts.

Out-of-game knowledge transfer

Video games are effective tools for learning, because they are fun (players are intrinsically motivated to play them) and because of their ability to induce players into a state of flow or a state of focused concentration. Flow is achieved when the challenge of the in-game tasks is balanced with the skills of the player.[47] The players become hyperfocused, often experience a distortion of time, and feel driven to continue playing, because they are having a good time. When in a state of flow, learning becomes optimized, as the player is hyperfocused on the in-game tasks and determined to complete them because their skills are being challenged. The social nature of games (i.e., playing with friends) can further reinforce this desire to continue playing.

While games are almost universally acknowledged for their potential to be used as effective learning tools, there is an open debate about players' ability to transfer this knowledge from the game to other contexts. It is important to not overstate the links between games in learning. While knowledge transfer from the game to other offline or online contexts does occur, the transfer tends to be quite narrow. This is part of the reason we do not see everyone who plays a first-person shooter (FPS) game display a new proficiency with firearms after playing, but we may notice an improved ability to see small changes in their visual environment. This is not to say that new skills cannot be developed. For example, many researchers have noted that leadership skills can be developed through online gameplay.[48] [49] However, games do seem to be more adept at honing preexisting skills, such as visual spatial skills,[50] creative thinking,[51] and problem-solving.[52]

Positive growth

Far too often, the discussion of video game effects is geared toward the negative, particularly addiction, aggression, and the assumed antisocial nature of gameplay itself. While these topics are worthy of discussion, the potential positive impacts of gameplay also deserve our attention.

It is time that games become more widely recognized as vehicles for positive growth, not the destruction of society. Rather than being considered antisocial, time-wasting activities, games are highly engaging, social spaces that have the potential to develop and hone a range of skills applicable in everyday contexts. They can also support the creation and strengthening of friendships and the development of skills in a way that is easily accessible anytime, anyplace.

MEET RACHEL KOWERT

Dr. Rachel Kowert is a research psychologist and research director of Take This, a mental health nonprofit that serves the gaming industry and community, and science content creator on YouTube, *Psychgeist*. She holds a PhD in psychology and an MA in counseling psychology. Dr. Kowert has dedicated her career to studying video games and the gamers who love them. As a researcher, psychologist, and parent, she strives to educate other parents about the potential dangers and unique contributions that video games can bring to our everyday lives. She has published multiple books and dozens of scientific articles on the subject. One of her most recent books, *A Parent's Guide to Video Games*, won an INDIES Award in science. She also published her first children's book in 2019, *Pragmatic Princess: 26 Superb Stories of Self-Sufficiency*. Follow her online at:

youtube.com/psychgeist
rkowert.com
twitter.com/DrKowert
linkedin.com/in/rachelkowert

CHAPTER 16

The Tree Tap Adventure

When I was two years old, my parents purchased a fixer-upper of a summer home on a tiny island about two hours from Toronto. While my family sanded, repainted, and renovated the cottage, I was often left to explore solo. For me, the island was my own little oasis, where my curiosity, independence, and fascination with the natural world grew.

To this day, there is an unassuming and, frankly, ugly book at the cottage. No one who visits ever pulls it off the shelf without being prompted to do so. It's a homemade work, crafted from yellowed drawing paper, with staples for the binding. The front has no writing, just some gold sparkle glue. I remember well the afternoon my father and I made it.

To help keep me occupied during those reno days, my father, a biology teacher, would task me with island exploration projects.

"Go around the island," he said, "and collect a leaf from every type of tree you can find, and when you come back, we'll name them together."

It sounds like a pretty mundane exercise, but to a five-year-old, having a mission like this was brilliant (both for myself and my parents). Every page of the book we created has one leaf taped to it and the name of the tree scrawled in messy handwriting below: juniper, red oak, white oak, birch, maple, baby maple, and so on. It's a childhood memory, a natural history survey, and a guidebook all in one. It was the spark that ignited the mobile game Tree Tap Adventure.

Early beginnings

I enthusiastically told this story to a friend and colleague, Jeremy, three years ago over coffee on a drizzly December morning. We met to discuss some ideas that had been brewing. Augmented and virtual reality (AR/VR) were gaining traction, and the technologies were becoming more accessible. We both come from a television production background and have worked on many great history and science documentary TV series. In AR and VR, we saw an opportunity to use these platforms to tell stories in new and possibly more engaging ways.

It's difficult to get the same response from audiences when comparing an adrenaline-pumping sequence of a hunting lion to one of a gray squirrel collecting acorns. The question for us was this: How do you elicit the same (or even greater) audience engagement with the more day-to-day events that happen in nature with critters that harvest nuts and seeds?

The keys to connecting with this audience, we believe, are in using new technologies like AR to literally augment the experience and gamify the content. In the same way that my father turned learning about leaves into a collection game for me, we can look at nature's common interactions and connections and turn these into simple games where educational content is built right into the activity.

One beauty of altered realities is the empathy and experience a player or observer gains by being able to step for a moment into the shoes of another. VR companies have done this well and are beginning to finally move beyond technology for technology's sake to thinking about how the medium can really be used to enhance how people see and experience the world through immersive storytelling. AR is getting there too, but we've really only scratched the surface of what's possible. However, we're hoping to inch things along with Tree Tap Adventure.

The adventure

Tree Tap Adventure is part collection, part role-playing, and part side-scroller, all blended together through storytelling to give players a sense of journey, immersion, and progression. We've designed the title to be played on a phone or tablet for two reasons: AR compatibility and mobility.

The game begins with a story and the player's mission. During a storm, an old oak tree that has been the home, shelter, resting place, and food source for animals over many centuries is suddenly lost. In the wake of the storm, the critters that once called the tree part of their home disperse except for two: a gray squirrel and a hummingbird. These characters find one remaining branch filled with acorns and ask for players' help in planting and growing the acorns into new oak trees and reuniting them with their forest friends.

The player progresses through a side-scroller game where players get to fly the hummingbird (and later other winged characters). These games unlock new habitats, with key critters, where the player can plant an acorn and then design and grow an oak tree that comes to life anywhere via AR. There are also augmented reality games within Tree Tap Adventure, where the player gets to step into the feet or paws of other characters and play single or multiplayer strategy games that speed up their overall game progression. Finally, when the player reaches a certain level, through partnerships with tree-planting initiatives, we will plant a tree in the real world alongside our digital forest.

Where possible, every chance to enhance the game with real science and information has been made. The side-scroller characters' flight patterns and styles match the species. The items collected and obstacles are real-world food items or predators. There are badges to collect with what we call "wow worthy" facts about the animals the players are uncovering and collecting. And the AR games have players perform real animal behaviors.

In addition, while keeping public safety in mind, we encourage the player to experience the AR portion of the game in a local park or a similar outdoor space. The player is also asked to move around with their device in those green settings. For those without a safe space, those with mobility issues, or where the weather simply isn't cooperating, we have created table-top AR games as well.

Tree Tap Adventure blends different genres in mobile gaming but falls under the blanket of casual gaming, a genre defined by short play length and limited complexity. Those who play in the casual genre want shorter play sessions, fewer rules, and simpler game mechanics in their video, online, or mobile games. Casual titles are designed to be played in shorter bursts of time and to provide an overall sense of entertainment without stressing the player out. The genre includes puzzles like match-three games, arcade games, and simulations like farming games. And the genre now includes AR.

Mass appeal and social community

The Tree Tap Adventures are also generally seen as games that appeal to mass audiences. With our goal of using the natural world as both the inspiration for and a feature of our game, this genre is the perfect fit. We want to create a fun, wondrous, and relaxing experience for players in the same way that a great nature documentary can inspire and entertain. We also want this game to appeal to as many people—young and old—as possible, and we're taking some inspiration and ideas from esports to help us with this.

In the same way that esports promote community and competition, we're also hoping to build a broad social community, organize competitive elements, and encourage teamwork through interactive play and the introduction of guilds.

Our strategy with our in-game and online presence is to develop a brand that is promoting outdoor play and social interaction. We have information and tips on our website and social media accounts for families seeking nature-based activities, so they can learn more about the natural world and ways to engage with their local community on these topics. We'll also be actively engaging with multiple online platforms and building a community of players and like-minded individuals to share tips that pertain to the game or the wider brand we hope to create.

With success, we would eventually like to increase the ways players can interact within the game and online. Guilds can be formed between friends that allow them to work together to progress and compete in game events. With this project and through our online community, we are aiming to build a brand beyond the game itself that promotes learning about nature, healthy social connection, and spending time outside.

Getting active

When we launched Tree Tap Adventures, we focused the competitive elements of gaming within the AR games. There are collection-based activities that ask players to run around seeking different items within a specific time and compete against a friend on the same device, a pass-and-play mode. We will eventually bring in global leaderboards for the AR and 2D games.

Since healthier bodies make healthier minds, in the AR games we have purposely asked players to get active. During early testing we noticed that this was really uncommon for people experiencing AR, but rather than eliminate it in favor of more familiar movements and gestures, we amplified it. We did this for two main reasons. First, between the ages of four and eight, fine motor skills and spatial awareness are developing in children. The more children are exposed to play that asks them to bend, move in multiple directions, balance on uneven ground, and increase their peripheral vision, the more advanced their coordination and observation skill sets will be throughout their entire life. Second, we all need more movement in our lives. Players of all ages can benefit from increasing their step count and stretching to collect AR objects on the ground. I've also discovered that time in green spaces is essential to my personal well-being, but it took me a little while to make that connection.

A career in science communications

My background and experiences are part of the driving force behind Tree Tap Adventure. While not knowing it at the time, and honestly confusing my family, I crafted a career in science communication. Not many kids decide to get a degree in biology and film and then a master's in international communications, but for some reason, I've always been passionate about sharing my love for science and nature with others, and you can't do that effectively without strong visual and communication skills. After college, while I was delving into the television industry, I also began working with a professor who was investigating the science and health curriculum in Canadian schools. Here, I was able to learn about how and what we teach children. Volunteer work with local environmental camps also gave me an insight into how important childhood experiences similar to mine are in developing necessary life skills.

What I've witnessed, however, is that the opportunities I had aren't accessible or available to many children around the world, for a whole host of reasons. For me, it comes down to knowledge and accessibility. Parents and educators are often not comfortable in the outdoors, purely because they haven't experienced it themselves and may be uncomfortable with the unknown. It's impossible to teach or be passionate about what you don't know, and for many, science is still one of those big, scary topics. Compounding this, city planners, governments, and their financiers have chosen to add more concrete and less green for short-term gains. The result is that many children are growing up without adequate exposure to natural environments, which can make them feel completely disconnected from nature and can negatively affect their mental and physical health. The phenomenon is described and documented as "nature-deficit disorder" by Richard Louv in his book *Last Child in the Woods*.

The benefits of nature on health and wellness

There are thousands of studies and books written about the myriad benefits of nature on health and wellness. For me, the most convincing element is that, as a species, humans have relied on and been in a relationship with the land and wilderness for hundreds of thousands of years. There's no way it's not connected to our well-being. Our stress levels drop significantly in nature. Even the smells have immune-boosting effects.

To combat nature deficit and bring people closer to the outdoors, we believe that through immersive storytelling, a blending of technologies, and cleverly executed education, we can bring back the endangered wild child. Through projects like Tree Tap Adventure, we want to use technology to give people a tool that allows them to take small steps toward increasing their comfort with the outdoors and nature.

Our hope is that, by gamifying educational content about nature and encouraging players to get outside, users will start to wonder—not at the animated characters in the game but at nature itself—and feel more comfortable exploring green areas near their homes and beyond.

We've created games to tell stories about critters that many people can find in their own backyard. Through the AR gamification, players can become these critters for a little while. We have created in-game prompts, will promote local park or backyard species observations through the game and on social media, and ensure all players know about our real-world tree-planting initiatives. In addition to learning by osmosis and through in-game facts, these AR games have been designed to promote developmentally advantageous movements and activity.

This type of AR, in particular, where players step into the shoes of another, can be useful in many areas of education, especially for children, where VR technologies are not recommended by health practitioners until they have reached at least thirteen years of age. From interactive fictional storytelling to natural history to ancient history, being able to empathize through another's experience is an incredible learning tool.

Jeremy and I joined the gaming world not as coders or tech-savvy people but as producers and writers who wanted to see how we could push the limits of storytelling through technology. Through our knowledge of science and the natural world, we were able to see connections that allowed us to embed this content within the gameplay itself.

Tree Tap Adventure began with a desire to share passion for the natural world by all involved. Through mobile gaming and immersive technologies, we hope these passions can spread to new generations and anyone looking for a casual game that is trying to make a difference.

MEET KALIN MOON

Over the last twelve years, Kalin has translated her diverse educational background in science, health, and media into a career focused on science and history-based documentary television, digital media, and science communication. She has worked as a research lead, writer, producer, and director, creating content for broadcasters that include VICE, Discovery, History, and BBC. She also has extensive experience with environmental and science communication, including serving as a volunteer with various Toronto-based outdoor organizations and through the Faculty of Education at University of Ontario Institute of Technology, where she published on science and health curriculum and co-created an educational website dedicated to children's health and wellness.

Tree Tap Adventure was created in partnership with Cream Productions, with funding support by the Canadian and Ontario governments and additional support from Toronto-based universities and colleges. Follow her online at:

instagram.com/kalinmoon

facebook.com/treetapadventure

linkedin.com/in/kalin-moon

treetapadventure.com

CHAPTER 17

Forming Social Connections

In 2019, approximately two-thirds of the global online population played digital games[1] for myriad reasons—namely, because games are enjoyable, enable escapism and immersion, and allow players to challenge themselves. Likewise, 2019 saw the continued rise of esports and digital game livestreaming—domains in which people engage for entertainment, to learn about their favorite game, to escape from the real world, to compete and challenge themselves, and to satisfy a need for power.

But gaming needs to be seen as more than just a pleasurable pastime or competitive hobby. It also nurtures well-being by helping players recover from stress, repair bad moods, build self-esteem, promote mindfulness, explore difficult emotions, and cope with challenging life situations like grieving a loved one or getting over a breakup. Beyond these individual benefits, adults and children also play games to socialize with others. The majority of adult gamers in 2019 played in multiplayer mode with others for an average of 4.8 hours per week online and 3.5 hours per week in person, because they feel that video games help them connect with friends and family.[2]

At the same time, there has been increasing interest and participation in esports, professional video game play performed for spectators and undertaken by expert players within the paradigms of competitive sporting contexts (e.g., leagues, sponsored teams, and bracketed tournaments). The meteoric rise of esports is rapidly changing the landscape of digital games, livestreaming, and how we conceptualize and understand gaming communities. This cultural shift is driven by the rapid growth of the esports audience—with spectatorship of esports potentially reaching 474 million viewers in 2021.[3] This growth is also reflected fiscally: The entire esports revenue landscape was estimated at $24.9 billion USD in 2020,[4] with the largest esports prize pool to date ($34 million) nearing that of the Wimbledon tennis championships (£34 million).

This rise of social gaming, alongside the rise of esports and livestreaming, is happening at the same time as decreasing social connectedness threatens our well-being.[5] Humans need to form lasting and caring relationships to feel like they belong, but the social connectedness has declined over the past decade. Loneliness harms our well-being, and with fewer people feeling like they have relatives or friends they can count on to help in a time of need, this represents a crisis in mental health. Research has shown that people who feel isolated have an increased risk of mortality, are subject to impaired executive functioning, and interpret neutral information in a hostile way.[6] For lonely people, the world is a more threatening and dangerous place. A Minister of Loneliness was even appointed in the U.K. in 2018 to help address the problem of social isolation.

Interestingly, loneliness is highest among eighteen- to thirty-year-olds,[7] which is the same age range of adults with the highest proportion of gamers.[8] Given the rise of multiplayer digital games and esports in a context of rising loneliness, it seems timely to further explore how the relationships that are formed and maintained through digital gaming and esports engagement—including playing together, interacting over streams, training and competing in teams, attending virtual and physical esports events and tournaments, and interacting about games over third-party systems (e.g., Discord)—can help gamers.

Games for good

Digital games—played together in person or online—can help us connect to others, maintain existing relationships, facilitate the development of trust with strangers, and even combat loneliness. Stereotypes about the antisocial, lonely gamer have long been shown to be inaccurate, with players viewing games as a social medium on which they want to form and maintain friendships. In one study, researchers showed that World of Warcraft players use the game as a platform to maintain existing relationships, form new ones, and even find romantic partners.[9] This study was the first to apply the concept of social capital to in-game relationships, a framework that introduces social networks as resources that, when fostered, return value to an individual in the form of social support and personal information-sharing that can improve well-being.[10] There are two kinds of relationships discussed in the social capital framework: bridging ties and bonding ties. Bonding ties refers to strong relationships in which people feel emotional and social support and are characterized by strong personal connections (perhaps lacking in diversity of perspective and context) that provide mutual and substantive emotional support. Conversely, bridging ties are characterized as tentative relationships that may lack depth but make up for it in breadth. They broaden an individual's social horizon, as they expose us to different worldviews, opinions, and resources.

Early research (2005–2010) has shown that relationships enacted within games like World of Warcraft, Second Life, and Counter-Strike are capable of generating social capital, but generally agreed that social gaming was more likely to lead to bridging ties (tentative relationships that lack depth but offer breadth) than bonding ties (strong relationships).[11] [12] [13] More recent work (2016–present) further investigated the properties of games and the gamers, demonstrating that playing with online and physical friends in Destiny built bonding ties; whereas, playing with online friends and strangers built bridging ties.[14] Furthermore, Depping and colleagues found that interdependent and benevolent gaming communities facilitated both bridging and bonding capital in games and that both were associated with reductions in loneliness outside of the game.[15]

We have also seen an increase in socialization through esports. Social integrative motivations have been identified as a primary predictor of engagement in professional play and video game livestreams (dominated, in terms of viewership, by professional players). Both bridging and bonding social capital built in esports clans has been found to be positively associated with offline social support in the form of advice, assistance, and listening.[16]

The context of esports allows professional players to both seek out and experience social support, emerging in the form of emotional and esteem support from other players. This support likewise positively influences the players' in-person interactions and relationships external to competitive gaming.[17] Likewise, fans are similarly motivated to engage with livestreams for the purpose of socialization, social engagement, sense of community, and meeting new people. In fact, these social motivations appear to contribute to greater participation than in other domains, with esports fans showing more dedication and desire to engage with esports content than in traditional (e.g., physical) sporting arenas.[18]

Despite these benefits, it is important to remain cognizant of the potential drawbacks of social play. We know that the same mechanics, games, and gaming contexts that foster social closeness in games can instead lead to toxic game environments or displace offline relationships, resulting in feelings of harmful social exclusion. One popular controversy that enjoys significant media attention concerns "problematic gaming" (characterized by a lack of control over gaming and time spent playing), which has been associated with a range of harms to our physical and psychological well-being. Finally, social gaming can become problematic when it exposes players to toxicity in online gaming, especially when players engage in anonymous and impersonal interactions or in environments (e.g., competitive esports platforms) where negative behaviors are normalized.

The potential value or damage that results from social gameplay and esports engagement can have a great impact on players, but existing, contrasting evidence makes it challenging to reconcile whether social play harms or helps well-being. Nonetheless, research does point to the numerous social and well-being benefits garnered from engaging in social and esports play. While we need to remain cautious of the potential drawbacks of social play, it is also important—in a climate of reduced social connection—to acknowledge, support, and encourage play environments that foster social connectedness and bonding for players.

Furthermore, it is necessary, so we can combat problematic gaming, game-related social isolation, and game-related toxicity while simultaneously promoting social gaming and esports as an appealing leisure activity that provides enjoyment, recovery, and social connectedness for the millions of gamers who benefit from its captivation.

MEET REGAN MANDRYK AND MADISON KLARKOWSKI

Regan Mandryk

Regan is a professor of computer science at the University of Saskatchewan and a Tier 1 Canada research chair in digital gaming technologies and experiences. She pioneered the area of affective physiological evaluation for computer games in her PhD research with support from Electronic Arts. With over two hundred publications that have been cited over ten thousand times (including one of Google Scholar's ten classic papers in human-computer interaction from 2006), she continues to investigate novel ways of understanding players and their experiences, but also develops and evaluates games for health and well-being and games that foster interpersonal relationships.

Regan has been the invited keynote speaker at several international game conferences. She has led games research in the Canadian GRAND Network. She also organizes international conferences, including the inaugural CHI PLAY, the inaugural CHI Games Subcommittee, and

CHI 2018, and leads the first-ever Canadian graduate training program on games user research (SWaGUR.ca) with $2.5 million of support from the Natural Sciences and Engineering Research Council of Canada. She was inducted into the Royal Society of Canada's College of New Scholars, Artists and Scientists in 2014, received the University of Saskatchewan New Researcher Award in 2015, the Canadian Association for Computer Science's Outstanding Young Canadian Computer Science Researcher Prize in 2016, and the prestigious E.W.R. Steacie Memorial Fellowship in 2018. Follow her online at:

linkedin.com/in/regan-mandryk-b69a9434
twitter.com/reganmandryk
goo.gl/PPifWA

Madison Klarkowski

Dr. Madison Klarkowski is an assistant professor with the Computer Science Department at the University of Saskatchewan, Canada. She specializes in games user research and player experience evaluation and has been a dedicated player of competitive games since childhood. To this end, it was perhaps inevitable that one of her first initiatives as an academic was to develop a program of research investigating esports. Madison hopes to pivot her research background in video game challenge, player experience, and player well-being to assess and support expertise in esports, inform understanding of esports communities, and explore the translational ability of advanced gameplay.

When Madison isn't studying games, she spends her time playing them, watching them, and occasionally remembering to go outside and get hopelessly lost on beautiful hiking trails. You can find her online at:

linkedin.com/in/mklarkowski
twitter.com/MadaPotion

PART 5

The Business of Esports

CHAPTER 18

A Look at Brands and Rights Holders

E ndemic brands—companies directly and inherently linked to gaming, such as software and hardware manufacturers—have long been a staple of the esports industry, with teams, tournaments, live events, and streamers sponsored or partnered with hardware companies. It made sense for these hardware companies, because they were directly engaging with their target audience and the people who needed to buy their products to have a good gaming experience.

A great example of this took place in the early 2000s, when Intel sponsored esports teams in the United Kingdom, Germany, Sweden, and France. This enabled Intel to promote their products in local markets and on a global level when those teams competed in international tournaments. Intel went one step further and sponsored several of the leading international tournaments, such as the Cyberathlete Professional League, in the United States, which, at the time, was the pinnacle of international competition. This enabled Intel to be associated with the leading teams and tournaments and to generate constant awareness of the Intel brand and products.

Since that time, Intel has continued to be heavily involved in the esports space and now has the title sponsorship of one of the largest and most watched global esports tournaments. The Intel Extreme Masters tournament entails a reported $100 million being spent on a multiyear deal with tournament operator ESL (formerly the Electronic Sports League), which operates the tournaments and live events around the world on behalf of Intel.

Nonendemic brands entering the space

For many years, nonendemic brands—those with no obvious inherent tie to gaming—were unsure about getting involved in the esports space, because a lot of the top esports game titles were shooting games. Then, titles such as League of Legends joined the landscape and started to build a large player audience and viewership. This sort of game presented an alternative for those nonendemic brands that were not able to activate against the shooting titles. As League of Legends grew further, Riot Games, the creators of the game, established structured leagues and broadcasts, and this further enticed nonendemic brands.

Esports is a way for nonendemic brands to do three things: diversify from traditional TV advertising, advertise to a different segment of the population, and build brand affinity with an audience with higher levels of disposable income.

Diversifying from traditional TV advertising has increased in importance due to research suggesting that some segments of the population, like those who watch esports, don't watch any traditional TV or sports on TV. Thus, the money spent by nonendemic brands on traditional sports sponsorship does not reach parts of this esports and gaming audience. Research also indicates that this gaming audience (players and viewers) is more educated, with more disposable income than other segments, which leads nonendemic brands to see it as a great new opportunity.[1]

Games like Fortnite are also entertaining a slightly younger audience, who will be the buyers of tomorrow. Because of this, car manufacturers are looking at advertising in esports as a long-term strategy so they can build relationships with an audience that already wants to purchase and the younger audience that could be future customers. This realization has seen more nonendemic companies getting involved in esports too, including Mercedes, BMW, Toyota, Kia Motors, Snickers, Mountain Dew, Coca-Cola, Sephora, Chipotle, AirAsia, the European telecommunications company Orange, Verizon, AT&T, Vodafone, SAP, Barclays Bank, Kappa, Champion, Nike, Adidas, and many more.

The level of involvement of nonendemic brands differs by brand and by geography. Some of these brands choose to sponsor teams to have consistent visibility during multiyear contracts. This mirrors what is already common in traditional sports for jersey sponsorships or naming rights. Other nonendemic brands are sponsoring tournaments to gain visibility with a critical reach in a short time with tournament branding and online viewership of the tournaments. Leading esports tournaments can attract hundreds of thousands of viewers to these online broadcasts. Today these broadcasts are even being localized for key markets and languages, enabling nonendemic brands to focus on the type of audience that matters most.

McDonald's Denmark, for instance, undertook what could be termed a guerrilla marketing campaign in Copenhagen. They didn't sponsor the tournament; instead, they used the areas close to the venue to attract these prospective customers. To get to the venue, attendees had to walk across several bridges, so McDonald's placed advertising banners along these bridges promoting their different product options.

The brilliant part of this campaign was the messaging used to describe a Big Mac or a box of Chicken McNuggets was directly related to the game being played in the tournament: Counter-Strike: Global Offensive, a shooting game where players had to buy new items and equipment at the start of each round. McDonald's played on this by aligning their products with different equipment scenarios. For example, if players don't have enough money in the game to buy all the equipment they need, it's referred to as an "eco" round. Similarly, if they have enough money and can get all the equipment and items they want, they call it a "full buy." McDonald's used this in their message to present a Big Mac Meal (with all the extras) as a full buy; whereas, a portion of fries and other single items were referred to as an eco-buy. They even had pictures of each product with the relevant game terminology beneath it so the event attendees could clearly see how each product compared.

This campaign generated lots of coverage and positive discussion on social media, because McDonald's had understood the game and the audience. And because of this, they were able to create something relevant and meaningful for their audience and reaped the positive results.

DHL is a global delivery company, like FedEx or UPS. For an event in Germany, they realized there was an opportunity to educate event attendees and viewers about how they operated by linking it to the game. Dota 2 was the game being played at this tournament event, and one aspect of the game is that items can be bought from an in-game shop and delivered to the players wherever they are on the map. DHL realized this linked to core elements of their business, especially in their warehouses, where they have little portable robots that follow their staff. And when products are collected from a shelf, the robot takes the product or package to the delivery point.

DHL created two parts to their campaign at the tournament event. First, they worked with a content influencer who walked around the event with one of the DHL robots and gave away prizes. This mirrored the scenario in the DHL warehouse. Second, they created some video content showing their robot inside the game acting as the delivery mechanism for the items the players had bought from the in-game shop. This combination of relevant campaign activities led to the audience chanting the name DHL in the main event arena.

Rights holders and esports

Rights holders are also starting to move into the esports space, such as those who own sports teams, tournament brands, or event brands.

This category can include holding groups, governments, and federations. Globally recognized rights holders include the NFL, the NBA, the English Premier League, FIFA, and Formula 1. It's become so effective that leading sports rights holders have chosen to expand their offering into the esports and gaming space for three reasons.

First, it enables those rights holders to engage with their existing fans in a different way. The NBA has created a league structure using the NBA2K game, with most of the NBA franchise teams recruiting gamers to represent them in the NBA2K League. Formula 1 has seen a similar structure using the game version of Formula 1, with each of the teams recruiting sim racers (the name for drivers in racing games) to represent them in the gaming championship. This gives Formula 1 fans an additional version of the team to support, just as NBA fans can in the NBA2K game.

The second reason rights holders have expanded into esports and gaming is because it enables them to access an audience that may not be fans of the traditional sport. Research suggests that a portion of the U.S. audience on Twitch (a game-streaming platform) doesn't watch any sports. For rights holders to access and engage with this audience, they need different mechanisms, and gaming offers an alternative.

The third reason pertains to branding and sponsorships. Having an esports and gaming version allows the rights holders to sell additional sponsorships, because they have more properties and inventory that a company could advertise on than if they just had the physical version of the sport. For example, the naming sponsorship of the gaming league could be separate from the naming sponsorship of the physical league.

During the COVID-19 pandemic, a lot of sporting leagues and clubs turned to esports and gaming when physical matches and activity were not possible. The English Premier League, for example, hosted an invitational event using pro footballers, while Formula 1 hosted a "Not the Real Grand Prix" series with virtual races using the official Formula 1 game. These virtual races had real Formula 1 drivers participating, along with a mix of other sporting stars, celebrities, and content creators.

Both examples were broadcast online across YouTube and Twitch. Sky Sports, in the United Kingdom, broadcast the virtual Formula 1 races on multiple channels, because they had no other content available when there were no physical races taking place. Other examples of sports rights holders using esports and gaming during the COVID-19 pandemic include the MLS, the U.S. professional soccer league, U.A.E. Arabian Gulf League, and MBS, the Saudi Professional League.

Another area that brands and rights holders are exploring is the blockchain and NFT space. NFTs are "non-fungible tokens"—essentially a digital asset that can appreciate in value due to limited quantity or rarity. The NBA has released a mobile app called TopShot in which users purchase packs of digital content. This digital content includes video clips from NBA matches, and each clip has an identifier of what quantity will be produced and a rarity level. The more rare the card, the more highly valued it will become with people bidding to purchase it from the owner. A key point here is that the owner no longer becomes the rights holder, the owner is the person who gained the video clip from opening the pack. This creates a trading market for the NFTs (the video clips that are digital assets) and introduces game-style mechanics, such as sets of clips to collect, challenges for clips of certain rarities, challenges for clips related to specific players or teams, and a range of other mechanics.

The learning gained from seeing what works in the games industry is now crossing over, and it won't be long before we see brands also using NFTs as a means of engagement. Brands could work with game owners to create special NFTs that act as boosters inside the game, or unlock special content, and the brands could exclusively distribute access to the Tokens through their own channels to boost engagement. This approach could also be introduced to the viewing audience of esports tournaments who have a chance to win NFTs related to the game they are watching.

We're still in the beginning stages of brands and rights holders entering esports, with many going through a cycle of learn–evaluate–commit.

As budgets continue to shift toward digital formats and decisionmakers become people who grew up with gaming and esports, the trend of brand and rights holder involvement will continue. Entry into any new market has its challenges and pitfalls to avoid, but with less brand clutter than many traditional sports, the new frontier is definitely esports.

MEET PHILIP WRIDE

Philip has been involved in the esports industry for over twenty years. His experience includes management of the world's best esports teams and operating national and international qualifier tournaments and events. As a semi-pro esports player in the U.K., he played the game Counter-Strike for ten years.

Philip has worked with global game publishers such as EA Sports, Square Enix, and Disney. At EA Sports Philip was the U.K. community manager for the FIFA game between 2009 and 2011. He has also developed esports strategy and campaigns for companies such as Intel, Microsoft, and Telefonica.

Philip's media work on esports includes articles for *PC Gamer* and *PC Zone* magazines in the U.K. as well as articles for the BBC Technology website. He also wrote the esports section in the 2008 edition of the *Guinness Book of World Records*.

More recently, Philip has been operating the specialist esports marketing agency Cheesecake Digital, which helps guide and educate brands, rights holders, governments, and event organizers about esports. Follow him at:

linkedin.com/in/philipwride

CHAPTER 19

AirAsia Flying High

Before I joined AirAsia, I was a college dropout and pursued my passion as an entrepreneur in the paintball industry, an extreme sport, for ten years. For the uninitiated, AirAsia is one of the largest low-cost airlines in Southeast Asia, with over 200 Airbus planes and over 20,000 employees. I worked in various roles such as esports, regional marketing, partnerships and business development, ancillary income, corporate culture, employee engagement, and internal branding. I stumbled upon esports and gaming by chance when a pilot came up to me and shared that our co-founder and Group CEO, Tony Fernandes, was aware about it. After conducting a lot of research, I realized the immense potential of esports in terms of its growth potential and wanted AirAsia as a brand to ride the wave. The number of eyeballs and projections was amazing and too difficult for any marketer to ignore.

Any brand or company that's not involved in esports as a part of its marketing initiative is really behind the curve. Even traditional ad agencies in Southeast Asia are lagging behind, but they're trying to play catchup now. The esports landscape in Southeast Asia is exciting, with the 2019 and 2021 Southeast Asian Games, also known as the SEA Games, having six and ten gold medals, respectively, for esports in a variety of game genres. The SEA Games is a biennial multisport event involving participants from eleven countries in Southeast Asia. The games are under the regulation of the Southeast Asian Games Federation with supervision by the International Olympic Committee (IOC) and the Olympic Council of Asia (OCA).

Even the Indonesian government is all-in for esports, by organizing the Esports Presidential Cup, the biggest competition for online gamers in the country. The Esports Presidential Cup is in line with President Jokowi Widodo's mandate to develop sportsmanship values, national values, and the economy and will play a major role in making esports mainstream in Indonesia. In Malaysia, the government allocated a dedicated budget for the country's esports industry; US$10.8 million of the country's national budget towards the development of the local esports industry for three years in a row from 2019 to 2021. The Ministry of Youth and Sports Malaysia has even drafted out a comprehensive five-year national esports blueprint for developing the esports industry and eco-system in the country.

Esports and employee engagement

It's not uncommon for companies to have football clubs, badminton clubs, bowling clubs, and so on. Therefore, why not create an esports club for employees? By creating esports teams internally, corporations can compete against each other. And that's exactly what we did at AirAsia. Chances are your employees are already into the gaming culture, so why not embrace it?

Naturally, there is a fit with an airline brand, as we believe the next generation will be flying around for esports events. My boss at AirAsia, Tony Fernandes, is surprisingly knowledgeable about esports. He even mentioned it in his book, *Flying High*. In June 2017, a pilot came up to me and said, "Allan, Tony knows about esports. And Tony knows about Twitch."

I thought, *Wow, my boss knows a lot!* I had to Google esports and Twitch. What caught my attention was that it was a high-traffic spectator sport. If I was going to propose anything related to esports, I knew I had to justify the return on investment (ROI). For example, I needed to know what specific genre captured the attention of a particular demographic and how many people were watching or participating in a particular esports title. And to be honest, even with the research I did, it took me a while to come on board. I just wasn't convinced, as it would require a lot of work to get internal buy-in from senior management. So, we did an internal survey on our staff via our internal communications platform, Workplace by Facebook. We asked around to see who was actually interested in esports and if they play any games. We had over two hundred responses, which was encouraging. But then we had to convince senior management about the potential of esports. And this was back in 2017, when esports was still relatively unknown in our country.

Well, senior management was game, so we started by creating a team jersey. I spent my own money, about 4,000 ringgit (US$960) for one hundred customized esports jerseys for our AirAsia Allstars Esports Club, to be distributed to senior management and key opinion leaders within the company. The program was still in its infancy stage. We didn't have an esports budget, so I couldn't even get reimbursed. But I took a chance and bought the jerseys and printed my colleagues' names at the back of the jerseys. I considered it a small investment in order to create internal awareness on esports. I gave one to Tony Fernandes, the co-founder and group CEO of AirAsia. It went viral internally and then, the next day, Datuk Kamarudin Meranun's (the co-founder and executive chairman of AirAsia) personal assistant messaged me. It turned out Datuk Kamarudin wanted his own esports jersey too! I went over to his residence with his jersey in hand and pitched him my proposal for AirAsia to get involved in esports. He was impressed with the "creating internal awareness on esports" via the esports jersey initiative. Thanks to his son, Ikhlas Kamarudin, who mentioned to Datuk Kamarudin that I invested in the esports jerseys, so much so that Datuk Kamarudin reimbursed me for them.

After that meeting, we started a pilot project with an internal team. People from all walks of life joined: engineers, cabin crew, and pilots— we shared one thing in common; all of them were gamers! We visited a local esports event organized by the government and participated in Dota 2 and FIFA. There was lots of media coverage, and the best part is that it became free PR for AirAsia.

We also organized internal tournaments to embrace our community. And it paid off. We held esports tutorials during lunch hours and organized our own internal esports tournaments. We even hosted esports trainings in the office after work hours. Morale was high, momentum was building.

I was touring with teams across the region, and we were gaining market recognition. So, we kept building and integrating with the gaming culture. We sent our employees around the region and played against the Big 4 accounting firms, which have their own esports clubs. Petronas, Malaysia's petroleum conglomerate, has about twelve Dota teams, and almost every college in Malaysia, both public and private, has their own esports club. We participated in in-college versus corporate esports tournaments

We signed sponsorship deals with big gaming brands such as Razer, Alienware, and Secretlab for our employee esports team, the AirAsia Allstars Esports Club. All three companies supplied equipment for the AirAsia Esports Zone, a dedicated gaming space built at AirAsia's global headquarters, RedQ.

In addition to operating our internal esports program, AirAsia acquired Mobile Legends's organization team, Saiyan, rebranding them as AirAsia Saiyan, and we also sponsored one of the best Dota 2 teams in the world, Mineski. AirAsia went on to sponsor the WESG SEA (World Electronic Sports Games Southeast Asia), an esports tournament IP owned by Alisports (the sporting arm of the Alibaba Group), a milestone moment for our brand in the esports world.

Not only did we become an active brand in the esports space, but we also started a growing trend wherein companies use esports programs to attract the younger generation as part of their employer branding program.

We are one of the first in the region to actually get involved on such a deep level. Our esports team, AirAsia Saiyan, competed in a title called Mobile Legends: Bang Bang, a mobile multiplayer online battle arena (MOBA) title that barely registers as a blip on the Western radar but is a phenomenon in Southeast Asia.

There's no Team Liquid or 100 Thieves of Mobile Legends: Bang Bang. It's all regionally based, and that's what makes it attractive to the local audience, to follow a team that is the same nationality as them. Having traveled extensively as part of my esports crusade, I was particularly startled by mobile gaming's status as a second-class esport in the West, while the opposite has been the norm for some time in Asia.

I went to an Indonesian esports tournament, and they had four mobile games on the center stage. The previous year, Dota was on the center stage, and mobile games were played on the bean bags. What a stark contrast in just a year. You can see all types of people playing a mobile game, versus a PC game, which is not so attainable. Though it has become something of a conference cliché, Southeast Asia remains the fastest developing region in esports. In fact, Malaysia lies right in the middle of the esports revolution. In 2018, it appointed Syed Saddiq Syed Abdul Rahman, a Dota 2 player and esports advocate, as minister of youth and sports, making him the youngest minister in the country's history.

While local telecoms look to plant their flags with white-label events, East Asian tournament organizers also have ambitious plans. They are looking for a stronger foothold in the Southeast Asia market. And what better way than to partner with a brand that's esports ready and esports educated? AirAsia fits the bill because we are a regional airline. It was the right time at the right place. Part of the activation is flying players to and from tournament locations, all of which fits into AirAsia's greater plan of building an esports tourism industry.

My advice to other brands is this: You should come in slowly but surely. You don't have to start with a big marketing budget for esports. Instead, allocate maybe 5 or 10 percent of your overall marketing budget toward esports and test it out as a pilot program. Obtain the results, and build a robust case study to obtain bigger budgets the following year. Also, most importantly, talk with the esports community to get their feedback and to brainstorm ideas. I spent a lot of time communicating with them.

Usually, big companies take two years before entering the esports space, one year for market research and attending esports tournaments, another year for budget approvals. AirAsia did it in less than six months, and we gained first-mover market advantage. If you are not from a generation that grew up with esports, you need to get out there on-ground and experience it in person. It is still a largely untapped market, and the customer lifetime value is every marketer's dream, especially with the hard-to-reach demographics of Millennials, Generation Z, and Generation Alpha. Marketers, it's game on!

MEET ALLAN PHANG

Allan Phang is the chief marketing officer at Galaxy Racer, the largest esports, gaming, and lifestyle organization with over 100 content creators across the Middle East, North Africa, and Southeast Asia, over 500 million followers, over 2.5 billion monthly views, and over ten esports teams in over 20 countries.

Allan is a keynote speaker for TEDx Talks and global conferences in the USA, Europe, the Middle East, and Asia. He was invited to share on exports with marketers, business leaders, and government officials. Allan's previous esports campaign in AirAsia was highlighted as a success story and case study in "World Federation Advertisers (WFA): Esports Special Report" and garnered global coverage. Follow him online at:

linkedin.com/in/allanphang

instagram.com/allanphang

CHAPTER 20

The Keys to Brand Success in Esports and Gaming

To say that the global popularity of competitive gaming is exploding is an understatement. Thirty million people are tuning in to Twitch to watch live gaming content on each day.[1] There were over 2 billion gaming-specific tweets in 2020 alone,[2] and Fortnite saw $2.5 billion in profits in 2020[3]—purely on brag-worthy cosmetic items. Cord-cutters, cord-nevers, and all the other segments of the Millennial and Gen Z landscape are forging a new kind of fan experience through gaming and esports.

What was once considered a niche activity for a passionate core is now recognized by entire industries, as gaming inspires and evolves entertainment—across sports, music, and film. These subcultural intersections that activate across fandoms and communities allow esports and gaming to set themselves apart as a highly valuable and dynamic convergence, due in large part to gaming's recent growth. Since 2020, there has been a 75 percent increase in gaming conversation on Twitter—49 percent of which consisted of new participants.[4] Alongside that, streaming hours watched per day on streaming services like Twitch, YouTube, and Facebook Gaming also saw an 80 percent year over year increase in 2021, with 97 million hours watched of live streams per day,[5] while digital spend on games increased 30 percent year-over-year.[6] This record-breaking growth across all forms of engagement—watching, playing, and socializing—not only showcases how gaming has become a more established mainstream experience, but also its flexibility and creativity as a platform. As a result, we've seen the gaming space provide a depth of innovative and first-of-its-kind opportunities for brands, entertainment properties, and game communities.

With more brands recognizing this audience's value, the expansive opportunity, and the cultural trendiness around gaming communities, we have seen steady growth of brand sponsorship in gaming and esports across a wide range of brand categories. However, some brands do not always have the tools and knowledge to necessarily find success as they dive into their first gaming initiatives. Esports is a fragmented and complex space, but if you seek out those early adopters who have taken the leap—or at least dipped their toes into the test-and-learn pool—you will hear success stories that speak to an intense, passionate, and engaged affinity group that represents the ultimate moving target on advertiser radars.

The old cliché that gamers are either kids with no purchasing power or social misfits is long outdated and is not a true representation of the value that esports and gaming can offer. In fact, 73 percent of worldwide esports fans are the highly coveted, digital-first 16- to 35-year-old millennial or Gen Z audience with significant purchasing power.[7] 34 million gamers in the U.S. play on average 22 hours a week, and half do not have a paid TV provider.

Due to the significant value, whitespace, and maturation of gaming, now is the time for brands to get involved. Here are some tips on how nonendemic brands can succeed in this vibrant space.

Finding the right opportunities: using fragmentation to your advantage

The landscape of gaming and esports features a multitude of popular and new titles, leagues, tournaments, and teams, each with a diversely unique community and fandom. At first, it may look intimidating and appear complex to navigate. However, this fragmentation is to a brand's advantage. With multiple entry points, marketers can secure the right partners, ideal assets, and points of flexibility to activate in a way that is more robust. Key performance indicators (KPIs) can be boosted by a multifaceted program, whether the brand is pursuing a test and learn or making a larger play in the space.

Finding the ideal partnership alignments in gaming is also based on an understanding of the nuances of the space. For instance, the League of Legends community that follows the leagues and teams has distinctly unique personalities and traits than fans who are supporting Call of Duty leagues and teams, which both differ from those actively watching content creators livestream Fortnite or Among Us, or an activation with the hottest new game releases on Xbox or PlayStation. In fact, in 2019, we only saw a 30 percent overlap between players who played both League of Legends and Overwatch, and a 20 percent overlap between League of Legends and Fortnite.[8] Understanding the personalities, demographics, and culture defined by each game title, as well as having a clear strategic vision on which communities and fandoms you're going to integrate into within the scene, are both crucial to effectively market to this audience.

Finally, it's important to also understand typical assets that you can achieve with each property. Partnering with an esports league gives you mass scale and hyperfocus around a specific game and its community—this includes assets like broadcast rights, onsite activation, and intellectual property (IP) rights—whereas an esports team can give you opportunities to activate across multiple titles with direct access to talent, allowing brands to activate with pro players and custom content. More brands are now choosing to activate directly with streamers—with more focus on gaming personalities and entertainment over the highest achieving players and most elite tournaments. In fact, there has been a 79 percent increase in sponsored streams on Twitch and YouTube[9]—the reason for this being the natural scale, ability for ownership with strong customization in content, and the experiential nature of livestreaming that amplifies a brand's role with deeper interactivity and gamification.

Engage to win: creating notable value

To build affinity within the space, brands should aim to drive value and increase engagement within their sponsorships and activations. Often in esports, we see brands settle for media deals and standard logo placements, which forgo the opportunity to cultivate first-of-its-kind branded assets that will drive deeper engagement and enthusiasm with the fanbase. Not only is there exceptional flexibility in esports that is difficult to find in traditional sports; esports audiences are also extremely receptive to sponsorships. In fact, 70 percent of esports fans believe sponsorships are good for the gaming industry, and 51 percent are actively demanding more brand involvement.[10] As such, brands have the opportunity to support and legitimize the core passions of each community, through a combination of social, in-broadcast, onsite, and talent assets to deliver what esports fans love: exclusive products, rewards, VIP experiences, and behind-the-scenes content. Because the gaming and esports scene continues to evolve with new trends, opportunities, and areas of growth, brands should continue to monitor the space for new areas to activate around novel and culture-forward trends and whitespaces.

Some great examples of win-win activations that take advantage of trends:

- Luxury in esports: Gucci partnered with esports team Fnatic on a unique collection of luxury team-branded watches, noting an increasing demand for more luxury and hyper-premium merchandise in esports.

- Beauty in gaming: MAC Cosmetics recognized an untapped and ignored female audience in gaming by activating at TwitchCon, featuring "camera-ready" makeup tutorials, meet and greets with women streamers, and giveaways.

- Anime x gaming crossover: Viz Media partnered with Team Liquid on an innovative line of merchandise, cross-promoting Team Liquid's brand with the iconic anime Naruto Shippuden—recognizing the powerful overlap between anime and esports fans.

- Integrated shopper marketing: Pringles expanded its league deal with the LEC (League of Legends' European league) with an on-pack program, allowing fans to win incredibly rare in-game character skins.

- Purpose-driven initiatives in livestreaming: Merck partnered with Twitch on a marathon livestream on World MS Day to fundraise, have informative conversations around MS and gaming, and feature gaming modes that replicated MS symptoms while gaming—showcasing the exceptional opportunity Twitch streamers have to develop unique programs.

Stretching the boundaries of innovation

The great news for advertisers is that there is still significant whitespaces for innovative activations, allowing brands to come in, create value, and develop completely ownable engagements. Especially during COVID-19, we saw gaming's inherent digital breadth and platform flexibility continue to drive creative solutions for brands and sports properties while growing its relevance to fans around the world. The distinctive virtual world of gaming is proving to be a creative playground for celebrities, gamers, sports leagues, and brands to stretch the boundaries of what's new and innovative. In fact, 58 percent of people surveyed say they want to be part of an experience to escape from everyday life.[11] What this statistic tells us is there is a demand for next-level engagement across the board.

In gaming, the brand's role in sponsorship can be transformed from a simple media asset into a value-driving live experience where the majority of viewership is taking place on streaming platforms like Twitch and YouTube Gaming. These platforms are not the equivalent of passive TV viewing, but rather offer interaction and engagement through live chats, real-time subscriptions/donations, and programmable interactive overlays that allow for a deeper, more customized experience.

These assets are already starting to be used with incredible success, as entertainment properties, celebrities, and brands transform live content into experiential content with first-of-its-kind interactions, such as:

- Virtual music performances: There has been a big trend in game concertans and performances, such as Ariana Grande in Fortnite, Block by Blockwest in Minecraft, and Lil Nas X in Roblox. These often serve as quintessential cross-culture gaming experiences that can go beyond the limitations of real world, while being more accessible for more fans to experience it.

- Film marketing initiatives: Streamer Dr Lupo interviewed Sacha Baron Cohen in character as Borat live on his Twitch stream to promote the film.

- Health and wellness promotion: Sweetgreen partnered with Valkyrae, the world's biggest female streamer, as a brand ambassador alongside other fitness influencers, for a custom bowl and healthy "sweetstream"—showcasing the opportunity for more healthy messaging in gaming.

From a personal experience, an activation that takes full advantage of the gamification opportunity on Twitch is a streaming event I managed with Momentum Worldwide for Mondelez's peanut butter cookie brand, Nutter Butter. We programmed the Day of Nuttiness "Twitch takeover" in partnership with StreamElements to create a twelve-hour marathon that celebrated the nutty culture and personalities of Twitch, featuring livestreamed gameplay and IRL content from nine top gaming streamers, including Fortnite World Cup winner Bugha, renowned DJ Steve Aoki, and big personalities like Ludwig, Mizkif, and Fuslie. We worked with each influencer to program nutty twists to amplify their typical content, integrating first-of-its-kind experiential engagements that allowed viewers to directly impact the content they were watching—while ensuring the content was consistent and unique to the influencers' communities. This included letting viewers vote live on challenges influencers would have to take within their favorite games, fill meters to get giveaways, and animated full screen explosions programmed to respond to viewers' comments. The interactive nature of this stream resulted in incredibly memorable and meme-able content for each streamer's audience with references to the event continuing in the months after. Due to this, viewership was four times higher and had eight times as many impressions than a standard influencer streaming activation.

And I would argue that we're just scratching the surface of integrating gamification through content. The possibilities are endless, as long as the gaming industry remains flexible and willing to try new initiatives. From a brand perspective, that's a pretty exciting notion.

Activate around culture, trends, and whitespaces

Gaming has not only become a major part of pop culture, but each major game title has also created its own individual culture that is defined by its community. As a result, we're seeing the beginnings of fabulous cross-culture collaborations within esports and gaming spaces—and brands have an opportunity to have a symbiotic role in this new trend.

In music, this trend is not just represented by in-game music performances, but game x music merchandise collaborations, music artist, and celebrity cameos in gaming ads and content, and musicians leveraging Twitch as a monetization platform.

With traditional sports, leagues and teams have not just invested in esports directly to create their own properties in esports; they've also looked to integrate their properties into the gaming culture. For instance, Twitch's sports broadcast rights include NFL Thursday Nights in the U.S. and the Premier League in the U.K., so they can broaden their fanbase and reach a cord-cutting audience.

In licensing and merchandising, luxury and streetwear fashion brands have become among the biggest and trendiest rising categories in gaming. In fact, U.S. esports fans of League of Legends are 83 percent more likely to consider themselves fashionable and are 92 percent more willing to pay for luxury brands[12]—showcasing their evolution from outdated gaming stereotypes as well as a willingness to spend on the things they love.

As more partnerships are being developed with major esports teams and gaming titles to create unique collaborations, marketers recognize the gap between a high-spending audience and the demand for quality merchandise. Important examples that we've seen include Nike's jersey deal with LPL (League of Legends' Chinese league) for a more performance-focused partnership, Fnatic's collaboration line with the traditionally female-focused brand Sanrio's Hello Kitty, Team Liquid's merchandise collections with Marvel that feature character-themed jerseys, FaZe Clan's collection with the NFL to fuse unique IP, and 100 Thieves' backpack design with Gucci. The most famous fashion collaboration to date is Louis Vuitton's partnership with Riot Games, featuring an LoL-inspired fashion line, in-game character skins wearing Louis Vuitton designs, and integration into the LoL Worlds music video and esports tournament—allowing for a multilayered activation that included gaming, esports, and cross-culture. However, despite the depth of drops, collaborations, and innovative partnerships, I still believe this is an area where we're still just scratching the surface, as premium merchandise in nerd culture is still a relatively newer phenomenon.

Change the game: reaching more women in esports

It is widely known in the industry that women make up around 41 percent of gamers; however, it has been asserted by some that this number is driven just by casual and mobile games. While the growth of mobile gaming in the past ten years has certainly contributed to this number, there is still significant scale in reaching the core woman gamer. Thirty-five percent of all Twitch users are women, and core female gamers spend an average of 4.39 hours gaming per day,[13] showcasing the size and depth of the opportunity. For many women around the world, this is not simply a casual hobby but a deep passion point.

Despite this, recent data shows that 62 percent of female esports fans do not believe that esports brands market to them, and 71 percent say women aren't being represented enough in esports,[14] with only 5 percent of positions in the games industry held by women, according to Women in Games. As such, brands face an untapped whitespace to develop more bespoke programs that focus on reaching more diverse audiences with targeted and inclusive activation priorities. But to create a more inclusive and welcoming industry, it will take a team effort from publishers, esports leagues, teams, platforms, and partners.

The good news is that 2020 saw a real re-prioritization toward diversity and inclusivity in the gaming and esports space, with major new initiatives that promoted women streamers and pro players. It was a remarkable year for women content creators like Valkyrae, whose massive growth launched her to win Streamer of the Year at the Game Awards, while rising creators like Fuslie joined esports organization 100 Thieves and activated with top brands like Lexus, Mondelez, Excedrin, Converse, and more. Esports teams now prioritize women talent, whether it's on the content creation side, such as FaZe Clan signing Call of Duty Warzone streamer Kalei, or the competitive side with esports team rosters. Riot Games' esports title Valorant has been the unicorn for inclusivity in esports, with dedicated all-female or coed teams from Cloud9, TSM, and Evil Geniuses that compete directly with all-male teams. This also led to amazing initiatives like the VCT Game Changers to create more opportunities for all-female teams to grow and compete in Valorant. These initiatives are crucial as women gamers want to feel seen, heard, and, most importantly, inspired. Representation in all media continues to be crucial for future growth in diversity and inclusivity, and gaming is no different: Female gamers want to see representation in games, livestreams, esports leagues, and professional teams.

When brands are marketing around women gamers, it's key to understand that brands do not necessarily need to focus on women-only esports teams or leagues to reach women—they're already fans of esports. While 22 percent of esports fans are women, it's critical to understand the nuances of each esports community and where women fandom is more common. For instance, there's significant female fandom for esports titles and leagues like Call of Duty, Valorant, Fortnite, and Super Smash Bros, and women are most interested in attending gaming events like BlizzCon, TwitchCon, and the Overwatch League Grand Finals.[15]

The Return of Live Events

While gaming and esports have proven to be somewhat pandemic-proof, the in-person, live experience in the long run cannot be replaced. Esports fans are the most likely to find streaming events and virtual alternatives appealing during the COVID-19 pandemic (compared to traditional sports fans and festival attendees). They are also the most likely to return to live events the quickest, the most likely to travel, and the most likely to feel esports events are their most missed experience.[16]

Attending major conventions like PAX or TwitchCon or the League of Legends Split or Overwatch League Finals remains the zenith of many fans' engagement within the community. Equally important, as these industry events become more ingrained in culture, the entire industry moves forward. Brands that can drive real business value from participating in gaming and esports in the future are the ones that will strike the right balance between live and online experiences.

The experiential opportunity in esports is still among the industry's major whitespaces: 50 percent of esports audiences are only "somewhat satisfied" with brand activation at gaming events, despite the fact that 81 percent of esports fans have or are willing to invest time and money by traveling to these major tentpole events. Because they have to travel, they're looking for opportunities that will extend and amplify their entire experience while deepening their personal engagement with their own passion points.

Focus on Credibility

The term that every brand interested in getting into esports will hear is "authenticity." However, this challenge is no different from traditional sports and entertainment partnerships. All subcultures have barriers, but if brands are identifying those points of value, publishers, esports organizations, and agencies will take an active role to ensure the communication, voice, in-jokes, real-time engagement, and individual tactics are resonating with those individual audiences.

My advice to brands is to not fear the space. Instead, embrace one of the fastest-growing cultural segments in the world with a strong vision and a dynamic approach. The definition of gamer continues to be redefined and evolve, as gaming is now at the center of some of the greatest innovation and creative executions that entertainment as a whole is seeing. Gaming is a space for connection and socialization, an industry to promote health and wellness, and an ecosystem driven by performance and personality. Its audience is high spending, high traveling, highly passionate, and highly diverse. The sponsorship opportunities of gaming are only limited by preconceived notions, which brands would be remiss to let confine their integration into an ever-expanding landscape.

MEET TATIANA TACCA

Tatiana is the Founder of Oni Vision, an advisory and consultancy practice focused on gaming, esports, anime, and livestreaming marketing and strategic partnership initiatives. As an independent consultant, advisor, and thought leader with 10 years of gaming experience, Tatiana consults with brands, gaming organizations, and entertainment properties on intersection with gaming to optimize on trends, whitespaces, and the most valuable opportunities in the gaming space.

She has developed deals with Twitch, Riot Games, FaZe Clan, Activision Blizzard, TSM, Cloud9, NYXL, and content creators, and worked with dozens of clients, including Funimation, Twitch, Dr Pepper, Intel, United Airlines, Mondelez, Zytara, Sweetgreen, Buffalo Wild Wings, eFuse, Coca-Cola, Kellogg's, Verizon, T-Mobile, William Grant, Samsung, and more.

Previously, Tatiana was at Endeavor and Momentum Worldwide, where she ran Momentum's esports and gaming practice—leading the global agency's strategic approach to the gaming space, and consulting across all brand clients as a subject matter expert in gaming. Before that, she was the marketing lead on 20+ licensed mobile titles, driving the core marketing strategies of each title's launch and update and working directly with the licensors, including Marvel, Disney, Pixar, NBA, NFL, MLB, Fox, Lucasfilm, MLS, and the Premier League. You can find her online at:

linkedin.com/in/tatianatacca

CHAPTER 21

The Future of Entertainment

I am the third generation in the entertainment business in my family. We have invested in cinemas, bowling alleys, arcades, hotel operations, and yacht rentals over the decades. Our movie operations have reached three countries, with 305 cinemas at its peak in 2011, becoming the largest movie operation in the Russia–Ukraine–Turkish region. After twenty-five years of movie operation, I have decided to invest in esports.

Entertainment for the new generation

I did this to capture new generations' preferences in entertainment. We see a lot of similarities between esports and the movie business, although there are unique differences. The entertainment business, for example, is starting to see more self-produced products. Anyone who is over twenty-five will have an entertainment preference that is very different from that of today's youth.

If you are over thirty-five, your entertainment options may focus on consuming content with your loved ones, like watching movies or playing board games together, whereas entertainment customers under twenty-five are simultaneously using two or three other screens (phones, iPads, etc.) while watching a movie in a theater or engaging in some other form of entertainment. Several surveys have shown that, during a movie screening, the younger generation is also texting and playing games or listening to music.

I have seen the rise and the fall of movie attendance around the world. Depending on the stage of development of the movie industry in a particular country, you have a developed market in the West that is declining in attendance and a newly introduced Eastern market that is rapidly growing. Almost half of the world's 180,000 screens were built in China in the last decade.

The main reason for going to the movies has always been the social experience and the exclusivity of the content. But, today, digital platforms like Netflix and pirated movies are eating up the market for cinemas, especially during times of global crisis like the COVID-19 pandemic. Movie theaters have survived over the years by offering something no other venue could offer: a big screen and a big sound (think IMAX for the biggest of both).

Smaller films and artistic movies are finding their way to digital platforms, as the interest level in this type of film is dropping sharply. The younger generation is less interested in movies that are not mainstream or blockbusters. I believe this trend will continue and that fewer movies on fewer screens is the future of the movie industry.

The survival of movie theaters is not romantic; it is totally materialistic. The highest per-person revenue for producers is still generated by a movie seat. That is why the entertainment industry is holding on while carefully looking at Netflix and other streaming platforms for their exclusive product to generate higher and higher revenue per person for them. So far, these digital platforms are still far from generating numbers higher than movie theaters. This may or may not change in the future and will determine whether movie theaters thrive or survive.

Esports is very similar to the movie industry. Both industries have mainly three segments:

- Production

- Distribution

- Exhibition

Movie and game production are very similar. Distribution is also similar: In both cases, the producers or platforms (movie theaters or a gaming system or direct distributor, like Steam) supply the games or movies to the consumer. Exhibition has been the main marketing and revenue-generation tool for the movie industry for over a hundred years.

Entertainment investing

The exhibition part of the distribution process, however, has been largely missing from esports. There are few in-person social venues to gather consumers that are similar to each other and fans of the same games. That's why, three years ago, we gathered twelve angel investors to create esports cafes. Esports cafes are similar to the internet cafes of the 1990s, which brought people the internet experience in a communal space, but focused on gaming.

Our esports cafes offer several thousand square meters of facilities for tournaments with professional gamers, special training rooms, and even a specialized hotel for esports boot camps. We have built cafes all over Turkey, Greece, Cyprus, and North Macedonia, and continue to expand into other countries with our international partners.

The esports market began with home entertainment, from a single computer hooked to the internet and people playing with their friends. Today, all games have teams and have attracted audiences at esports events and on streaming services such as Twitch. At esports cafes, we supply the highest caliber of equipment to gamers who are interested in developing their talents by exercising long hours with their team members. Today, there are different houses for teams who are preparing for competitions, boot camps, and several million-dollar awards at tournaments.

As you may very well know, esports is the new buzzword for many entertainment investors. There are people investing in teams, and just like soccer clubs or horse race investors, they are trying to find the best teams to play the best game by training them. They count on sponsorship money to operate as well as competition awards as a profit center that may or may not be realized.

There are also people investing in arenas, which are used once a week on the weekends and stand empty all week, with the main revenue coming from the rental of facilities. Currently, several of them are built around the world, but event ticket income and sponsorships are rare commodities. If they cannot produce the impact on the industry they promised with the renewal of sponsorship deals, the business model is very vulnerable.

Game producers are supplying the game to the market, and if the game or its in-app purchases are sufficient, they make a profit. But it is a very crowded market. It is very hard to show your product to the customer. Usually, everyone talks about the top five games, and that changes every year with some exceptions. There are another hundred titles that are still in the mainstream. In fact, at Esports Cafe we keep updated versions of around 1,400 games.

There are also many leagues that are trying to market the game they feature to the fans. These leagues are successful competition-boosting marketing events. Even some TV stations are airing them and attracting more people than mainstream sports events. The successful events trigger more fans, and they trigger even more tournaments at the professional and amateur levels. This spiral is growing even now, with home tournaments.

All these business models are quite young, and most of them depend on sponsorship revenues, which may or may not happen in the market, depending on the economic situation of that market. This market is very unorganized so far. Everybody wants to invest in esports, but no business model without sponsorships has seemed feasible so far.

Esports Cafe

The business model of Esports Cafe is based on the rental of equipment, sponsorship revenues, and the sale of food. Ultimately, we will create a platform to bring together all esports fans and teams. This experience, like going to the movies, has to be exceptional compared with home entertainment. The event creates the opportunity for an outing and social interaction. This is why we must have the latest esports tournament-caliber equipment for rent, areas for the professionals to exercise, and others for viewers to come watch a weekend game while enjoying high-quality food and entertainment in a cafe with their friends.

Internet cafes were more popular in the East than the West. This may be because computer equipment was more affordable in the West. However, today, many esports players come from countries like Korea, where the internet cafe culture created a game industry and a social platform where these people could meet, even for dating.

Esports cafes are coming to upscale this experience. They are the future of gaming and social entertainment, because they will act as a hub where customers can meet like-minded people. They will also serve as a place where new players can be discovered. Our AI software constantly analyzes the game-playing habits, equipment, and food preferences of esports players to enable better performance. This software will be able to tell you how and when you are playing better, as well as what game you excel most at, which equipment suits you, and even what drinks help your game. It will also keep track of who is developing to be worthy of a top league team.

There are several types of games trending right now. These include team play, which requires more than one person and more than one station. This means the player's house, with a single computer, is not sufficient to play these games with friends. Gathering with five friends in an esports cafe, or for a team preparing for a tournament, is the ideal venue for entertainment for the young generation.

These players can also create their own streaming broadcast as they're playing, which is another area that is growing very rapidly. We have invested separately in YouTubers popular in gaming, because we spotted that most of the players would like to see other players playing their favorite game. Even games like Minecraft, which are quite slow and seemingly not much "sport," attract millions to watch famous players play. Today, we have gamers who have millions of subscribers.

The new reality of entertainment

This is the new reality of entertainment, and millions are flocking not only to stadiums to watch a live esports game but also to their favorite games on YouTube, instead of watching a movie or a TV show. Turkey's top YouTuber, Ener Batur, is twenty-one years old. He started his channel in 2017 and reaches over 15 million subscribers today. The top Turkish comedian, Cem Yılmaz, is fifty and hasn't yet passed 2.5 million subscribers. The *Magnificent Suleyman* TV series, a worldwide hit, has only 1.5 million subscribers. These are just some of the proof that the mainstream entertainment choices are changing, as are the entertainment habits of the next generation.

At no time in history was it this easy to broadcast your own content to billions of people with a smartphone or a PC. With any social platform, you can broadcast to the world for free. Players who are content producers on platforms like Twitch, where youngsters watch and donate money, are prospering rapidly.

Twitch was purchased for $1 billion by Amazon. Facebook and YouTube are scrambling to engage by transferring these content creators to their platforms with million-dollar transfer fees. Free content broadcasting could eliminate many industries, from camera crews to uplink systems and satellite services to digital TV broadcasters, just to name a few. The list will grow according to the choices of youngsters and technological advances.

It is a new world order, and the COVID-19 pandemic has doubled the size of the market for online gaming, changing everything we learned about entertainment. More people are playing and watching esports than basketball. Soon, it will catch up with the world's top attraction: soccer. The esports market feeds on the creativity of new generations, and new games just keep fueling the growth. It's time to embrace the change and adapt to entertain.

MEET A. ADNAN AKDEMIR

Adnan was born in Istanbul, Turkey. He is a third-generation entertainment entrepreneur. After receiving his MBA at National University, he attended UCLA Film School. In 1993, he returned home and founded AFM Cinemas, which has become the leading movie theater in Turkey.

Adnan introduced the quality cinema experience to Turkey, which created a national boom in the industry. In 2001, he cofounded the International Istanbul Film Festival to rejuvenate the Turkish film industry by creating a prestigious international event. In 2004, AFM Cinemas became the first entertainment company in Borsa Istanbul. He also cofounded the first Turkish film distribution company, Kenda, with top Turkish producers, to support local productions. Within three years, Kenda became the main driver behind half the market share of local content in Turkish cinema.

In 2008, Adnan sold the majority of AFM Cinemas to Russia's largest private group, Alfa. Adnan became their CEO and established Eurasia Cinemas, which has grown to 305 multiplex cinemas and is looking to become the leading movie chain in the Russia-Ukraine-Turkey region.

Adnan started AFM Online, investing in "only digital entertainment ideas." Some of his successful startups include www.ilsvision.com.tr, the largest YouTube MCN in the MENA region; and Fitas Digital Republic FDR, an esports cafe chain that is growing internationally. He started playing esports with Sinclair ZX 80 in 1982 and still enjoys daily World of Tanks Blitz skirmish.

He is an active member of YPO Gold. In 2012, Adnan received a Red Cross Golden Mercy Medal for his lifetime contributions. He can be found online at:

linkedin.com/in/adnan-akdemir-91603a35

CHAPTER 22

Galaxy Racer Esports

My journey with gaming pretty much began with my journey in Dubai. I moved to the city twenty-three years ago and very soon after cofounded and built the first game development company in the Middle East right here in Dubai.

Our first title was a PC-based hack-and-slash game called the Legend of Zord (no relation to Zork). Most players called it Prince of Persia 3D's poor cousin, and the fact that we shot an Arabic music video to promote it (complete with a belly dancer) did not help! In fact, I was recently contacted by someone on LinkedIn who had bought the game all those years ago, and he said that over time, he came to realize the game was so bad that it was actually really good and apparently it had developed a cult following!

Still, the fact that this was the first-ever game fully developed in the Middle East was in itself a great accomplishment, and this helped lay the foundations for the gaming industry in the U.A.E. and the wider Middle East.

Fast-forward to today, and I have had the good fortune to have worked on amazing entertainment projects, ranging from producing animated films to building world-class theme parks. This journey has allowed me to build strong relationships in the entertainment industry ranging from film (Hollywood and Bollywood) to gaming (Japanese, American, and

European markets). These relationships put me in good stead when I decided to venture back into gaming a few years ago.

This time, however, rather than build a new company from scratch, I decided to go the investor route. Therefore, with a group of like-minded co-investors, I have invested (and am currently investing) in companies in the gaming industry, which cover the entire gaming ecosystem (developers, publishers, platforms, etc.).

We typically act as strategic investors. For example, one of our portfolio companies is a mobile game developer and publisher based out of Los Angeles. Their specialty is in building mobile games based on well-known Hollywood movie franchises. This is where I was able to add strategic value in obtaining these IP licenses for them. We now work with most major Hollywood Studios—DreamWorks Animation, NBC Universal, Skydance Productions, and so on.

While looking at different investment opportunities, I have had a lot of offers in the last few years in the esports sector. Despite being heavily invested in the gaming industry, I was skeptical of esports—specifically around the business models. I am incredibly old fashioned in a business sense, in that, if I cannot figure out a way to make money in a particular business, I simply *do not* want to be in that business! Major tech companies that have never made a cent of profit but have obscene valuations continue to baffle me.

Over time, however, and after spending a lot of time meeting a lot of folks in the esports industry and studying it in great detail, I was finally convinced about the merits of esports and where potential business opportunities lay. However, by the time I was ready to invest (end of 2018, beginning of 2019), I was a bit late to the party. In established territories like North America, Europe, and the Far East, there were only two choices: back a struggling startup or buy into one of the established teams, most of which had eye-watering valuations, the likes of which would put a lot of top-flight football clubs to shame! There was basically nothing out there that would be considered value for money or that came into my ideal investment scenario, which is medium risk and high reward.

By this time, I was quite determined to get into the esports business. So, in the summer of 2019, I decided to finally roll up my sleeves and build my own esports organization, my first direct foray into building a company in the gaming and tech space, over seventeen years after I'd left my previous one! My initial plan was to focus on the Middle East, because most areas like the U.S. or Europe had become too saturated, whereas the Middle East and South Asia are one of the last untapped markets that have huge potential for growth in gaming and esports.

I was particularly intrigued with developing talent from this region, because several Tier 1 esports athletes in Europe and the U.S. were originally from the Middle East. However, what the region lacked was infrastructure, funding, and a highly competitive scene. Therefore, it was clear that the business model was to back top-quality talent from the region and provide them with world-class Tier 1 support.

That is how Galaxy Racer Esports was born. However, even after starting the company, I still felt that something was missing. The plans to build a world-class Middle Eastern organization were coming along well, but my gut kept telling me it was not enough. But all that changed when GIRLGAMER walked into my life.

As is usually the case with me, inspiration for my greatest achievements and ideas has come in the most unlikely of places and situations, and it was no different this time. A freak combination of a typhoon, a cancelled flight, an unscheduled car service, and a chance meeting at a bar led to my first meeting with the founders of GIRLGAMER and the beginning of a partnership. The encounter opened my eyes to the world of women in gaming—everything from the challenges female gamers faced, to the lack of investment in the sector, but most importantly to the huge potential that lay with this demographic.

This was my eureka moment—female esports. I instantly knew this was the missing piece in my quest to build an esports organization with a difference. The first thing that I did was secure rights to host the

GIRLGAMER World Finals for the next five editions of the finals. I promised the founders we would fund and put on the biggest edition of GIRLGAMER ever held, and we stuck to that promise!

Most people thought I was crazy making the kind of investment that we did. The exact words I heard from a friend who is a well-respected figure in the esports industry were "It's an esports event . . . for girls . . . and in Dubai? Are you nuts that you're spending this kind of money?" And the reply I gave to him was "Exactly! It *is* an esports event *for* girls and *in* Dubai."

The GIRLGAMER World Finals held in February 2020 was the single largest international esports event for women ever held. The event drew in millions of viewers from all over the globe, and I was vindicated.

GIRLGAMER allowed us to debut the first Galaxy Racer Esports team, which also happened to be the first-ever female professional esports team from the Middle East. This feat, along with the sheer scale of the event, caught the attention of the world's media. This made Galaxy Racer the youngest-ever esports organization in the world to get a front-page feature on CNN International.

Galaxy Racer had arrived on the esports scene with a bang!

GIRLGAMER also served as the perfect scouting ground for us to start growing our roster of teams. Soon after the World Finals were held, Galaxy Racer signed on players from the teams that won the CS:GO and LoL finals, as well as players from the runner-up teams.

While the COVID-19 pandemic caused havoc to most industries globally, gaming and esports have seen tremendous growth. Indeed, with a lack of live sports during the peak of the 2020 lockdown (late spring to early summer), there was a large surge in terms of "sports" fans switching to "esports" to watch competitive matches. I was also able to quickly readjust my strategy for esports during the lockdown.

While in the past, a significant part of our investment would have included building a physical location and setting down infrastructure, we decided to focus purely on talent acquisition, building a world-class support team and an extremely strong scouting network.

Today our organization has three main verticals: competitive teams, tournaments, and content creation. Our quick expansion has led us to become one of the world's fastest-growing esports organizations. Between April 2020 and May 2021, we have grown our roster, stayed true to our development policy, launched monthly online tournaments, and launched our content-creation vertical.

Competitive teams

In just over a year, we grew our total roster from one to thirteen teams. Galaxy Racer currently owns thirteen teams competing in CS:GO, League of Legends, Dota 2, PUBG Mobile, Call of Duty Mobile, Rocket League, Valorant, and Fortnite.

True to our philosophy, our rosters are equally made up of male and female athletes. The organization is especially known for its diversity. The seventy-five male and female athletes represent twenty-two different nationalities. The teams are spread across Europe (Eastern and Western), the Middle East, South Asia, and Southeast Asia. The organization has a full base of operations in each of these four regions. Both teams (male and female) are at the absolute top of their game, and each of our rosters is at least a Tier 2 if not a Tier 1 team.

We have also stayed true to our development policy. We foster young talent, but we couple them with a world-class performance team consisting of coaches, analysts, and sports psychologists. This has allowed an extremely young esports organization like us to get results that are making the competition stand up and take notice.

Tournaments

In addition to being the local partners for GIRLGAMER, Galaxy Racer has launched monthly online tournaments that we host for League of Legends, CS:GO, and Fortnite. While professional teams do participate, these tournaments are primarily aimed at up-and-coming amateur teams and amateur talent that have the potential to turn professional. These tournaments offer a fantastic opportunity for regional talent to be scouted by professional organizations.

Content creation

We launched our content-creation vertical in September 2020 and have acquired some of the biggest gaming content creators on YouTube in the Middle East and South Asia. We are currently the largest gaming content-creation house in the Middle East and South Asia. As of this writing, the content creators we have acquired in the last nine months have over 157 million direct followers. The content they produce on YouTube alone generates a staggering one billion views per month! Our goal is quite simple: to be the largest gaming content-creation house in the world.

I genuinely believe we have only just written the first chapter in Galaxy Racer's journey. I am excited about where this could lead. It's taken a long time, but I finally found an endeavor that has ignited the same passion that I had twenty years ago!

MEET PAUL ROY

Paul Roy is a serial entrepreneur and a twenty-year veteran in the media and entertainment industry. He is the chairman of the Riva Group of companies with interests ranging from theme parks and animation to VFX and video games.

In the theme park sector, Paul led the creation and execution of most of the major theme parks in Dubai, including IMG Worlds of Adventure, Motiongate Dubai, Bollywood Parks Dubai at Dubai Parks and Resorts, and HUBzero.

Paul pioneered the video game industry in the Middle East and built the first game development studio in the region twenty years ago, which produced the first-ever PC game from the Arabic-speaking world. The Riva Group is currently investing in various mobile game developers and publishers across North America and China.

One of the companies is Firefly Games, in which Riva Technology and Entertainment (the holding company for Riva) owns a majority stake. Firefly Games is engaged in producing mobile games based on famous Hollywood brands like Terminator and DreamWorks Animation. The first game under Firefly Games was released in Q4 2019 and is called Terminator: Dark Fate.

Paul is also the CEO and founder of Galaxy Racer Esports, one of the largest esports and content organizations in the world with thirteen teams, multiple tournament platforms, 120 content creators, and over 500 million followers. You can find him online at:

linkedin.com/in/paul-roy-09072b6

CHAPTER 23

Gaming in India

We were interested in making a game with Indian mythology and with unique characters. The way we make the games in my company is to start mainly with a story-based structure for the game and to take real models and actors and use them as the game's 3D models. This is a technology we've used in our game-making process since early 2005. With limited resources, we created a studio with a VFX background and then started taking 360-degree pictures of actors and models. We hired them so that we could make digital humans that looked exactly like them, and we sometimes enhanced their dress and looks according to the need of the games.

While making Mahabharat and Ashwathama, we took several local actors and models from India and slowly started taking models from countries outside of India, like Russia, Ukraine, Africa, and so on. This gave us an edge to start another venture, cosplayseller.com, where people dress up as game, comic book, or movie characters in real life.

Slowly, with growth and interest from the media and entertainment industry, I invested in glamworldface, a platform where media people connect with business. When we started hiring models to become characters in a game, it was really hard for us to convince them and to make them understand what we were doing. We were probably too early for the market. But then, after Ashwathama released, they understood what we wanted to make. Now, the movie industry started approaching us to make games for them. We did several movie-based games with real stories and actors, like Boss2, Tushagni, and Nilanjana, and we made our own story-based game called Fight of the Legends.

Investing in game and game studios takes a lot of time to get the desired result. Before making any game, there has to be a market study and an understanding of the demand. Sometimes we can create demand while creating a real ecosystem. The ecosystem plays a vital role in making any title successful, and that boosts up game studios to win. We made eight VR game titles and partnered with publishers to market them.

Back in 1998, I started a training institute, where I trained lots of students in arts, logic, and programming, and those students are working in various industries now, not only in gaming but also in tech, animation, web media, design, programming, networking, and system security. My company became a hub for training and production at the same time.

In 2008, we started India's first gaming club on a university campus and started doing workshops in various colleges to teach people about gaming and new technology, while creating educational content. In 2009, we started training online, using the internet and video calling and desktop sharing. It started with animation, programming, and game development training for students in Asia, and slowly, we adopted cloud technology to automate it and enhance the experience for the students. It's a teacher-to-student relationship, which is not your typical training approach. We embrace the old Sanskrit culture, where knowledge is shared from person to person instead of only focusing on developing skills.

Esports is on a whole other level, a different league. We create blockchain-based solutions focused on esports. For example, blockchain-based platforms can offer advanced layers of security that other betting platforms may lack.

That's mainly for clients, not really our own games, but it is making a mark in Asia slowly. With proper strategic investment, if the ROI is right, and the founders can get community support, this can become a huge market. Things are happening fast, as the digital world is keeping a steady pace and making a mark in the real world. I'm sure that in time, we'll see augmented reality (AR) glasses powered by blockchain with AI integration while we drive, walk, or run. And these glasses will understand our needs and act accordingly. They'll even take care of our banking, and that's very much connected with gaming technology.

Venture capital funds have invested $438 million in Indian gaming startups since April 2020, topping the combined funding of the last five years (mint). Dream11 alone accounted for $225 million in venture funding.

India's esports boom is drawing big corporates. Tech Mahindra announced in Feb 2021 that it would organize a global chess league. This move makes Tech Mahindra the third Indian big corporate to enter esports after Airtel and Reliance Jio (mint).

Consider these other numbers:

- Over 50 percent of India's population is below 25 years of age.[1]

- India is the second largest internet consumer with over 560 million internet users.[2]

- In 2020, India rose to the number one spot in mobile game downloads, clocking 7.3 billion installs.[3]

- The real money gaming segment is expected to grow at a CAGR of 40 percent from 2020-22, whereas, the esports segment is expected to grow at a CAGR of 36 percent over the next three years.[4]

India is all set to become the industry leader of the modern world due to the increase in general interest and investment in the gaming culture.

MEET ARIJIT BHATTACHARYYA

Serial entrepreneur, programmer, and VR specialist, Arijit has over twenty-three years' experience helping startups, entrepreneurs, and governments across the world solve problems using entrepreneurship, technology, and innovation.

Arijit founded Virtualinfocom, one of India's first game development and VR app development companies and has created more than fifty-four superhero and comic book characters. Arijit always knew that the Indian animation and gaming industry's future was rooted in being able to produce original intellectual property. His special interest in creating original Indian content for global audiences yielded great success through creations such as Shaktimaan the game, fight of the legends (series), Ashwathama the immortal, Sukhu Dukhu, Lalkamal Nilkamal, Desert Drift, Saudi Arabia with love, and 3D racing, to name a few.

As founder of Entrepreneursface, Arjit helps entrepreneurs start up their business by coaching them from the ideation stage to execution. You can find him online at:

linkedin.com/in/arijitbhattacharyya

CHAPTER 24

Mobile Esports: New Opportunities for Gamers and Developers

y first project as a games industry analyst was a white paper study of the mass-market potential of mobile esports.[1] The key question was: What does the growing popularity of mobile gaming in esports mean for the esports industry going forward, given the size of mobile gaming's audience? What we found was striking, if unsurprising. Mobile esports is a huge market, with the potential to bring esports into the mainstream in ways the PC and console esports can't on their own.

In large part, this is a question of numbers. Esports fans can be broken up into three categories: people who play esports games but don't watch esports content, people who consume esports games and esports video content, and people who watch esports content without actually playing any esports games themselves. In most calculations of esports audience size, these three groups stay in similar proportions to one another. What this means is the player base is a big factor for the success of esports video content. The larger the player base, the larger the overall audience. So, if you compare the potential audience for PC esports to the potential audience for mobile esports, mobile simply has a much higher ceiling for total possible audience size based on the player numbers.

I remember reading a Reddit thread shortly after we published this study in which someone shared an article about our findings. I was thrilled to see a project I had worked on getting attention out in the world, but some of the reactions of serious Western esports fans were a form of gatekeeping. One of the top comments read, "Choose one: mobile or esports." What the person meant, I must assume, is that mobile games aren't suited to becoming esports. If your only experiences with mobile games are match-three games or Angry Birds, you might be inclined to share this opinion. This told me two things. First, many die-hard esports fans didn't really appreciate the complexity of the global esports industry and what a big role mobile already plays. And second, there is a lot of growth still waiting to happen in the esports industry, where huge segments are still developing.

Understanding where mobile esports fit

Historically, esports games represent the highest level of gaming for a core audience of serious enthusiasts. Esports in Korea, the U.S., Europe, and China were driven primarily by hardcore PC gamers.[2] Mobile games, on the other hand, are generally designed to be accessible, to run on smartphones, to appeal to the widest number of players, and ultimately to facilitate microtransactions. Their controls are necessarily simpler, and mobile games are often built with monetization and accessibility as their core principles, rather than high-level, head-to-head competition. For this reason, mobile games have historically been designed for a more casual audience. Mobile esports titles begin to bridge this gap, bringing serious competition to a more accessible platform.

In a market that favors console and PC gaming, like the U.S., mobile gaming and esports can seem pretty far apart. However, gaming culture is global, and regional audiences have different approaches, different demands, and different limitations for the games they play. Understanding the history of mobile games and the growing culture around mobile esports, especially in Asia, sheds some light on the complexities of the esports industry and helps to illuminate the future of esports as a global phenomenon. While mobile esports is still slowly growing in the U.S. and Europe, the mobile esports industry in Asia is already well established and has surpassed the PC and console esports industries there in many ways. Obviously, not all mobile games are trying to be esports games, but more and more are. So, while mobile esports is still developing in some markets, it's just a matter of time before they start to influence the global esports industry.

Where did mobile esports come from?

To understand the significance of mobile esports, it's useful to understand where mobile esports fits into the broader history of esports. Modern esports traces its roots to Korean gaming competitions in the early 2000s,[3] but it really began to take off a decade later as platforms like Twitch and YouTube made esports productions more globally marketable. With the success of MOBA games like Dota 2 and League of Legends, mobile game developers began to take an interest in this market segment by designing mobile games that looked and felt like PC esports titles.

In 2014, Vainglory, the first notable mobile esports game, was released. It featured complex controls (for a mobile title) and sought to cater to the kinds of serious gamers that were playing LoL or Dota 2. Other mobile esports titles followed suit: Honor of Kings/Arena of Valor launched in 2015, Mobile Legends: Bang launched in 2016, Clash Royale launched in 2016, and Hearthstone launched for mobile in 2015. Mobile developers sought to get into the esports action, as esports had a proven track record of improving engagement and player spending in both time and money.

Another factor in mobile esports growth was the ubiquity of mobile technology. While a high-level gaming PC or a current-generation gaming console represents hundreds of dollars in investment, nearly everyone has a mobile phone. This means that mobile esports games are much more accessible to the average gamer. This also helps to explain why mobile esports have done so well in Asia.

The rates of console ownership and PC ownership in Asia remain low, especially when compared to the U.S. or Europe. Instead, many Asian gamers rely on icafes to play top PC games. However, nearly everyone in Asia has a smartphone. In fact, smartphone penetration rates have risen dramatically across the region in the last decade, making the smartphone the leading gaming device in the region. As of 2019, there were 1.2 billion mobile gamers in Asia, or more than half of the world's mobile gamers.[4] When framed this way, it makes sense that all these gamers would want to play serious, competitive games on the device most accessible to them.

The excitement around esports and the accessibility of mobile games have turned mobile esports into a huge industry in Asia. For example, between 2018 and 2019 mobile esports prizes in Southeast Asia tripled. In China, Honor of Kings now challenges League of Legends for the top streaming audience and has way more players streaming the game themselves. Honor of Kings, Mobile Legends: Bang, Peacekeeper Elite, and PUBG Mobile all have their own esports leagues, on par with PC esports in the region, thanks to serious investment from publishers, operators, and sponsors. When our company, Niko Partners, talks about esports in Asia, we note that, by most metrics, mobile esports has already surpassed PC and console esports. In short, it's not a question of whether mobile esports will shape the global esports industry but of where, when, and how.

Why are mobile esports important for the future of all esports?

To understand the impacts mobile esports are having on the esports industry more broadly, it is useful to highlight some of the things that set mobile esports games apart from console and PC games. As the mobile esports industry continues to grow, these strengths will either be implemented more widely or help mobile reach new audiences.

Mobile esports games have serious viral potential. Mobile battle royale titles such as Peacekeeper Elite, PUBG Mobile, Free Fire, and Fortnite Mobile performed strongly in 2019, in addition to the continued strength of MOBA titles Honor of Kings/Arena of Valor and Mobile Legends: Bang Bang. When a mobile game gets going, it can build a big audience very quickly. For example, when PUBG Mobile launched in India, it became an overnight phenomenon, thanks to being free to play, the large number of mobile users in India, and a cultural phenomenon around the game's launch. This kind of viral sensation wouldn't have been possible for a PC or console game in this market. Esports requires a lot of investment from operators and sponsors, so viral excitement does a great job of incentivizing this kind of investment.

Mobile esports games represent a high degree of genre diversity, ranging from casual titles (Pokémon GO, Battle of Balls, Puyo Puyo) to mid-core and core titles (Mobile Legends: Bang Bang, Honor of Kings, PUBG Mobile). While popular PC and console esports genres have been ported to mobile, there have also been a number of mobile-specific esports games or genres to emerge. For example, Pokémon GO relies on mobile platform affordances to work and couldn't simply be ported to PC or console. But this is not just a matter of technology; the size of the player base for mobile and the native touch interface of most mobile devices have given rise to more mobile-first esports titles that bend or break traditional esports genres.

Mobile gaming means players can get in on the action wherever and whenever they want, and this allows mobile esports to benefit from internet infrastructure. It becomes easier to organize small-scale participatory esports events, to facilitate esports tie-ins at retail locations, and to build on existing app integration. Instead of hosting a tournament in an icafe or an esports venue, you can host tournaments anywhere that has a stable mobile connection. This opens up a lot of new possibilities for the kinds of tournaments you can host, which is important, as esports seeks to build new partnerships with sponsors and brands. Already, retail locations are using mobile esports in ways that tie in to consumer practices. Moreover, as the smartphone becomes an increasingly important part of modern life, the integration of esports gaming into the app ecosystem on your phone provides a lot of new opportunities for the industry. From streamlined payment systems to livestreaming applications, app integration allows esports games and businesses to benefit from the utility of your mobile phone.

Mobile esports will precipitate a shift from a limited number of high-profile, spectator-focused esports productions toward a much larger number of open tournaments carried out regionally and locally. Historically, esports have been spectator-oriented events. And while this will remain the core of the industry, there is a growing value to letting more players get in on the action.

Already platforms are designing ways for regular gamers to play in esports competitions. We are seeing this in schools, colleges, smaller local tournaments, and online tournament platforms. Mobile esports will expand this market segment, allowing even more amateur gamers to play in or organize their own tournaments.

Mobile games have lower barriers to entry, more balanced demographics, and higher install rates in comparison to PC and console games. This allows for better economics and higher dollar-to-player value in producing tournaments. Another part of this equation is demographics. Mobile gaming reaches a much wider demographic than PC gaming across age and gender. Women have historically been underrepresented in esports both as players and as fans. Mobile esports is a chance for the industry to improve its coverage and to reach a part of the gaming population that has not been well served by console and PC esports. Numbers are a big factor in the power of mobile esports. We are already seeing how powerful the mobile esports audience can be across Asia. There are a lot more gamers on mobile, and this translates to higher revenue for mobile titles. Because esports remains a publisher- or operator-driven industry, the value these players generate translates to higher investments back into esports.

Mobile esports is not going to replace PC or console esports anytime soon. What mobile offers is a way for the industry to grow in new directions. As games industry analysts, we think about how different parts of the market fit together and how changes in one area affect another. In this respect, mobile esports benefits from a number of platform affordances that are helping this segment of the industry grow quickly. Just as mobile esports games and business models have drawn heavily from the success of console and PC esports, there are a lot of lessons and advantages mobile esports can bring to the industry.

MEET ALEXANDER CHAMPLIN

Alexander works as the esports senior analyst at Niko Partners, specializing in market trends and insights for Asia. He received his PhD from the Department of Film and Media Studies at the University of California, Santa Barbara, with a focus on esports and livestreaming. His academic work focuses on video game spectatorship industries. He has published and presented work on esports studios, esports franchising, and examining video game livestreaming production cultures. Find him online at:

linkedin.com/in/alexander-champlin-30759a95

CHAPTER 25

Putting Esports on the National Agenda

The combined prize pool of Dota 2, CS: GO, Fortnite, League of Legends, and StarCraft 2 was around $500 million in 2019,[1] which is larger than the annual turnover of many enterprises. That same year, the NBA Finals prize pool was $22 million,[2] the golf Masters Tournament was $11.5 million,[3] and FIFA Club World Cup was $16.5 million.[4] Dota 2' s The International exceeded each of them, with a total prize pool of $34.3 million.[5] To put this in perspective, the global gaming industry was more than the combined size of the global movie and music industries. At $146 billion in 2019, the global gaming industry is expected to bring in three times the combined earnings of the movie and music industries by 2025.

There is no denying the fact that gaming in this age is not a game anymore. Gaming is a career and a profession with phenomenal opportunities not only for the professional players but also for esports tournament organizers, team managers, coaches, peripheral providers, sponsors, shows and expo organizers, and—believe it or not—national economies.

You may be surprised to know that games like backgammon, checkers, senet, and nine men are more than 5,500 years old. It's even more surprising that all of these games originated from the Middle East. Believe it or not, the Middle East has continued its pedigree and legacy in the esports arena as well. As we speak, countries like Saudi Arabia and the U.A.E. have some of the best professional esports teams competing at global tournaments, and they're winning regional and Asian tournaments.

Let's take a step back and analyze why esports is gaining such traction in the region. If you look at the basic and fundamental enablers of esports in a country, there is a young (read "tech savvy") population, high-speed internet connectivity, mobile penetration, availability of a gaming infrastructure, and a reasonable per capita income. The Gulf Cooperation Council (GCC) countries have all of these and in abundance. In fact, 60 percent of the population of GCC countries is under thirty years of age. The smartphone and internet penetration is 60 percent, and it's expected to reach 85 percent by 2025.

Keep in mind that countries like the U.A.E., Saudi Arabia, and Qatar have more than 90 percent internet penetration and over 120 percent smartphone penetration.[6, 7, 8] I don't think I need to convince you on per capita income in these countries. As of now, China, the U.S., Japan, South Korea, and Germany are the top five countries in terms of the size of the gaming industry. Saudi Arabia is ranked nineteenth, and the U.A.E. is ranked thirty-fifth in terms of revenue in the gaming market.

If you look at the bigger picture of esports from an economic perspective, you will see there are two sets of countries—those that are pioneers in developing the games and other necessary technology and those that are buyers and consumers of these games and technology. It's easy to understand how the ones in the driver's seat are gaining the economic benefits. For decades, countries like China, the U.S., the U.K., Germany, and Japan have always been pioneers of development and innovation, and they have successfully developed an ecosystem that supports and promotes that. It's a monumental task for other countries to get there in a matter of a few years. On a brighter note, there are several other opportunities in the esports industry for other countries that go beyond the development of games and technology, including organizing expos, shows, and mega-events; hosting competitive tournaments; and organizing regional leagues.

So, are we saying that esports is an industry that regional economies can potentially focus on? No, we're saying the development of the esports industry *must* be a part of the national agenda for regional countries. It's clear that esports is a massive, yet less understood, industry. This could be because gaming started as a casual activity, then was tabooed as a waste of time, energy, and money.

Back in 2015, the Entertainment Software Association (ESA) reported that the U.S. games industry had approximately 2,500 game companies employing 220,000 employees at an average salary of $97,000 per annum for game developers. The report also claimed that the U.S. game industry contributed $11.7 billion to the U.S. GDP.[9] Note that these are the figures from 2015, and the gaming and esports industry has grown multifold since then.

Making the esports industry's development a national agenda wouldn't just be about esports. It would support a plethora of other industries, including hospitality, travel, tourism, logistics, transportation, manufacturing, and technology. In turn, this will bring in sustainable and long-term economic developments.

Latency is the biggest turnoff for gamers. To counter that, gaming companies are setting up regional and in-country servers. Many of them are even taking up large spaces in data centers to eliminate the latency issue. Valorant launched dedicated regional servers with Amazon Web Services (AWS) in Bahrain. Valorant is no Dota 2 or League of Legends yet, but imagine if other major titles also followed suit.

On the other hand, the U.A.E. has established itself as the go-to place for trade shows, expos, and flagship conferences. The country has hosted several gaming expos and conferences in the past few years, which definitely brought in an additional economic value. However, there are other—and bigger—opportunities to capture in the areas of innovation, development, and production, but these require a more robust strategy, including planning, and a fundamental shift in the approach.

First, they will need to centralize the control and ownership. That is, there must be a single government body or department dedicated to achieving this goal. Countries aspiring to emerge as a leader in the esports industry will have to have a centralized body to drive this change. One of the first steps such a department will have to work toward is transforming the entire thought process, culture, and outlook toward gaming and esports, which will have to begin from a very basic level, starting with the education system. Programs would be needed to drive awareness about esports as a potential career to help shift the mindsets of others.

The second step would be to develop and implement strategies to move a country higher up the esports value chain to get it involved in the production of games. This would need a robust ecosystem and an over-haul of the educational courses and curriculum. Introducing subjects and courses in school that support creativity and sharpen cutting-edge technology skills would be pivotal.

As we know, the best of the games have an average development cycle of five years or more. This means there is a significant amount of financial investment required in developing games, with a longer ROI cycle. The regional game development studios will need a strong fund-ing engine in the form of venture capitalists, private equity investors, and government support.

There is no denying that esports is a sunshine industry and there are several opportunities for the ecosystem players. The GCC countries have most of the building blocks to establish themselves as a prominent player in this industry. Countries like Saudi Arabia, the largest country of the GCC region, as well as United Arab Emirates, have been quick to realize the potential of this industry, develop strategies, and proceed with implementation. Both the countries have made several announcements about their plans to capitalize on the massive economic opportunity that esports is. For example, Dubai Economic Department (DED) recently hosted the global championship of PUBG Mobile, which had a whopping prize pool of $2 million. Similarly, Saudi Arabia has set up Saudi Arabian Federation for Electronic and Intellectual Sports (SAFEIS) with a goal to establish Saudis among the most accomplished gamers around the world and for the country to be a global gaming hub. These certainly are the steps in the right direction of stamping their presence in the list of top esports and gaming economies. For regional economies, this is just the beginning of exciting gaming times.

MEET SAURABH VERMA

Saurabh is a casual gamer but a serious gaming and esports enthusiast. He has been gaming since childhood and was active in competitive gaming during his teen years. Today, he is regularly beaten by his teenage son in most of the games they play. In his corporate life, Saurabh is a senior director and regional head for the information and communications technology (ICT) practice of Frost & Sullivan, Middle East. He has also worked with several clients, including government bodies, to develop roadmaps for the development of the esports industry and ecosystem and promote esports as a national development agenda for regional governments.

Saurabh is regularly featured in leading media publications and conferences on various ICT technologies, esports, and gaming. He was recently invited for a fireside chat on esports at CABSAT.Virtual 2020. Find him online at:

linkedin.com/in/saurabhverma2

PART 6

Careers in Esports

CHAPTER 26

The Esports Economy

For the unsuspecting or those late to the party, esports has become a part of the mainstream of society. Where esports was once only a small subset of sports culture, it has grown into its own standalone industry. Esports has hit this lofty level primarily due to the social engagement found uniquely among gamers. Livestreaming their own gameplay has turned each participant into their own content curator and procurer. Despite not being face-to-face with their audience, fans on gaming-specific streaming platforms like Twitch and YouTube Gaming have a direct connection to the players and teams.[1]

Accepting the premise that sport reflects societal characteristics, we look to identify those people, events, or acts that impose change on society. These changes can only be facilitated when society acts as a reflection of the institution being changed—in this case, sport as an institution.

Traditionally, we have seen game changers or influencers in traditional sports—such as baseball, football, and college athletics—have an impact beyond their sport and cause societal change. Jackie Robinson, arguably the most influential athlete of the twentieth century, broke the color barrier in baseball in 1947 and single-handedly changed race relations in sports and society. Today, every minority athlete owes their success, salary, and influence to Jackie's courage. On January 12, 1969, Joe Namath led the NY Jets of the AFL to a stunning upset of the heavily favored Baltimore Colts. The Super Bowl was born. Fifty-four years later, Super Bowl Sunday—with its pageantry, economic impact, and viewership—is celebrated around the world. In college athletics, Title IX changed the game—literally—for female athletes. In 1972, this legislation deemed that women were to be treated equitably and fairly. This opened the door to equality in education, in the workplace, and in society. More women enrolled in college and entered the workforce as a direct result of Title IX.

Similar to traditional sports, game changers exist in the history of esports and gaming. Many people have seen the explosion of esports across the globe, but few recall when the first game-changing moment occurred in esports and gaming. No, Ninja was not involved. The esports industry's first game changer took place on October 19, 1972, when the first video game tournament in the sci-fi rocket combat game Spacewar! was held at the Stanford Artificial Intelligence Laboratory in Los Altos, California. The event unleashed on an unsuspecting world the enormous potential of computers and the unfettered creativity they offered and their ability to change society. No one could have expected how important that event would be nearly fifty years later.[2]

The change was not immediate, but that doesn't make its impact any less impressive. From its humble beginnings, the world of esports has grown faster than any traditional sport ever did. Now, competitive computer gaming is a spectator sport and a worldwide phenomenon that not only rivals traditional sports but, in many cases, has also surpassed them.

A 2021 report on the growth of esports by market research firm Newzoo lends statistical credence to esports' impact: Revenues are estimated to reach an impressive $1.1 billion in 2021, showing year-to-year growth of over 14 percent.[3] The highest-grossing individual esports revenue stream worldwide is sponsorship, set to generate $833.6 million in 2021.[4] The global esports audience will grow to 728.8 million in 2021.[5] A closer look at the esports industry will reveal different game changers in the form of people, philosophy, and business enterprise. These game changers have altered the trajectory of esports in areas such as the economy, social impact, business opportunities, sponsorships, events, and academics.

The esports economy

The transformation and game-changing element that created the esports economy occurred with the maturation of the gaming industry. As a result, business leaders decided the time was right to invest in the esports ecosystem. Venture capitalists and private equity firms doubled the number of investments in esports between 2017 and 2018, going from thirty-four to sixty-eight, per Deloitte.[6]

In terms of total dollars invested, investments were up to $4.5 billion in 2018 from just $490 million the year before, a staggering year-over-year growth rate of 837 percent, per Deloitte. These investments touch on the entire esports ecosystem—from esports organizations to tournament operators and digital broadcasters.[7] By making these financial investments into the esports economy, these financiers are betting on the economics of esports to continue to rise and bring them a return on their investment.

Esports business opportunities

In traditional sports, business opportunities abound in media, merchandise sales, sponsorships, player endorsements, team value, and mega-events. From this model, esports now offers similar business opportunities to entrepreneurs to create their own niche in the esports industry. Justin Dellario, the head of esports at Twitch since 2016, has been instrumental in making Twitch the world's leading streaming service and community for gamers. He is responsible for Twitch Esports programs' business and strategy in operations, strategic partnerships, development, and innovative growth.[8]

In a recent interview, Dellario stated, "Esports and Twitch are kind of synonymous; it's very much in our DNA. The growth of esports and the growth of Twitch have pretty much moved along at the same pace."

To further his mission to create business opportunities in esports, Dellario added, "We don't just think about our role in esports as one to just be strictly a distributor, but we think in a lot of ways about how we can help grow the space and create value for other segments as well."[9]

Athletes in traditional sports have also pursued opportunities in esports. Former Los Angeles Lakers star Rick Fox has become an advocate for esports and for the opportunities in the industry. As a gamer and esports franchise owner, Fox is changing the game by making esports business ventures more mainstream. Meanwhile, prominent professional sport owners, such as Robert Kraft and Fred and Jeff Wilpon, have seen the financial value of esports from fan engagement to competitions and have invested in (or own) esports franchises. Meanwhile, famous sport venues—such as Barclay's Center and Madison Square Garden in New York City and the Staples Center in Los Angeles—are selling esports competitions to capacity. In Texas, where everything is bigger, Esports Stadium Arlington, with one hundred thousand square feet, is the largest dedicated esports facility in North America, with esports event hosting and production capabilities.

Esports sponsorships

The world's largest brands have taken notice of the rise of esports and the rising participation and viewership numbers. Sponsorship opportunities continue to rise, as sponsorships of teams, players, and events continue to drive revenues. Nike and the League of Legends Pro League have entered into a $144 million deal similar to those in traditional sports, where the players, coaches, managers, and refs wear only Nike gear during gameplay.[10] Coca-Cola has partnered with Riot Games as sponsors of the League of Legends World Championship.

One unique element of the sponsorship included having over two hundred cinemas host simultaneous viewing parties for the 2016 League of Legends World Championships throughout the U.S., Canada, and Europe.[11]

The biggest game changer in esports sponsorships is streamer Tyler Blevins, known to his fans as Ninja. He became the first gamer to truly capitalize on his popularity by signing various endorsement deals. While many of his deals were endemic (products or services found directly in the industry) in nature, the game changer occurred with his deal with Adidas, the world's second largest sports brand. For the first time, a gamer-influencer crossed over into nonendemic brands (businesses whose products or services are not directly linked to the industry) more commonly found endorsing athletes and spending their sponsorship dollars in traditional sports. Through this endorsement, Ninja has the same—or bigger—name recognition as the world's greatest athletes, Roger Federer and LeBron James. The unique game changer of this sponsorship has Adidas looking to add products in both the physical and virtual worlds.[12]

Adidas made the deal with Ninja because of his impressive social media following. Before his move to Microsoft Mixer, he had over 14 million Twitch followers, and his Twitch videos received tens of thousands of views.[13] His Twitter page has 6.7 million followers.[14] While the Mixer platform recently merged with Facebook Gaming, Ninja's largest video streaming influence can still be found on YouTube, with 24.2 million subscribers.[15] Because Ninja creates his own content, brands have flocked to him for endorsement deals to allow them direct contact and connection with Ninja's loyal fan base.[16]

The esports personality crossover into mainstream media was reinforced when Sasha Hostyn, better known as Scarlett, one of the top StarCraft players in the world and the most accomplished woman in the history of esports, recently commanded a lengthy profile in *The New Yorker*.[17]

Whether of a team, league, player, or event, sponsorships have changed the game in the esports industry. User content, social engagement, and star power have all combined to make gamers highly sought-after properties for both endemic and nonendemic brands within the esports industry.

Events

The game changer for esports events happened in 2019 in Queens, New York. While there have been bigger events and larger crowds at other esports events around the globe, Epic Games' Fortnite World Cup finals changed the game in the United States. The esports industry was suddenly on everyone's radar. Even nongamers were attracted to the size of the crowds and the $30 million prize pool. The Fortnite finals selected the USTA Billie Jean King National Tennis Center's Arthur Ashe Stadium, home of the U.S. Open in tennis, connecting esports to traditional sports in their choice of venue. The twenty-three-thousand-seat facility sold out for all three days, and the nearly seventy thousand fans watched a sixteen-year-old from Pennsylvania, Kyle Giersdorf (aka Bugha), earn the winner's share of $3 million, as more than two million concurrent livestream viewers watched the finals.[18]

Increased prize money has significantly helped the growth of esports events. In 2000, the total prize money from twenty-seven tournaments barely topped half a million dollars. Fourteen years later, organizers shelled out more than $35 million in prize money over nearly two thousand tournaments, not counting lucrative sponsorships.[19] In 2019, the above-mentioned Fortnite World Cup offered $30 million all by itself. As prize money continues to increase, the mega event will continue to shape the future of esports competitions, signaling that esports is the future of sports entertainment.

Collegiate academics

Becker College changed the academic game when they announced a new bachelor of science in esports management in 2018. Recognizing the economic and professional opportunities generated by the burgeoning competitive gaming industry, Becker's esports management major will equip students with the knowledge and experience needed to excel in one of the fastest-growing sectors in the sports and entertainment industries.[20]

Following this, Caldwell University, in their School of Business and Computer Science, developed the first esports business management major degree program in the state of New Jersey. As Caldwell esports professor Neil Malvone stated, "The esports business management focus is to provide a program that prepares students to lead and manage in the business of esports management through hands-on and experiential learning."[21]

Following the lead of Becker College and Caldwell University, more colleges are now preparing students for careers in esports through courses and degree programs. We are now in the midst of another societal revolution causing its sport members to switch their allegiances again to another new sport. Game changers within society should be readily identifiable and, more importantly, significantly impactful. The game changers foretell the revolution, and we should embrace the change.

MEET RAY KATZ AND NEIL MALVONE

Ray Katz

Ray Katz is co-founder and chief operating officer of the Collegiate Sports Management Group (CSMG), a college-sports-focused properties group that drives the business performance of college athletic conferences and schools, providing them with a successful growth strategy and generating revenue to support their athletic departments and initiatives. CSMG specializes in marketing and media rights, revenue generation, content creation and distribution, strategy and negotiation, asset valuation, NIL (Name, Image and Likeness), sponsorship sales, licensing, and esports. Katz is a highly accomplished executive and entrepreneur with over twenty-five years in the industry and is frequently referenced in leading media outlets, including Bloomberg, Thompson Reuters, and Associated Press. He has diverse experience working for the National Football League, Young & Rubicam, The Lord Group, The Walt Disney Company, and Madison Square Garden. His expertise ranges from sports marketing disciplines to research and analytics. He can be found at:

linkedin.com/in/raykatz

Neil Malvone

Neil A. Malvone is the executive vice president, partnerships and chief esports officer at CSMG and CEO/founder of Cutting Edge Sports Management (CESM). At CSMG, Neil heads up the esports division and is involved in media, marketing, and event operations. In 2021, Neil and CSMG created their own game changer in the collegiate esports industry by hosting the first Collegiate Esports National Championship (CENC). The CENC was the largest collegiate esports event in the history of collegiate esports and incorporated many groundbreaking firsts including play-in tournaments, a selection show, high school teams, 2-year colleges and 4-year colleges participating, eCommerce and licensing revenue streams, Name, Image, and Likeness adoptions, and an international college showcase. CENC was broadcast on three Twitch channels and on ESTV. The event garnered 500,000 social media impressions and had 577,000 minutes of streams watched during the 4-day event.

On the traditional sport side, Neil is engaged in all aspects of sport event planning, including event creation, revenue generation, sponsorship sales and activation, and social media. As the founder of CESM, Neil developed the Dream Bowl and the Historically Black Colleges and Universities (HBCU) Spirit of America Bowl football showcase events. HBCU-Dream Bowl Weekend features non-Football Bowl Subdivision (non-FBS) and HBCU athletes in a one-of-its-kind event specifically for players from around the country. The games enhance CESM's mission to celebrate football, social progress, and Americana.

In 2019, Neil was named vice chairman of the National Junior College Athletic Association Esports. Neil continues to develop collegiate esports national championship events for the NJCAAE and the Eastern College Athletic Conference, the two national governing bodies for esports, with a focus on production, media rights, streaming, and sponsorships. Neil is also a notable professor of sport business, sport law, and esports business management at the master's and undergraduate levels throughout the New York metropolitan area. At Caldwell University, Neil created the first esports business management degree curriculum in the state of New Jersey. You can connect with him on LinkedIn at:

linkedin.com/in/neil-a-malvone-5317295

CHAPTER 27

Building a Gaming Company

In seventh grade, I used Adobe Flash to design and animate a cat. After hitting the "run animation" button, the cat burst into motion, legs churning. I was delighted . . . until I realized I couldn't stop it. My poor cat was doomed to eternal running. My mission was clear: I needed a "stop" button. So, I created one, using this code:

```
Function goClick(e:MouseEvent){
    gotoAndStop(2);}
```

Now I could create a button, and the cat finally froze. But I had forgotten all about cats, amazed and excited by what the code could do. Fascinated with code, I began to create small games and posted them online and on the mobile stores, which led me to eventually start my own company and learn the complexities of advertising and marketing. Now, like then, if I don't know the code to do something, I learn it, and I'm happy that hundreds of thousands of people enjoy my 130-plus games. I was lucky to get the chance to work at Electronic Arts, N3TWORK, Sony PlayStation, and Google on game projects to get a better sense of what gamers and users want to see in large-scale games and related applications.

After being in the gaming industry for eleven years now, I've been lucky to have over 9.2 million people download my games and see what

I've made. Being selected to be on the *Forbes* 30 Under 30 list in my junior year of college was the first moment that I felt like I really did belong in the industry and finally was able to speak about what I loved to do more publicly. Since the industry is very predominantly male, my dream is to make it a kinder and more diverse place for people by continuing to speak at events like the annual Game Developers Conference and Games for Change. I was lucky to have entered at an age where I didn't realize that I'd be a minority and have felt so lucky to have mentors like Kate Edwards and Kelly Wallick and Laura Warner, amazing women who have boosted my own self-confidence and helped me grow in this industry.

Many think that video games offer no benefit to society and that they, in fact, detract from it. That's why I started a mobile fitness gaming company, Talofa, with my dad and brother. We wanted to use games as a medium to inspire people who have never run before or found the motivation to continue running. As a runner, I've found that my friends always tell me that running is intimidating, difficult, and boring, even though there are so many mental and physical health benefits that it provides. Run to My Heart is a game that I'm currently creating that will help get players into running and guide them into a healthy running routine. This game combines immersive audio with a social community mobilized around a narrative fantasy universe. My hope is that players who run with Run to My Heart will form virtual communities paralleling traditional run clubs even within the confines of their homes during the COVID-19 pandemic. Not only that, I hope that with my team of seventeen, we can create a diverse and inclusive game that serves players of all fitness levels and body types and that they can see themselves in the characters in our game. As a game that ties in real sports to gaming, I can see how competition that forms around Run to My Heart can parallel those of esports, competing with each other live while getting more fit in their real lives.

I know that as a female software developer, I can inspire other girls to start learning coding skills. I want to use this opportunity so that I can focus my efforts on bringing the gender gap to a close. I want to be able to continue creating games and applications that can affect the people around me, and I want to be able to reach audiences that I've never even dreamed of reaching.

When I taught video game development at my elementary school, I found that girls and boys were usually equally curious about how I make my games, and sometimes the girls were the ones who seemed the most interested. Questions like "Can you teach me how to make games like you?" always motivate me to keep making games and to continue to reach more and more girls who love games. Now that I'm the CEO of a gaming company and creating games for others full time, I want to become a leader who can inspire and create a change in the industry.

Sometimes I still think about that poor cat I made. Now I'm the one in constant motion. But unlike my experience with the virtual cat, I hope I never find my "stop" button. There's way too much to do.

MEET JENNY C. XU

Jenny is a *Forbes* 30 Under 30: Games recipient, long-distance runner, artist, programmer, gamer, farmer, and CEO of Talofa Games. She's passionate about the intersection of fitness and gaming and is currently developing a social running game at Talofa Games. She also solo develops horror comedy mobile games for her indie game company, JCSoft Inc.

In her free time, she runs Abs with Jenny, a gamified virtual fitness class that has taught over 430 people and raised over $10,000 for charity. After graduating from MIT with a computer science degree, she's worked in the intersection of AR and fitness to explore how gaming motivates healthy habits. In her ten years in the gaming industry, she's created 130-plus games for web and mobile with ten shipped titles on the mobile app stores with over 9.2 million downloads. She's also completed internships at Google, Electronic Arts, Sony PlayStation, and N3TWORK. Connect with her at:

linkedin.com/in/xujennyc

CHAPTER 28

Forging a Unique Career Path

Let me make something perfectly clear: I never aspired to work in the game industry. I was about seven years old when I saw and played the original Pong arcade machine, and while I have been an avid gamer ever since, I never viewed game development as a career goal.

Without a doubt, part of that is due to the fact that in those early days of the game industry (the 1970s and 1980s), there wasn't any formal education path to learn the skills of game creation—most of the pioneers of that era sort of stumbled into their game-making paths from various other disciplines. So, while I really loved playing games, my goals were set much higher right out of high school: I wanted to be an astronaut! I was four years old when humans stepped on the moon for the first time in 1969, and I watched it on my grandmother's black-and-white television in awe and wonder.

Over time, what I came to realize is I have far too many interests and that I'm curious about too many things. From wanting to be an astronaut, to aspiring, pursuing, and then becoming a storyboard artist for Lucasfilm so I could work on a *Star Wars* movie, to dabbling in history and entomology. I finally found my intellectual home in geography, not only because I have always loved maps and travel and learning about other cultures but also because geography encompasses so many broad areas of knowledge. However, like most people, I never completely abandoned my other interests. I simply moved them aside to focus on something else. Ultimately, what I have really wanted out of my career path—more than anything—was *confluence* and *impact*.

In the field of geography, we use the word *confluence* to describe the junction of two or more rivers—basically a place where different flows come together and join into one larger force. Similarly, what I have always wanted out of my career was to somehow find a way for my core passions to not only coexist but also complement one another and combine into something even greater. As for impact, I think that is straightforward. Like most people, I've wanted my work to make a positive contribution to my field of interest, the people around me, and the world at large.

At this point you may be wondering what all this really has to do with video games. Like any good cartographer, I'll strive to map out that answer for you.

In hindsight, it's not surprising to me at all that the various influences on my life and my career were always present from my very earliest memories. The spark may have started with the moon landing, but that burning passion quickly grew, thanks to watching countless hours of science fiction on television like the original *Star Trek*, *Twilight Zone*, *The Outer Limits*, and *Land of the Giants*. And the very first movie I remember seeing in a theater was *2001: A Space Odyssey*—that pretty much set the tone for what was to follow in my life. I also had a whole phase of obsession with Ray Harryhausen's amazing stop-motion animation films like *Jason and the Argonauts* and *The Mysterious Island*, which drove my friends and I to create our own stop-motion animated films in high school using a Super 8mm film camera and clay models.

Even at this young stage, I already had an eclectic mix of interests around technology and the creative arts and maintained a fascination with the fictional worlds and narratives as well as the technical process of creating them for film and television. This obsession was taken to a whole other level in 1977 when the first *Star Wars* movie was released. At the very impressionable age of twelve, my whole conception for what was possible had changed. I had seen amazing worlds on screen before, but nothing even remotely close to the *Star Wars* universe. To this day, I sometimes find it hard to impress on younger people—for whom *Star Wars* is just another escapism option among many—how revolutionary it was for my generation.

And yet the calling to real space, via an aerospace engineering program at Cal Poly State University in San Luis Obispo, pulled at me first. It didn't take long for my quantum dislike of calculus to convince me to shift to an industrial design program at Cal State Long Beach, as I had learned that many of the Lucasfilm storyboard artists at that time had obtained their amazing skills in industrial design—and some at that very same school. I already had the artistic aptitude (it helped that my mom was an artist as well as a teacher), but I wanted to learn that specific conceptual art style—and I did it within two years. And now, finally on a path to an interesting career—on a complete whim and to the shock of those around me—I suddenly decided to change my academic major to geography and cartography.

As the industrial design program was going to add at least a year or two to my undergraduate work, I had decided early on to pursue a minor degree in geography. The subject matter had always positively haunted me, going all the way back to an old globe I used to study intensely as a kid and the fantastic "Create a Country" project in junior high—which was arguably my very first experience with world-building. *And I absolutely loved it.*

What I would come to realize many years later is that geographers make for excellent world-builders, because we spend so much of our time deconstructing the "real world." We strive for a deep understanding of how global systems interact and affect one another—from the physical environment (e.g., climatology, plate tectonics, biospheres) to the human environment (e.g., geopolitics, economics, cultures, languages).

Any map you have ever seen is a world-building exercise on the part of the geographer/cartographer. They are taking specific variables from the "real world"—such as terrain elevation, vegetation types, road networks, and populated areas—and reproducing them in a carefully planned and generalized format to make it easier to understand these phenomena and their spatial relationships. Some of these map worlds are intended for general use—such as helping you drive from point A to point B or finding a store to shop at—while other maps are thematic and intended to express a specific variable—such as population density, political affiliations, or relative temperature.

I fully understand now that geographers are indeed a type of world-builder, but after I completed my undergraduate degree, worked for a year as a cartographer, and then entered graduate school, I still had no idea what I was getting into. Yet my subconscious knew better, to the point that my master's thesis in geography was on the topic of using VR technology (which was nascent at that time) to leverage more human sensory inputs to create more intuitive maps and greatly increase our comprehension of spatial phenomena. Once again, my longtime interests in cutting-edge technology and creativity found their way back into my work.

Shortly after completing my master's thesis, our geography department at the University of Washington in Seattle received a call from Microsoft. The company was looking for a cartographer to build all the maps for a new product called Encarta Encyclopedia. Being newly married and a "starving" graduate student, I took the contractor job, because the work sounded interesting and the pay was quite good.

I fully expected to complete the three-to-six-month contract and then return to my doctorate studies in geography. However, Microsoft kept extending my contract. And then eventually they offered me a full-time position in a new kind of role they asked me to create—a geopolitical strategist. My job would focus primarily on helping the mapping products (Encarta World Atlas, Streets & Trips, etc.) navigate complicated and sensitive geopolitical issues—such as how to portray certain disputed areas of the world (e.g., Jammu and Kashmir) or what's the proper place name for certain features, countries, and so on.

As I put my PhD on hold and dove into this new role at Microsoft, it didn't take long before people had heard about my role in the company. It was slow at first, but I started receiving random emails from the Windows team, the Office team, Internet Explorer, and many more, all asking me practical, business-oriented questions related to geography, geopolitics, and cultures, like "What's the correct flag for this country?" "Is it acceptable to make an icon out of this gesture?"

What was really cool is that I could actually answer most of these questions and help them out without having to do much additional research. It dawned on me that an information technology (IT) company like Microsoft really needed someone with my unorthodox, non-tech expertise, and I could actually be useful—even as a geographer.

But I wouldn't fully realize my usefulness until a few years into the job, when I saw the company make a couple of very serious and similar errors in the Korean market in two different products—Encarta World Atlas and the original Age of Empires. The issues happening within a few months of each other caused a huge disruption for Microsoft's business, and it could have been so easily avoided if the product teams had been talking to one another. This incident sparked an idea for a cross-functional, company-wide team that would coordinate the knowledge about these sensitive geopolitical and cultural issues and help educate employees on best practices. I called this team Geopolitical Strategy, and, after significant effort, I was granted permission to create and lead the team.

Up to that point, I had consulted on Flight Simulator and a couple of other game projects but not in a formal capacity. But now as the manager and lead subject matter expert of the Geopolitical Strategy team, I had a formal mandate to help all products across the company—which included *all the games* created by Microsoft and its studios. And suddenly, I was working in the game industry without even realizing it at first. But the more I worked on various games—from Halo and Fable to Age of Empires and Forza Motorsport—I found that my world-builder mentality as a geographer fit perfectly with the world-building exercise of creating a game. I quickly developed a greater camaraderie and affinity for the game designers, narrative designers, and creative team.

Working on video games is actually how I finally found my confluence. Everything I valued and in which I was interested—new technologies, leveraging the imagination, world-building, and creative collaboration—I discovered in the game space. In essence, I had created my dream job, performing culturalization consulting on video games, without even really intending to do so.

It's no surprise then that when I left Microsoft in 2005, I did so not because I disliked my work. On the contrary, I felt I had achieved as much as I could for the company and simply felt it was time to move on and help other companies, with the intention of focusing primarily on the games sector. And although I still maintain a decent percentage of my consulting work outside of games, helping companies like Google, Facebook, Huawei, National Geographic, and others, the majority of my time is spent working on what I love and with people whose skills I so greatly admire.

At the same time, over the past decade or so, I've also expanded my focus to help the game industry be a better place for its amazingly talented people. So I've focused on advocacy efforts like running the International Game Developers Association and the Global Game Jam, and I serve on several boards and in advisory roles that focus on creating a more inclusive industry that values its people and treats them well.

What I really hope you take away from this is that every passion you have, every interest you maintain, and everything you've ever been curious about are all valid parts of who you are as a creative individual. While we typically select a singular career path to focus on, and many who pursue a career in games tend to follow well-trodden paths as programmers, narrative designers, artists, and so forth, it is also completely possible to blend multiple interests into your field of study and career.

As individuals we are all a very unique outcome of so many variables—both internal and external—that shape our skills and experiences. So, if you don't find yourself fitting into an existing path, then create your own. It requires persistence, diligence, and a certain high level of passion about your convictions and how you can contribute. You may attempt various avenues and fail, but don't let that deter you.

When I created my Geopolitical Strategy team at Microsoft, I had to pitch the idea to *five* different VPs before I finally received the approval to move forward. It took seven months of rejection, rethinking, rewriting, and seeking guidance from various mentors, but I never relented, because deep down I knew the company could benefit from this new kind of resource.

In the end, no matter what your background is—geographically, culturally, linguistically, or otherwise—the game industry can be a place for you, even if you need to forge that new path on your own. You will ultimately enjoy the destination far more because it's of your own making, but don't forget to also enjoy the journey—which for all its ups and downs can be just as satisfying.

By the way, many years after I had aspired to work on something *Star Wars*–related, and long after I thought that aspiration was no longer attainable, I ended up working for four years on the game *Star Wars: The Old Republic*. Granted, I was in a completely different role than I imagined as a teenager—a culturalization consultant and not a conceptual artist—however, the circle was now complete.

MEET KATE EDWARDS

Kate Edwards is the CEO and principal consultant of Geogrify, a consultancy for content culturalization; the executive director of the Global Game Jam; and the former executive director of the International Game Developers Association. In addition to being an outspoken, award-winning advocate that serves in several advisory/board roles, she is a geographer, writer, and corporate strategist who pioneered the field of content culturalization in games.

Formerly as Microsoft's first geopolitical strategist in the Geopolitical Strategy team she created and managed, Kate protected the company against political and cultural content risks across all products and locales. Following thirteen years at Microsoft, she has consulted on many game and non-game projects for BioWare, Google, Amazon, Facebook, LEGO, Ubisoft, and many other companies. Kate is also a columnist for *MultiLingual Computing* magazine. *Fortune* magazine named her as one of the "10 most powerful women" in the game industry, and she was named by GamesIndustry.biz as one of their six People of the Year. She was most recently honored with the Ambassador Award at the Game Developers Choice Awards at GDC 2020. She was also profiled in the December 2018 publication *Women in Gaming: 100 Professionals of Play*. Find her online at:

linkedin.com/in/geogrify
twitter.com/geogrify

CHAPTER 29

The Rise of the Gamerpreneur

"That's the funny thing about the video game industry. The deeper you get into it, the less time you have to play games yourself."

—BOBBY BAIRD

Bobby Baird is the director for strategic partnerships for a huge, enterprise-focused data analytics firm. He joined a marketing firm out of college as an account manager, dealing with large corporations to help promote their goods and services. When an opening came up after the owners of the company started a new business focused on data analytics for esports and streaming companies, Bobby was promoted to his directorship. Still in his early twenties, the sky is the limit for Bobby in terms of professional growth. A huge gamer his entire life, Bobby turned his passion for video games into a career when he entered the business world.

But Bobby is not unusual. Hidden behind society's constant drumbeat that video games create violent offenders, make us lazy, and turn us into slaves of the television, individuals like Bobby are rising up and deciding to take their futures into their own hands in the ways they know how, even if their friends and family believe they are wasting their time.

Dispelling the myth

Gamerpreneurs—individuals who are working to dispel the myth that society has laid upon gamers everywhere of the lazy, unmotivated basement dweller—embody a different philosophy of life and business than any I had met before in the corporate world. In my search for more of these gamerpreneurs, I have met countless individuals who completely break the mold by standing out as entrepreneurs, job holders, and salespeople.

My own path to becoming a gamerpreneur began relatively late in my life. Never in my wildest dreams did I ever think I would enter the gaming industry in my thirties—quite to the contrary. After growing up being told there was absolutely no future with video games, which I had spent the vast majority of my waking hours playing as a child and teenager, I went to college, then law school, and ended up becoming a court administrator for a county court before going into private practice and becoming a partner at a twenty-eight-year-old law firm at the ripe old age of twenty-seven. Once I hit that ceiling of advancement, I figured it was time to go into the world of entrepreneurship, so I started a new law practice with my wife. That practice became one of the fastest growing in Northeast Ohio before I decided to branch out and become a business coach and consultant.

The funny thing about all this success was that I came to realize that most of it was due to the skills and experiences I had developed from playing video games. Persistence, patience, problem-solving, critical thinking, and more were all honed and trained while playing games.

It wasn't until years later that I realized that, despite my enormous success in life, I was simply not happy. In fact, I was pretty miserable dealing with businesses and business owners who did not mesh with my personality. I was a gamer at heart, and so I had to find other gamers to work with. So, I set out to find different businesses and business owners to hire me, gamer-owned businesses, and video gamers. Very quickly, it became apparent to me that—despite the stigma society has placed on gamers—there are countless gamers out there who have started their own businesses, and scores more who hold steady, well-paying jobs.

Mentoring 101

My job is to show all these wonderful individuals, full of passion and life, the basics of how business works, how to produce content and products that will sell, how to promote themselves in ways that make them irresistible to their target audiences, and how to profit off of proven systems and processes that others are already using in the business world.

I'm sorry to say, for the most part, these are skills that gamers have not been exposed to, and lack of business acumen is the reason so few people seem to take gamers seriously. However, I show them the tips and tricks I've picked up over the years dealing with businesses, large and small, including funding deals worth millions of dollars. Then we shape their dreams into real businesses that exceed their wildest imaginings.

David Harvey was one of my very first coaching clients. David had a rough childhood and found his escape in video games and skateboarding. When he first found an opportunity to break away from poverty, he took it. David started by selling skateboards out of the back of a pickup truck. Within just a few months, he moved into a retail location, built up a loyal following, and was earning over $150,000 per year. Before long, he moved into distribution for retail stores, and he is now building partnerships all over the world selling merchandise. He still plays video games in his spare time and realized that gamers were a fantastic demographic for him to focus his marketing efforts on to further expand his business.

Turning passion into a career

However, it isn't just young people who are gamerpreneurs. Adam Gerstin is in his late forties and is a lifelong gamer. When Adam isn't getting his fix from gaming, he enjoys live action role-playing, also known as LARPing. Adam began his career as a digital marketer for businesses, focusing on search engine optimization through Google and other search browsers. When Adam reached a point in his life where he had enough business to live a comfortable life, he realized he needed more fulfillment, and that took him back to his gaming roots.

Adam started and self-funded a venture called LFG Nexus, a new social media tool that allows gamers of all stripes to find others—online and in their local communities—to play with. Adam built a team of like-minded entrepreneurs and now manages the day-to-day operations of LFG, while still managing to squeak in some game time when he's not otherwise working to promote his enterprise.

There are millions of people striving to turn their gaming into a full-time income source, and a few have. However, the majority of them understand that it's still aspirational. In fact, it is incredibly difficult to earn a living from simply playing video games full time. This is why most of them do it in their spare time rather than dropping out and sitting in front of the computer all day. Even among professional gamers, the vast majority hold down steady jobs. Ranging from auto mechanics and copywriters to program developers, all but a handful of gamers have "regular" jobs.

To be a top competitor in this industry, you must get in the game at a young age, when your reflexes are at their best. But it's important to remember that once someone has aged out, they do not necessarily wither away and die. Instead, many of these gamers who go into the industry in a professional player capacity turn their experiences into an advantage. They get to see the multibillion-dollar video games industry from the inside, since they're playing at a young age. Then, a good number of them end up in consulting positions after they have done their tour as players.

Johnny Ryan Weaver, for example, is the founder of Click Gaming. Johnny was a multiyear champion at Halo 2, a first-person shooter game. Johnny played at the highest levels but realized that there would come a point when he would age out. When that day came, Johnny moved into consulting. Now he is working with large corporations to help them establish their own esports tournaments as promotional campaigns. Johnny secures venues, establishes an administrative team, organizes a content schedule, and oversees the operations of these events, often with budgets ranging in the millions of dollars. He also works with children to help them see there can be a future beyond the controller in gaming.

Universal skills

Not every gamer ends up turning their gaming passion into their career. Eric Didier, chief creative officer of Urban Misfit Ventures, is an example of a gamer who recognized his skills were better suited to influencer development and marketing. Eric helped found a digital marketing enterprise that works with businesses, salespeople, and entrepreneurs to position themselves as separate and apart from their competitors. Of course, Eric credits his creativity and vision to his time playing video games.

Only a few years ago, I believed the line that my own parents had told me that "there is no future in video games." If I had not believed them, I would have considered going into the burgeoning field of esports law. Justin Jacobson did just that. He graduated around the same time that I did but was not fed the same line. Instead, he saw the industry for what it was: a vast, untapped market with endless potential. Now, he is with the Jacobson Firm, P.C. Justin is one of the few attorneys promoting themselves as practicing in the field, and his business is booming.

However, even if he hadn't gone into esports law, he could still practice any other type of law he would like. In fact, every person I've mentioned so far could have lucrative careers in any industry they put their minds to. That's the wonderful part of gamerpreneurs: The skills they have developed are universal. Whether it's their ability to communicate quickly and effectively or their ability to persist in the face of repeated rejection (how many times did they practice this while playing a game and losing over and over again?) or their ability to create inventive solutions (if you haven't seen some of the works of art made by players in games, you're missing out), gamers everywhere are dispelling the myth of the lazy, unmotivated basement dweller.

A gamer's potential future is also not limited only to playing games professionally for an esports team or on a stream. In fact, the vast majority of video gamers I have encountered barely have time to play at all. They are so focused on steering their successful businesses and careers that playing games has become a luxury. The skills they develop and nurture through video games can manifest into an abundant life. Other gamers have done it. And you or your gamer child can too.

––––––––––

MEET BRADFORD CARLTON

Bradford Carlton, J.D., is a business coach focused on video gamer–owned businesses. Bradford realized he needed to get involved in the gaming and esports world after recognizing that gamers are often raised under the assumption that their gaming hobby is a weight dragging them down, rather than an asset to further their growth. Now, Bradford works with gamer-owned businesses, showing them the fundamentals of business, sales, and marketing. Bradford is the founder and host of The Gamerpreneur Podcast and co-owner of DBD Esports, LLC, an esports-focused marketing company. You can learn more about Gamerpreneurs and their mission to help gamers by visiting: www.the-gamerpreneur.com. Find Bradford at:

linkedin.com/in/bradfordcarlton

PART 7

The Future of Esports

CHAPTER 30

Asia: The Heart of Global Esports

Asia is the heart of global esports, with China at the epicenter. Esports in Asia is more than just big tournaments for PC competitions with huge crowds in arenas. It is a way of life. It is the essence of social entertainment and the essence of competition. In some countries it's even a national sport. Esports includes large professional tournaments and small amateur tournaments for PC and mobile games. Esports is also a driving force behind the use of internet cafes, where teams can play side by side and the spirit of competition abounds. Esports is supported by national governments, is embraced by the tourism industry, and is the new darling of consumer products companies hoping to advertise to more than a billion gamers in Asia, more than half of whom are esports enthusiasts.

For several years esports and esports games have been the leading driver for the growth of the video game industry in Asia. Games played in esports have mechanics that are attractive to competitive gamers, and they also have incentives built into gameplay, encouraging gamers to improve to become more competitive. Esports offers players the ability to watch pro gamers practice and compete, and then return to their own PC or mobile phone and practice what they saw. This all leads to esports games having longer lives than many non-esports videogames.

In 2020, the esports industry globally took a turn, as did all industries, due to the COVID-19 global pandemic. Remarkably, tournament organizers were agile enough to quickly shift from tournaments in offline venues, such as arenas and internet cafes, to online experiences played remotely and streamed to viewers everywhere. It was not without challenges to make sure all competitors were playing fairly, but by and large the shift from arena-based play with live audiences transferred nicely to online-only experiences.

China was the first country to allow in-person esports tournaments to resume. The Esports Beijing 2020 Series Events were held in Beijing in August of 2020, with the Honor of Kings World Championship Cup Final held with a socially distanced crowd of avid fans in Beijing's Wukesong Arena. One thing is for sure: The enthusiasm for esports has not waned, be it in person or online.

Types of games popular for esports in Asia

Multiplayer online battle arena (MOBA) is the main genre played in esports. MOBA leads the esports explosion in Asia and is the top-grossing esports genre in the region. Top MOBA tournaments attract the largest esports audiences. **Notable titles:** League of Legends, Dota 2, Honor of Kings/Arena of Valor, Mobile Legends: Bang Bang.

Digital collectible card games and auto battlers are turn-based strategy games that have become popular in recent years. They are particularly well suited for mobile devices, with their slower pace of play and touch interfaces. **Notable titles:** Hearthstone, Auto Chess Mobile, Teamfight Tactics, Clash Royale.

Real-time strategy games like StarCraft were integral to the development of esports in Asia. They are enjoying a resurgence as mobile and mid-core titles. **Notable titles:** StarCraft 2, Age of Empires, Warcraft 3.

Sports, racing, and fighting genres are integral to the success of mobile and console esports. Japan's esports industry is built around these kinds of games. They also appeal to mid-core gamers, capturing an audience that core esports titles may not. **Notable titles:** QQ Speed, Crazyracing: Kartrider, FIFA (franchise), Tekken, King of Fighters.

Battle royale titles experienced explosive growth in 2018 and 2019, supplanting MOBA as the most popular genre in several Asian markets. While less popular than battle royale titles, traditional first-person shooter esports are still popular in esports competitions, and we likely will see a small increase with the release of Valorant. **Notable titles***:* Counter-Strike: Global Offensive, Peacekeeper Elite, PUBG Mobile, Garena Free Fire, Fortnite Mobile, CrossFire Mobile, Valorant, Rainbow 6: Siege.

Internet cafes and tournament venues

Asia is unique worldwide in many ways, and one of these is that the internet cafe society is rich and vibrant. Some geographical regions require icafes for utilitarian reasons, because disposable income is too low for a robust PC and broadband connection at home, or the telecommunications infrastructure has yet to be fully built out to the homes. Without speed, a gamer will lose, so they seek access to the fastest connections and reliable telecommunications services. Game developers and publishers understand they must partner with world-class telcos to have safe, quick, and efficient transport of the data packets that make up the digital games played online. Uptime is of paramount importance for successful games.

Gamers go to internet cafes for three main reasons. The first reason is that their favorite game, which is served over a robust network, is not optimally played in their home environment. The internet cafes download client software for many client-based games and offer Steam and other premium platforms. The second reason is that icafes often set up esports competition zones, where the tables and PCs are lined up 5v5 or other ways for team-based play, and sometimes there are spectator seats.

And the third reason is that icafes offer a social venue to go on a date, hang out with friends, form casual teams, practice, play, get to know each other, and have fun chatting while gaming.

How and why Asian gamers embrace esports, including streaming video

One of the major aspects of esports is that gamers play and view their favorite pros for entertainment and for training on how to improve. Asian gamers, to a further extent than other markets, are motivated by the 4 Cs: competition, completion, community, and challenge. These gamers love to play a game that is challenging that everyone is playing, exchange social posts about their victories or tips on how to play, and wrap up a session of the game in a reasonable amount of time (as opposed to a perpetual-universe game). Those 4 Cs actually embody esports games, and these motivations, supported by Niko's data and analysis, are proof that esports is here to stay in Asia.

Other than hearing of a game, watching ads about a game, attending tournaments as a participant or a fan, and practicing playing, gamers everywhere are enthralled with streaming video. Streamers are gamers who share their screens online so that viewers can watch, learn, and engage with them. These streamers are key opinion leaders and major influencers, without even trying to be. Streaming is so popular that there is significant competition in the segment of streaming platforms.

Asia is home to a robust ecosystem of streaming video platforms that support esports and gaming content. Over 510 million viewers consume esports content at least once a month. While Western platforms such as Twitch and YouTube also serve Asia, regional and local platforms are more popular and contribute to a more diverse and specialized ecosystem. These platforms have become even more important to the esports industry, as many esports events moved online during the COVID-19 pandemic.

Increasing competition between platforms for key markets is driving deeper platform segmentation as each seeks to establish its niche. This is also generating competition for esports media licenses and broadcast exclusivity, one of the major revenue streams for esports. Competition between platforms benefits esports productions, which rely on media rights as a revenue stream. China is the most diverse streaming market in Asia, and growing diversity among streaming platforms across the region is increasing esports' value and visibility.

The leading streaming sites globally are Twitch, Facebook Gaming, and YouTube. In Asia, those three are popular in many countries, but all countries also have their own local favorite streaming platforms. And in China, those three global giants are not permitted. The local leading streaming sites by country are Douyu, Huya, Bilibili, and Tencent Video in China; Garena Live, NimoTV, CubeTV, and Bigo Live in Southeast Asia (SEA); AfreecaTV, NaverTV, and KakaoTV in South Korea; OPEN-REC.tv, Niconico, and Mildom in Japan; and Loco and Rheo in India. As a new media industry we expect this landscape to continue to shift and grow, but as streaming has become an essential part of gaming and esports, the role of livestreaming and esports is only going to get bigger.

The intersection of tourism and esports

Asia is a region of many countries. My company, Niko Partners, conducts market research on the video game industry in eleven of them. It is easy to travel between countries, particularly within Southeast Asia. There are budget airlines and budget hotels, and avid gamers like to use both. Cities and countries are embracing esports to build arenas, attract gamers, attract consumer product sponsorship, and build an industry that will generate revenue and taxes to plough back into the local economy.

China has created esports zones, esports cities, and so forth with government support. Indonesia and Malaysia embrace esports and building venues around them, also with government support. Most

Asian countries have done this, in fact. Singapore has even seen the Singapore Tourism Board try to partner with esports tournament organizers to bring tournaments to their country and build travel packages around them. For example, there may be a budget airline, a budget hotel, and a tournament ticket package offered together and marketed by the Singapore Tourism Board.

Colleges and universities in esports

So much of an industry has developed, that universities and colleges across Asia (as in other regions) have completely embraced esports. Most major esports leagues in Asia have corresponding collegiate esports teams. Tencent (based in China) operates collegiate leagues for hit esports titles of today, such as League of Legends (LoL), Honor of Kings, PUBG, and Peacekeeper Elite (China). Similarly, Garena (based in Singapore) operates collegiate leagues for LoL across SEA.

Many universities are developing their own varsity esports leagues, which operate separately from publisher-operated collegiate esports leagues. Universities across Asia have introduced programs in esports and esports management. Universities in China, Chinese Taipei, Philippines, and Thailand introduced esports management programs in 2019. Another trend sees universities developing esports professionalization programs, designed to train esports players.

Governments across the region are investing in national esports development, and many of these collegiate esports programs dovetail with national support for esports. Collegiate esports and esports management programs are pipelines for training and developing national esports professionals. Collegiate esports are usually organized by esports organizations for college students. Varsity esports are university sanctioned organized competitions.

The 2019 League of Legends International College Cup finals were held at the 2019 Esports and Music Festival in Hong Kong. Six of twelve teams in the tournament were from Asian universities. China's Jimei University won the 2019 world title.

The spillover to create pan-entertainment, such as TV shows, theme parks, and more

The bottom line of being successful with esports is to engage as many gamers and create as many fans as possible. This is done by the ubiquitous usage of games in internet cafes, tournaments, streaming platforms, and beyond. The esports teams are owned and sponsored by investors or private companies, and these companies endeavor to get sponsors from consumer products and other endemic or nonendemic companies. Licensors want to leverage the popularity of such games, because so many gamers and fans follow them. Therefore, the games' IP often is desired to be licensed for other uses, such as theme parks, TV shows, books, or versions of games for other platforms (e.g., a PC game is adapted for mobile use). This is true for esports titles and for non-esports titles.

Esports is a global industry, and Asia is leading the way for innovation and enthusiasm. The games, the venues, the consumer intersection with sponsorships and tourism, and the spillover to other forms of entertainment make up this collective industry formed around games that were made popular by the 4 Cs. Gamers in Asia are motivated to play esports, and it is clear the industry is here to stay.

MEET LISA HANSON

As the founder and president of Niko Partners, a market research and consulting firm covering video games, esports, and streaming markets in Asia, Lisa Cosmas Hanson is one of the leading experts on esports and video games in Asia. Lisa founded Niko Partners in 2002 and has since honed her expertise on the Chinese and Southeast Asian games industries that has benefited Niko's clients: companies that are global leaders in game publishing, game services, hardware, and investments. Before founding Niko, she served as a lead strategist at Viant and as a director, worldwide quarterly PC tracker, and senior analyst for Asia Pacific at IDC Research. Lisa began her career as an equity analyst at Marusan Securities in Tokyo.

Lisa's expertise in esports includes multiple published reports and data trackers covering esports in Asia, as well as numerous custom projects. She has also presented speeches and keynotes on esports at industry events, including ChinaJoy, the World Cyber Games, and the Esports Business Summit.

Lisa appears regularly in *The New York Times*, *Business Week*, *Forbes*, *The Wall Street Journal*, *Dow Jones*, *Reuters*, *BBC*, *Bloomberg*, and *Financial Times*, among others. She is based in the U.S. but travels to Asia regularly. Find her online at:

linkedin.com/in/lisa-cosmas-hanson-49193

CHAPTER 31

A Space to Develop

As incredible as this sounds, especially in the light of the global COVID-19 pandemic, the esports market is expected to grow both in viewership and revenue, seeing a giant leap by the year 2022. With more games in established genres added to this competitive market, thus logically the number of participants grows, and the esports market will continue to be lucrative for advertisers to spend their money effectively, which will enable publishers, organizations, and players both amateur and professional, to engage as a collective with an ever growing, fully engaged audience.

In Canada, the numbers reflect a similar growth. According to Newzoo, 1.5 million Canadians now watch esports at least once a month.[1] There are three esports-specific spaces—physical arenas to play, spectate, and broadcast esports competitions—in three different provinces, with a fourth just announced in the largest city, Toronto. Esports teams continue to be formed, along with esports analytics companies, broadcast companies, and more. All of them reach beyond Canada, working with publishers, organizations, and teams, in and outside of the industry, creating a truly global ecosystem.

I was asked to speak at the FIST Global Series event in 2019 in Toronto. I started by saying, "You aren't going to like what you are about to hear," and I will caution you now: You probably won't like what

I am about to say. I commented about how little we still know about the esports community and the different games, and how everyone is still guessing. It was not the usual *esports is amazing, hop on the train, make money fast!* message. It was—and still is—an honest, hard, and frank look at the industry. There is a need for physical esports spaces, not just at the level of the 2,500- to 10,000-seat stadiums currently being constructed, but also of varying sizes to accommodate other uses.

Where we are today

First, COVID-19 has pushed the pro and amateur games online, which has been a blessing and a curse. Tournaments have been easier to host, and a lot of money is pushed, or held back, to specific needs by investors, because the costs to host in person versus online are night and day. But the sponsors have been tighter with dollars, and the quality, at times, has been lacking, so the more important issue is consistency. Each individual tournament or event has made it frustrating for teams to play at a consistent level, making adjustments a challenge. Add in player or roster changes to stay at the top in an ever-changing landscape, and you create a recipe for much frustration.

Second, the investors are pushing their visions of the business model, rather than allowing the real driver, the publisher, to do so. Publishers are trying to grow their product and cannot do so in a consistent manner when competing tournaments change the rulesets, the team rosters change, and games and characters are updated. All of this is frustrating for viewers as well. They watch because they love the game and certain teams or players, but each tournament offers challenges that are easily jumped on in Twitch chat by the community.

This is why physical spaces are so important. Yet, the space by itself is not enough, nor is a space dedicated merely to the public enough. Esports players, viewers, and fans latch on to teams and games. A publisher is needed to be a business partner, with top talent playing in the space. There also needs to be a presence in the schools. Much like any professional space, whether NFL, NHL, or NASCAR, if the best players and leagues do not go to the spaces, you cannot expect a space to succeed. With solid partnerships with developers and publishers in place, how does this solve the issues facing esports and the many diverse communities?

These spaces solve the problems in three ways. First, they give confidence in the space to the local communities and the many diverse gamers who are loyal to their games or teams. Second, they allow the best to train and play in the space that the professionals play, thus creating a farm system for the esport. This is essential to the success of the space as, much like other sports' high-performance training programs, the best can receive this training in a setting that allows them to succeed. This is why the top esports teams have their own facilities. However, because there are thousands of esports teams and players, those who are the have-nots of the industry need access to the same level of training, resources, and growth potential. The third problem a space solves is the most important one, which is validity for esports— still a niche market—for sponsors, influencers, and advertisers. With millions of dollars waiting to be spent, KPI statistics and ROI are still showing strategic growth.

"Even before the pandemic, esports enjoyed a fast-growing viewership as well as a coveted youthful audience that has become increasingly difficult to reach via more traditional media. By some measures, esports audience sizes have become comparable to traditional sports audiences— the largest esports league, League of Legends, boasts higher viewership than MLB, the NBA, or the NHL."[2] This consistency is necessary, as the publishers create the ruleset of each game, giving the ability to adapt and train with other teams at a high level with no outside or online issues, such as internet connectivity.

Third, as in life, there are the haves and the have-nots in esports. Esports organizations listed publicly or long established and with capital resources have major advantages, forcing newer or less-well-funded teams into a feeder system model. This is bad for the ecosystem. There is a reason there are more than thirty teams in major sports leagues. To have only fifteen to eighteen top organizations in North America specifically hurts the communities, because it does not promote growth. Instead, it promotes collusion within the esports disciplines they play in. Tournaments with only the top teams create a gap and division that limits the ability of other investors and owners to grow and to see returns on their investments, both personally and professionally.

Why have spaces failed?

Unlike the South Pacific and Asia, most consumers in North America own PCs or gaming consoles, so the need to connect weekly or even daily is satisfied from home rather than in person. Simply put, North American gaming spaces are going after the wrong demographic. They are after the consumer, who likes to stay at home, instead of the publishers, who can draw those players out to see a show. They have changed their business model but still haven't found the right market.

Where esports is going

Publishers need to have control of their product, not allowing random events or tournaments to dictate inconsistent showcases of their product. Imagine the NFL, the NHL, or the MLB allowing different organizers to create select tournaments with select teams. What chance would organizations like the Jacksonville Jaguars have of getting invited to the big game or qualifying for the Super Bowl? By having a standard ruleset, these small market teams have the chance to compete, and the league gets more games, more advertising opportunities, and more variety for the fans.

My company, PxlBrd Arena, is building three spaces in the United States (expected to open in 2022), designed not for the consumer but for the B2B market. We are working with publishers, teams, and developing pros in their respective ecosystems. At the end of the day, publishers need the resources to build an esport and its ecosystem. Often, new publishers with investment dollars spend anywhere from $450,000 to well over $2 million to develop and host events to grow their brand. Our space provides these publishers, small and large, a space to do so but at a far more accessible cost, allowing them to stretch their budget while having access to equipment, training programs, software, and more to push and create their own ecosystem. It also allows smaller esports teams to use the space on their budgets, giving them access to the same resources that are usually reserved for the more established and well-funded teams. This two-pronged attack allows for growth, development, high-performance training, custom events not limited to single titles, corporate events for team building, and more. We plan to deliver a multipurpose space that is a community center. This is a kind of space that does not exist yet and that is lacking terribly in the ecosystem.

Esports is going to continue to develop and grow. It is going to continue to make more money. It is going to continue to baffle and frustrate investors looking for solid investments or unicorns. Esports is also here to stay. Working with it, understanding the space, and forming the ecosystems within it are the key not only to succeeding but also to making it a successful venture and space for everyone.

MEET DAN CYBAK

As the original founder and former CEO of Myesports Ventures Ltd. and "The Gaming Stadium," Dan has realized his dream of taking the esports experience from the highest level to everyday players and businesses. Now working with his new team of consultants, esports organizations can get expertise and insight into this vast and ever-changing business! Dan managed the project from inception to build out, to open, using a client-based needs assessment and program delivery with the objective of helping players identify programs best suited to meet their needs. He is excited to see the future of esports in North America grow and to be a key figure in a part of that growth. You can find him online at:

linkedin.com/in/dan-cybak-516b3651

CHAPTER 32

New Tech and the Future of Esports

You've probably heard of the game Minecraft, even if you haven't played it yourself. It's the best-selling video game of all time, having sold more than 176 million copies since 2011. Today, Minecraft has more than 112 million monthly players, who can discover and collect raw materials, craft tools, and build structures or earthworks in the game's immersive, procedurally generated 3D world. Depending on the game mode, players can also fight computer-controlled foes and cooperate with—or compete against—other players.

For most gamers, the only thing better than playing is being able to share the experience. And since the early days of PC and console games, people have been eager to come together and compete, conquer challenges, and join a global community of players and fans. In the last decade, esports—organized video game competitions between fully fledged professional teams or amateur players—transformed gaming on a global scale by turning it into a spectator sport. Esports events and tournaments engaged the community in an entirely new way by going beyond the game itself to invite fans into an immersive live experience, whether in person at local events or shared with millions via livestreaming platforms such as YouTube and Twitch.

By helping foster a dedicated audience of player fans, esports has propelled many of the world's top titles like Fortnite, PlayerUnknown's Battlegrounds, and Mobile Legends: Bang to unprecedented levels of success. But more importantly, it's revealed that driving meaningful user engagement is about more than designing a great game. It's about competition, completion, challenge, and community.

Mobile esports

As mobile technology catches up to its PC and console counterparts, mobile esports is quickly taking the spotlight, and gamers are stealing the show. That's where mobile technology has been a game changer. Anyone with an internet connection and a mobile phone can participate in the world of esports, whether they're competing at home or watching a livestream while waiting in line at the store. With the hardware barrier to entry lifted, mobile has increased accessibility and exposure to a multitude of multiplayer games.

Following the global explosion of esports, mobile games started to transition from simpler titles that only required a single click or swipe to mid-core and hardcore titles with complex control schemes. Mobile game developers looking to build on the success and style of PC esports shifted their focus from massively multiplayer online role-playing games to the hottest esports genres: multiplayer online battle arenas, shooter and battle royale games, and strategy and auto battlers. Thanks to the ubiquity and evolution of mobile technology, more fans and players can be a part of the growing esports community, and mobile esports productions and audiences are poised to quickly outpace PC esports on a global scale.

While the COVID-19 pandemic has temporarily limited the number of local tournaments hosted at internet cafes, retail stores, and shopping malls, gaming and streaming have only grown more popular during quarantine. Mobile's ease of access has allowed esports fans to stay connected, despite the physical distance, and as quarantine restrictions continue to loosen, gamers will be able to access the venues that have fueled esports fandom for years.

Cloud infrastructure

As game development and esports are evolving across geographies, game studios, big and small, are trending toward building multiplayer, free-to-play games, across multiple platforms. As a result, cloud infrastructure is increasingly becoming one of the most critical components of development and operation of a video game.

Gaming requires some of the most sensitive and resource-intensive infrastructure. Game developers must optimize their code to shave microseconds from each function. They often need to simulate physics, understand user input, apply game logic, position 3D model assets, and paint high-resolution textures. On the server side, milliseconds matter when gamers are competing against each other in fast-paced, competitive FPS games. Network performance and server stability is a requirement when thousands of players are competing against each other in real time.

A hit-driven industry

In addition to the technical challenges, game development is inherently risky. Statistics indicate that the majority of games fail to meet expectations. Gaming is a hit-driven industry, and success in one title does not guarantee success in the next. As a result, game developers proactively seek solutions that mitigate their risk. For example, most widely adopted gaming platforms and services (e.g., Unity, Unreal, and Play-Fab) are those that reduce the upfront financial risk by providing free or freemium services to developers during the development phase. Game developers gravitate toward services that reduce risk during development and in the operation of their game.

"The game industry today . . . Here are some
things worth noting. There are no billion-dollar
movies anymore. There are no billion-dollar
books or TV series or radio stations. There are no
billion-dollar billboard companies. The top 10
games are all over a billion dollars. To start with,
if you want to be in any form of content, by far
the largest business you could fantasize, that you
could ever achieve something in, is games. It's the
world's biggest revenue source for IP today. "[1]

—JOHN RICCITIELLO, UNITY CEO

Esports and leagues are a fast-paced, fast-growing industry where no longer can you afford to take two to three years to develop games, and new content needs to be added constantly to appeal to the industry. The global games market reached about $146 billion in revenue in 2019 and is expected to keep growing rapidly as cloud gaming rises in popularity, with mobile gaming accounting for about 45 percent of the market, and with $67 billion (roughly a third of revenue) spent on development and operations expenses (e.g., cloud hosting, managed game services). Mobile gaming is expected to generate $90.7 billion in 2021, growing +4.4 percent year on year. This is more than half of the global games market, as the segment is less affected by the effects of COVID-19 than PC and console gaming. [2][3]

Modern game development has shifted games from products to services. With this shift to hosting games online and continually iterating and updating to keep players excited and engaged, there's an increased need for a powerful infrastructure to keep up with the enabling of innovative, real-time experiences.

The role of new tech on the future of esports is key, as the biggest growth opportunities are in AI and machine learning, live ops and business intelligence, and community and player engagement. AI and machine learning have become crucial technology, with the need to translate text to speech in real time with localization features, improve outage prediction and traffic management, offer game balance testing, find overpowered situations and dominant strategies, and add more social interactions while moderating content and analyzing sentiment.

There's not much built out for games in either live ops or business intelligence, and in the future, they can be seen as interlinked: Great business intelligence will help improve live ops and vice versa. Investments in this area will lead to increasing engagement, retention, monetization, and acquisition, predicting player behavior, optimizing ad spend, and streaming data. Community and player engagement is seen as the lifeblood and future of sustained gaming, seeking localization to improve player support and player life cycle, and embedding accessibility features building for everyone.

World-class mobile technology and infrastructure

While PC and console games once had the upper hand on factors like connection speed and graphics, new developments—including improved mobile hardware, cloud gaming, and 5G networks—are bringing mobile esports up to speed with its predecessors.

In the last few years, there has been increased investment in gaming smartphone hardware and peripherals to improve the experience for mobile esports gamers. Manufacturers Asus, Huawei, and Xiaomi have already created dedicated gaming smartphones with enhanced features, including ultrafast display, high-speed processors, and console-inspired designs.

Cloud gaming

Cloud gaming will narrow the graphics and performance gap between mobile and PC or console games, therefore allowing mobile gamers to play higher-spec titles. Cloud gaming (e.g., PlayStation Now, Microsoft's Project xCloud, GeForce Now, Tencent Instant Play, and Google's Stadia) is expected to build gradually over the next few years, offering developers the opportunity to reach and engage new gamers as the market steadily grows.

5G technology will reduce latency for players and result in a better overall user experience. 5G also provides new tools for game development through edge and cloud computing.

Microsoft is a recognized leader in the cloud infrastructure market providing enterprise scale and reliability. Microsoft owns fifteen game studios that run on Azure (Compulsion Games, Rare, The Coalition, inXile Entertainment, Double Fine, Obsidian Entertainment, Undead Labs, The Initiative, Turn 10 Studios, Minecraft, World's Edge, 343 Industries, Ninja Theory, Xbox Game Studios, and Microsoft Casual Games).

Success Stories

Here are some customer success stories: In Rainbow Six Siege, Ubisoft uses Azure Autoscale to keep up with spikes in demand across the globe, ensuring they can give players the performance they need without worrying about provisioning servers. Next Games handled over one million game downloads and thirty-one million gameplay minutes during the release weekend of The Walking Dead: No Man's Land using Azure Cosmos DB as a core component of the game. Game Insight used Azure Premium Storage to get an extreme performance boost and shift from five database servers to two for the game 2020: My Country. Tencent Games transforms the traditional front end of PC games into back-end microservices using Azure Service Fabric to help reduce complexity when building new games, avoid repeated development workloads from dependencies, and update new features within game apps independently. Hitman, from IO Interactive, uses numerous Azure services—such as Azure App Service, Azure SQL Database, Azure Service Fabric, and Azure Stream Analytics—to collect and analyze telemetry data from live gameplay, support game logic and player sessions, and more.

Educating new generations

At Microsoft, we believe that we need a culture founded in a growth mindset that starts with a belief that everyone can grow and develop, that potential is nurtured, not predetermined, and that anyone can change their mindset. We need to be always learning and insatiably curious. We need to be willing to lean into uncertainty, take risks, and move quickly when we make mistakes, recognizing that failure happens along the way to mastery.

Gaming Concepts curriculum

That's why we believe gaming and esports can also have a role in educating new generations on curiosity and team play, and we have designed a course for educators from all subject areas who would like to know more about esports and how it leads to improved learning outcomes within cross-curricular educational settings. Using the Gaming Concepts curriculum, educators can use the high-interest platform of esports while teaching.

In a recent global survey of educators, 64 percent said they lack the resources or time to support students' well-being, though 80 percent believe it to be vital for student success.[1] Given this link between social and emotional learning and student success, it is unsurprising that the Gaming Concepts curriculum as implemented in schools has been shown to increase student attendance by more than 10 percent and GPAs by an average of 1.4 points. Gaming Concepts fosters social and emotional intelligence while teaching college and career-ready skills. It was written by educators for educators and requires no prior gaming experience.

Coupling esports curriculum with an after-school esports program offers inclusive gaming communities to all students, addressing toxicity through in-person accountability, building better relationships with technology through organized play, and creating a clear future through STEAM and industry opportunities.

Engaging a growing community of gamers

To tap into the world of mobile esports to engage a growing community of gamers, developers should plan for mobile, as audiences are larger and more diverse, and mobile technology sparked esports communities in corners of the world where PC and consoles couldn't.

They also should branch out to appeal to gamers' new interests, showing more genre diversity than PC and console games. Now is a great time to experiment with creating atypical genres, gameplay options, and in-game features to entice a wider audience.

Developers can also give gamers the power to participate in esports competitions building or sponsoring tournament platforms for popular games, incorporating esports tournament brackets into their own games to stoke new competition. They could even use streaming platforms to promote small esports events or encourage streamers to host their own tournaments.

As the market continues to develop, we should expect to see media rights, team franchising, and sponsorships become cornerstones of mass participation from devoted players and fans. The future of esports and gaming promises to be exciting and to offer gamers new engaging and interactive experiences.

Are you ready to ride the next wave into the future of gaming?

MEET ROBERTO CROCI

With over twenty years' experience working for the likes of Microsoft (who recently announced plans to acquire Activision Blizzard for $68 billion) and Google, Roberto Croci's passion lies in innovation, startups, and people. Relationship-driven, he has bridged the gap between corporates and startups across more than twenty countries, helping them develop real solutions that solve real-world problems.

A leading innovator in developing ecosystems where startups thrive, Roberto's expertise and candid approach have kept him in demand with major tech companies throughout his career. In his current role as the managing director of Microsoft for Startups, Roberto is building Microsoft's new division from scratch, including spearheading its expansion and innovation strategy, with the vision to foster a collaborative startup ecosystem to create a better, brighter future for people around the world. Connecting the dots between startups, government agencies, and private sector organizations, Roberto helps organizations adopt the innovation mindset and leverage the technology and nimbleness that startups provide.

With an ability to cut through the noise, he works directly with startup founders and encourages them to "think differently" and to "be more curious." Roberto also sits on the Advisory Board of WeSoar.ai and Miami Ad School.

A graduate of Harvard Business School, Roberto is passionate about leadership and mentoring young people, helping them develop an entrepreneurial mindset to search for solutions to problems they see in their community, in their country, or across the globe. Roberto wants to inspire one million students and entrepreneurs to build homegrown tech startups that become global unicorns. Follow him online at:

linkedin.com/in/robertocroci

CHAPTER 33

Virtual Esports: A Mom Embraces a Virtual World

For most of the past twenty-four years, I was a conservative home-school mom. We didn't allow computer games, and I'd never heard of esports. If someone had told me that, one day, I'd be playing games for pleasure and helping build a VR esports industry, I would've thought they were crazy. But, sometimes, the best things in life come when we're not expecting or even looking for them.

In April 2017, my family encouraged me to try an Oculus Rift at a Best Buy store demo. I agreed, because they said I could go sit in the car afterward, but it never crossed my mind that the experience would change my life. It still gives me chills when I recall that "wow" moment. Thirty minutes later, I was walking out of the store with my newly purchased treasure.

Over the next few months, I played VR daily, and then a few months later, I joined the beta for a game from Ready at Dawn called Echo Arena. I fell in love with the zero-gravity environment, with an arena where teams competed to put a disc through the opponent's goal before the opponent scored their goal.

I was cautious about meeting people online, but I really enjoyed the budding community. There were only about fifty of us who played regularly, so we all knew each other, and it became a family of sorts. We'd see who could find bugs, learn new tricks, argue about playspace abuse, discuss harassment in gaming, and so on.

A few weeks later, Oculus and ESL announced the VR Challenger League, a VR esports league that would feature Echo Arena and The Unspoken. My friends and I formed a team and started practicing. Ultimately, my team qualified for nationals at Oculus Connect later that summer, so I headed to California while many people back home in Tennessee were convinced I was flying to my death at the hands of "gamers I met on the internet."

One of the best things about that trip was being able to talk with others who loved the game and the possibilities for the new industry of VR esports. There weren't many of us, but we were passionate, and we had a vision for the future of competitive VR. My perspective was a bit different from the others' because they were all familiar with esports. I knew nothing about it, so my only frame of reference was with traditional sports, such as basketball or football.

While traditional esports require concentration, quick decision-making skills, hand-eye coordination, and incredibly fast reflexes, VR esports add in a component of physicality. It's a beautiful combination of athleticism and technology as players duck, dodge, and jump in immersive realities. Even in FPS, players will move their bodies to step around the side of a building or lie down prone to take a sniper position. Many actions that are done in traditional esports with a keyboard or controller are done in VR via physical movement.

The growth of VR esports

The first VR esports leagues were founded in 2017: the Oculus-funded and ESL-run VR Challenger League, which was also sponsored by

Intel, as well as the community-driven VR Master League. The VR
Challenger League was popular among the small group of dedicated
VR esports, but it remained small mostly because there simply weren't
that many people with VR headsets, especially compared to the numbers in traditional esports.

During that first year of the VR esports leagues, there were other
challenges, as well as learning opportunities. While you do encounter
hackers as you would with traditional esports, for VR, there is also the
issue of playspace abuse. By that I mean some players would purpose-
fully move in physical reality to gain an advantage in the game. At that
time, the headsets that could be used for competitive VR games—HTC
Vive and the Oculus Rift—also required external sensors, so sometimes
they'd be knocked over or blocked.

Another issue that came up that first year related to harassment. The
esports industry doesn't exactly have the best track record in regard to
its treatment of females or anyone who—to be quite blunt—isn't a young
white male. Although there has been a recent trend to keep that in
check, and leagues have actively begun to ban players who violate code
of conduct standards for games and competitions, some esports players
who grew up in the traditional gaming environment came to VR with
the attitude that they could do whatever they wanted.

In 2018, two new VR leagues came onto the scene. The Collegiate VR
Esports League was formed in January that year to provide a fun, competitive league, tailored to the needs of college students. Their first season
started in the autumn with six participating colleges, and when season
three began in the fall of 2019, there were fifteen colleges participating.

The Virtual Athletics League also came onto the scene in 2018 with
a worldwide tournament featuring a popular rhythm game called Beat
Saber. This league was established to help arcades learn how to build
VR esports communities and host events among their customers.

VR esports continued to grow throughout 2019, and competitions
became increasingly common. Since most events were focused on

players in North America and Europe due to ping issues, the owner of an arcade in Israel founded the League of International VR Esports to fill in the gaps, allowing any player (home or arcade) from any region to participate. There have definitely been some challenges with this, but they continue to find ways to adjust so anyone interested in competing will be able to do so.

Connecting people

After my initial experience at Oculus Connect in 2017, I decided to start writing about some of the benefits of VR esports.

When they were younger, I'd tell my kids that we didn't allow computer games in the house because they made people angry or they'd destroy their eyesight. I'd also told them that gamers grew up to be antisocial single people who lived in their parents' basements. Obviously, as I learned more about esports, I began to respect the industry and the people involved in it, realizing that most of my presumptions were incorrect.

In fact, there are tactical decisions that vary for each game, countless hours of practice, and challenges to be overcome. I decided to use my expertise as a journalist to write about the benefits of esports, such as communication and leadership skills, team-building skills, and problem-solving skills. In my writing, I also mention that with VR esports, you have the physical component, so it's great exercise!

Events started to pop up around the globe, so I'd write articles about those events, and I traveled to as many of them as I could afford. One thing that struck me was the diversity of VR esports players. There were people of various races, religions, and ages. All of us came together at events and focused on the games and the industry we loved rather than the things that might deter us from being friends in traditional settings.

When we're in VR, people focus on the player's personality, but many of the labels we apply to others are ignored. I have a saying: "In VR, we drop the labels and focus on the person behind the headset." Once you know the person and enjoy their personality, when you meet in physical reality, it's a unique experience, because you've already had contact in immersive reality. The presence of VR that enables you to hear someone and see their body language makes it more possible to develop deep relationships in immersive reality.

During the COVID-19 pandemic

Of course, in 2020, the world was largely shut down due to the COVID-19 pandemic, but the crisis has actually increased participation in and awareness of VR esports, as people have tried to find ways to stay healthy and engaged with others while in quarantine. VR is a perfect way to meet with others and still have social interaction. For those with a competitive nature, VR esports is an excellent way to engage in a community where they're able to exercise, compete, and create fellowship, despite the restrictions of the outside world.

The introduction of the Oculus Quest also had a positive impact on the growth of VR esports. Players no longer need an expensive gaming PC to play competitive VR. Echo Arena remains one of the most popular VR esports games, and when it came to the Quest in beta, the community more than tripled in size over just a few months. The community Discord group that had only five thousand members in January jumped to over eighteen thousand by July. These numbers would probably be even higher, but COVID-19 has made it increasingly difficult to obtain headsets, as workers who would normally be making necessary components have been put to work making respirators and other necessities.

The past few years have been a time of transition in my family. My children are grown now, so they're finding their way in life with jobs, relationships, military service, and so on. These days, they enjoy laughing about the fact that their mom has become a gamer.

Meanwhile, I continue to enjoy playing and promoting VR games. It's exciting to see how quickly the industry is growing, and while I never anticipated I'd one day be a professional VR esports player and journalist, it's an honor to be a part of the wonderful world of VR esports!

––––––––––

MEET SONYA A. HASKINS

Sonya Haskins is a respected journalist, esports player, and community leader in the field of virtual reality. She was the first female player to qualify for the VR League North American Regional Championships and helps manage social communities for some of the largest VR esports communities.

In 2019, Sonya founded VR Community Builders, a nonprofit organization created to encourage the growth of positive, inclusive environments in immersive, social, and physical realities.

A native of East Tennessee, Sonya has traveled to numerous countries and visited three continents to talk about the positive impact virtual reality can have in the world. She has written eight books, and you can find her work on various blogs and news outlets, including VR Fitness Insider, where she serves as a VR esports editor. Reach out to Sonya online at:

twitter.com/sonyahaskins
sonyahaskins5@gmail.com
linkedin.com/in/sonya-haskins-99223ba1

CHAPTER 34

Investing in the Future

As both players and entrepreneurs in the games sector and with games careers stretching back decades, I and my fellow Hiro founders have seen the games sector evolve dramatically. Driven by technology disruption and globalization, we believe that games and games technology are the future and that games are eating the world—in a good way.

Games used to be a niche nerdy product, just for young guys in Western markets and Japan. Now, they are a vast global sector, the largest sector of entertainment, serving players in almost every country worldwide from every demographic.

Play is deep

Play is a fundamental human behavior that all humans do as children to develop resource management, strategy, planning, and social skills. As children and as adults, we take pleasure from play, and games in 2021 are a global digital platform for bringing humans together in play.

As human societies have evolved and become safer and wealthier, this childlike evolutionary necessity has become a source of pleasure in time-rich societies and a massive global industry.

Games as an industry have gone from niche to mainstream over the past ten years. Driven by the rollout of smartphones and the development of emerging markets, this industry has gone from one hundred million players of video games in the mid-1990s to two hundred million in the mid-2000s to around three billion now. So the games industry has gone from niche to mass. And we believe games will now go from being mass market to being an absolutely central pillar of the mid-twenty-first-century economy and society and our lives.

As investors in the games industry, we seek out games technology founders and game content creators who are building the future. We believe that games and games technologies will be at the heart of next-generation societies. Our fund, "Hiro Capital," is so named for the hero you become when you play a game or sport; for the hero you are when you found and build a company; and because we are inspired by Hiro Protagonist, lead character in Neal Stephenson's Snow Crash, a hacker gamer human who codes the Metaverse and saves the world against the odds.

We believe that games are becoming not just the largest sector of entertainment and the new form of media for Gen Z, but also that games studios and games technologies are the foundational pillars of the Metaverse—a new human-computer and human-human communications ecosystem. Games are where the tech for next-generation human societies is being built. Games like Fortnite and Roblox and platforms like Oculus, Google Stadia, Huya, and Unreal Engine are the beginnings of next-generation social networks that are immersive, social, user-generated, and visual. These ecosystems' growth is as big a change and investment opportunity for 2020–2040 as the emergence of the internet and mobile phones was for 1990–2020. As a sector-focused early-stage investor, this is incredibly exciting.

Metaverse tech trends

Games are being evolved, grown, and disrupted by an interconnected set of technology trends. These trends have been in development for decades: Multi-user computer worlds were conceived by Alan Turing in the 1940s, and the first multiplayer video games were played on government mainframes in the 1960s. But now, thanks to Moore's law, battery efficiencies, new image technologies, and massive improvements to networks, we are reaching escape velocity and entering the Metaverse. The on-ramp to the Metaverse includes:

Mobile devices and device delivery neutrality

Games and esports were traditionally delivered to audiences on specialist devices (arcade machines, power PCs, or games consoles). Increasingly, with super computers in our pockets, all esports and all games are available to watch, consume, analyze, and play on apps or browsers on smartphones and on any internet-connected device.

Streaming, 5G, and the cloud

The build out of cloud-based data centers worldwide and of the associated architectures that move the processing of video and complex code to the cloud transforms the economics of delivering games and esports, making it ultimately available everywhere at very low cost. It also means games developers and games and esports software and content creators have access to cloud-based development environments and tools and can scale and globally deploy innovations rapidly with minimal capital expenditure. The rollout of 5G and the increased bandwidth and smarter network architectures that it enables accelerates these trends.

Globalization and new geographic markets

The money and business markets for video games and sports were traditionally concentrated in the U.S., Europe, and Japan (with much smaller and more local ecosystems in emerging markets). Now, the audience and player base for huge sports, like soccer; for niche sports, like bouldering, UFC, and skateboarding; and for games, like Fortnite and League of Legends, and Clash of Clans, is increasingly global, with global tournaments, global distributors, and an increasingly global audience. China, for example, is now explicitly striving to become a leading football nation, and Chinese games platforms are now the world's largest. India, Latin America, and Africa, meanwhile, have large and enthusiastic middle-class player and audience bases and still have a decade of continuing expansion from GDP growth and smartphone penetration.

Big data and machine learning

Cloud-delivered games and digitally streamed esports generate vast stores of real-time and post-match data on players, games, and the audience. Increasingly this is beginning to be mined and analyzed through machine learning for team and athlete coaching and improvement, advertising and ecommerce personalization, social network connections, news and updates, betting and predictions, and product and game improvement.

Wearables and the internet of things

Games and esports are starting to be transformed by wearables. New game wearables (e.g., VR glasses, game controller wearable rings, gamer smartphone peripherals, and esports wearables, such as fitness and health trackers, esports-specific sensors, and AR glasses) are mostly still early stage and not yet at mass-market maturity or cost. These technologies will become mass-market products during the 2020s. They have the effect of bringing games off the chair into the real world and of bringing real-world analog sports more and more into digital and simulated online environments.

AR, VR, and MR

Augmented reality, virtual reality, and mixed reality are emerging technologies in which many of the most compelling use cases will be in games and esports. In VR, your entire body becomes the game controller, and you move through an infinite imaginary world, bringing fitness and games together. Beatsaber and FitXR are full body multiplayer rhythm games that already have large player bases. Meanwhile, Pokémon Go is an early AR game that already has over 200 million users. AR and VR technologies are not yet mass market, but 2022 will see the launch of new VR headsets from Apple, Sony, Facebook, and others.

Digital goods and NFTs

Since the early 2000s, starting in Korea's online gaming ecosystem, gamers have been prepared to pay real money for purely digital in-game items such as cosmetic items or power-ups. Now, the market for digital "skins" in games is $50 billion annually and growing. Parallel to this, since 2015, the crypto world has developed "non-fungible tokens," which are unique or limited-edition digital artworks and collectibles that can be bought and traded on the blockchain. Now, NFTs and Game items are beginning to converge with many startups developing multiplayer game worlds containing digital real estate and blockchain tradeable commodities, fashion, and art.

Investing in games

The gaming market is a competitive one. At Hiro, we see around two thousand opportunities in the gaming investment space every year, and we invest in less than 1 percent of what we see. What we look for when we invest in a game studio or game technology company is a multitude of different factors, which boil down to three key criteria: the quality and resilience of the team, the defensibility of the technology or content moat, and the scale size of the market they are targeting.

We also apply a set of strong environmental, social, and governance filters, seeking factors like whether the investment is a force for good, encourages learning, fosters a creative community, is inclusive, has little environmental impact, converges the real and digital worlds, and is honorable. We believe that games, sports, and technology can be a general force for good; we do not invest in toxic or addictive content. We invest in new technology that is positive.

We are in a phase of massive acceleration for video games and digital sports. It's a story of super-strong growth in every dimension and in every geography—in user numbers, games sales, revenues and profits, console sales, VR headsets, streamer views, visits to In-Game live events, etc. People fall in love and get married in games, do school classes and university graduations in games, and have come out of lockdown fitter and stronger thanks to home and VR fitness training than they had ever been before. As an investor, it is extremely rewarding to see our sector macro-thesis so emphatically confirmed.

Playing games and sports serves an evolutionary purpose: allowing humans to model and practice for reality. We look for creators making fun, innovative, challenging games. Many games and sports allow people to come together to have constructive and good-humored fun and to create and express themselves. We look for those platforms.

We are active sports players and fans as well as games players. We love the real world as well as the digital one. We like tech that brings these worlds together and gets people up and out of their bedrooms. We strive to be good people and, because of that, we like to work with and invest in good people.

Fundamentally, we believe that games and esports will be a central pillar of entertainment, economic, and social life in the mid-twenty-first century. Therefore, we seek out and invest in those innovators who are building that very future.

MEET LUKE ALVAREZ

Luke Alvarez is the founder and managing partner of Hiro Capital, Europe's leading games and esports venture capital fund. Luke has twenty-nine years in technology and twenty years in digital games. He has founded and invested in games and technology companies around the world. He was the cofounder and CEO of Inspired Entertainment Inc., a Nasdaq-listed mobile games and virtual sports technology leader with operations worldwide.

Luke was a founding board member of The Cloud, the U.K.'s largest public access Wi-Fi operator, and of Gematica SRL, one of Italy's first government gaming concessions. He was a case leader at the Boston Consulting Group, earned a first-class honors in philosophy at the University of Cambridge, and was a Fulbright Scholar to the University of California, Berkeley.

Luke is passionate about games and storytelling and their interaction with the future of technology. He leads Hiro's investment strategy and compliance and focuses on Hiro's digital sports, social network, and game technology investments. You can connect with him online at:

linkedin.com/in/luke-alvarez-699988171

Acknowledgments

This book was made possible because 38 individuals from around the world were willing to share their insights and knowledge about the esports/gaming space with you, the reader. Some of the authors I know well, but the majority I didn't before I reached out to them, usually via LinkedIn. The fact that they were willing to put pen to paper, or fingers to keyboard, is something I will always be grateful for, underscoring how inclusive this sector is and can be for those who are willing to learn, understand, and perhaps even take action as a result.

The other experts that bring a book to life are those on the publishing team. So firstly, a shoutout to Ruby Newell-Legner, an exceptional individual who put Greenleaf Book Group on my radar. I am a big fan of you, Ruby! At Greenleaf Book Group, starting with Executive Editor, Jessica Choi, I am still certain working on the title of this book with me was probably a thorn in your side, but thank you for doing so with grace and believing in the end product. Lindsay Bohls, thank you for the myriad of scheduling changes! To my first-ever editor, Nathan True, you have no idea how working with and being guided by you bolstered my confidence! Thank you, Diana Ceres and Kirstin Andrews, for your editorial eye. Tyler LeBleu and Lindsey Clark, you brought it over the finish line! There is a place in heaven for editors and project managers! I am also sure that finding endorsements for an unknown author is difficult. Sam Alexander, thank you for a solid brand strategy; there were some early mornings Zooms for me, but it was well worth it to brainstorm with you. Chelsea Richards, you are the bomb. Home run after home run! Kim Lance, you are a cover designer extraordinaire. It was so difficult to choose, and I am still vacillating, if you can believe it!

I was introduced to Terry Virts through a very special friend, Linda Szasz. So thank you Linda, because you know how incredibly special you are to me (with or without the introduction to an astronaut!). Terry, if I could do somersaults, that is what would have happened when you graciously agreed to write the Foreword! Glad we broke bread a few times together in Dubai!

I need to acknowledge my good friend and one of the contributing authors, Paul Roy. When Galaxy Racer was a concept in his mind, Paul fascinated me with his vision for what was missing in the MENA region and how much opportunity there was as a result. Well Paul, you certainly have built an amazing empire. Onwards and upwards!

I am so grateful to have family, friends, and colleagues who support me in all I do and everything that I could possibly manifest. Starting with my parents, Howard and Sou, thank you for supporting me when I decided all those years ago to start my life as an expat. To my sister Susan, my brother-in-law Gary, and nephew Garrett in Toronto, and also my brother Robert and sister-in-law Nora, you are why I look forward to coming home in the summer and winter every year! All my love to Ray Everett, my incredible husband and growing LinkedIn influencer! Max Chow Everett, I am so proud of you and what you bring to the world. I would need another book to express how much you both complete me.

And thank you to all my friends and family from around the world and to all the various organizations that I have the privilege to serve and work with. I hope I am adding value most days! And I would be remiss to not thank my LinkedIn connections, FB friends, and YouTube, Instagram, and Twitter followers!

Notes

PREFACE

1. TrendWatching. "After the Virus: 10 Cross-Industry Trends Accelerated by the Covid Crisis." March 2020. https://info.trendwatching.com/10-trends-for-a-post-coronavirus-world.
2. BrainyQuote. "Sydney J. Harris Quotes." Accessed May 17, 2021. https://www.brainyquote.com/quotes/sydney_j_harris_101958.

CHAPTER 1

1. Berube, Alan. "Black Household Income Is Rising across the United States." The Brookings Institution. October 3, 2019. https://www.brookings.edu/blog/the-avenue/2019/10/03/black-household-income-is-rising-across-the-united-states/.
2. Nieves, Emanuel. "Black and Latino Households Are on a Path to Owning Zero Wealth." *Prosperity Now,* September 12, 2017. https://prosperitynow.org/blog/black-and-latino-households-are-path-owning-zero-wealth.
3. World Health Organization (WHO) (@WHO). "#BeActive and stay #HealthyAtHome! Here are some physical activities you can do at home during #COVID19 outbreak." Twitter, March 25, 2020. https://twitter.com/WHO/status/1242738384772239360.
4. Sinclair, Brendan. "Developers Drag Rockstar over 100-Hour Weeks on Red Dead Redemption 2." Gamesindustry.biz, October 15, 2018. https://www.gamesindustry.biz/articles/2018-10-15-developers-drag-rockstar-over-100-hour-work-weeks.
5. Rivera, Joshua. "What It's Like to Work on Ultra-Violent Games like Mortal Kombat 11." Kotaku, May 8, 2019. https://kotaku.com/id-have-these-extremely-graphic-dreams-what-its-like-t-1834611691.
6. Jenkins, Henry. "Reality Bytes: Eight Myths about Video Games Debunked." PBS.org, accessed May 17, 2021.

7. Williams, Marian. "What Can VR Therapy Do for Dementia and Alzheimer's?" Being Patient, September 2, 2020. https://www.beingpatient.com/virtual-reality-for-dementia-alzheimers-vr-therapy/.

8. Newzoo. "Key Numbers." Accessed May 19, 2021. https://newzoo.com/key-numbers/.

9. Krush, Alesia. "eSports May Soon Overtake Traditional Sports." ObjectStyle.com, November 17, 2020. https://www.objectstyle.com/agile/esports-may-soon-overtake-traditional-sports-analysis.

10. Besombes, Nico. "Esports Related Professions." Medium, July 29, 2019. https://medium.com/@nicolas.besombes/esports-professions-e402a1c3ab92.

11. Takahashi, Dean. "Hitmarker: Esports Jobs Grew 87% in 2019." *VentureBeat*, February 8, 2020. https://venturebeat.com/2020/02/08/hitmarker-esports-jobs-grew-87-in-2019/.

12. Wijman, Tom. "Global Game Revenues Up an Extra $15 Billion This Year as Engagement Skyrockets." Newzoo, November 4, 2020. https://newzoo.com/insights/articles/game-engagement-during-covid-pandemic-adds-15-billion-to-global-games-market-revenue-forecast/.

13. Bay, Jason W. "All Careers in the Video Game Industry." Game Industry Career Guide. Accessed May 17, 2021. www.gameindustrycareerguide.com.

CHAPTER 2

1. Schütz, Martin. "Science Shows That eSports Professionals Are Real Athletes." DW.com, December 3, 2016. https://www.dw.com/en/science-shows-that-esports-professionals-are-real-athletes/a-19084993.

2. Tassi, Paul. "The U.S. Now Recognizes eSports Players as Professional Athletes." *Forbes*, July 14, 2013. https://www.forbes.com/sites/insertcoin/2013/07/14/the-u-s-now-recognizes-esports-players-as-professional-athletes/#4fd545613ac9.

3. Tassi, "The U.S. Now Recognizes eSports Players."

4. Schütz, "Science Shows."

5. Modesti, P.A., I. Pela, I. Cecioni, G.F. Gensini, G.G. Neri Serneri, and G. Bartolozzi. "Changes in Blood Pressure Reactivity and 24-Hour Blood Pressure Profile Occurring at Puberty." *Angiology* 45, no. 6 (June 1994): 443–50. https://doi.org/10.1177/000331979404500605.

CHAPTER 3

1. Schultz, Colin. "19th Century Concern Trolling: Chess Is 'a Mere Amusement of a Very Inferior Character.'" *Smithsonian Magazine*, November 10, 2014. https://www.smithsonianmag.com/smart-news/19th-century-concern-trollingchess-mere-amusement-very-inferior-character-180953281/.
2. Cannon, Tom. "Youth Game Addiction: The Darker Side of Gaming." Red Brick Research, October 21, 2014. https://www.redbrickresearch.com/2014/10/21/youth-game-addiction-the-darker-side-of-gaming/.

CHAPTER 4

1. ESPN Stats & Info. "Average Age in Esports vs. Major Sports." ESPN, September 17, 2017. https://www.espn.com/esports/story/_/id/20733853/the-average-age-esports-versus-nfl-nba-mlb-nhl.

CHAPTER 5

1. D.C. Funk et al. "eSport management: Embracing eSport Education and Research Opportunities." *Sport Management Review* 21, no. 1 (2017). http://dx.doi.org/10.1016/j.smr.2017.07.008.
2. Law, Julienna. "China's Esports Professionals: Long Hours and Low Pay, But Love for the Job." RADII, May 28, 2019. https://radiichina.com/chinas-esports-professionals-report/.
3. Hitmarker. "2019 Esports Jobs Report." https://s3.hitmarkerjobs.com/2019+Esports+Jobs+Report.pdf.
4. Woods, Bob. "Amazon's Twitch leads a booming esports six-figure-salary job market in coronavirus era." CNBC, May 19, 2020.
5. Venero, Bob. "Why the Rise of Esports Is Good for Schools, Students and Even Employers." *Forbes*, February 6, 2020. https://www.forbes.com/sites/forbestechcouncil/2020/02/06/why-the-rise-of-esports-is-good-for-schools-students-and-even-employers/.
6. Bull, Chris. "Esports Education Investments Endure and Grow Amidst Budget Restrictions." Futuresource Consulting, September 23, 2020. https://www.futuresource-consulting.com/insights/esports-education-investments-endure-and-grow-amidst-budget-restrictions/.
7. Bull, "Esports Education Investments."

CHAPTER 6

1. Johnson, D., C. Jones, L. Scholes, & M. Colder Carras. *Videogames and Wellbeing: A Comprehensive Review.* Melbourne: Young and Well Cooperative Research Centre, 2013.
2. Aarseth, E. et al. "Scholars' Open Debate Paper on the World Health Organization ICD-11 Gaming Disorder Proposal." *Journal of Behavioral Addictions* 6, no 3 (September 2017): 267–270.
3. Freitas, B. D. A., R. S. Contreras-Espinosa, & P. A. P. Correia. 2017. "The Benefits and Risks of Sponsoring eSports: A Brief Literature Review." In *eSports Yearbook 2017/2018,* edited by J. Hiltscher & T. M. Scholz, 49–57.
4. Shaver, P. R., M. Mikulincer & J. Cassidy. "Attachment, Caregiving in Couple Relationships, and Prosocial Behavior in the Wider World." *Current Opinion in Psychology* 25:16–20 (2019).

CHAPTER 7

1. ViewSonic. "Why Esports in Schools Is a Good Thing." January 25, 2021. https://www.viewsonic.com/library/education/esports-schools-good.
2. Kensington. "What Is Esports? The Next Step in Inclusive Education." March 18, 2020. https://www.kensington.com/news/ergonomic-workspace-blog/what-is-esports-the-next-step-in-inclusive-education.
3. Shenandoah University News. "SU Student Honored For Esports Leadership: Chris Kumke Earns Award From National Association Of Collegiate Esports." July 28, 2020. https://www.su.edu/blog/2020/07/su-student-honored-for-esports-leadership.
4. https://nacesports.org.
5. NAC Esports. "NASEF and NACE Partner to Provide High School – College Esports Connections to Benefit Students." March 2, 2021. https://nacesports.org/nasef-and-nace-partner.
6. Takahashi, Dean. "Hitmarker: Esports Jobs Grew 87% in 2019." *VentureBeat,* February 8, 2020. https://venturebeat.com/2020/02/08/hitmarker-esports-jobs-grew-87-in-2019/.
7. W., Bryan. "Varsity Esports: How US Colleges Are Earning Major ROI & Gamers Score Big Scholarships." Game Designing, last updated February 4, 2021. https://www.gamedesigning.org/schools/varsity-esports/.
8. FinancesOnline. "Number of Gamers Worldwide 2021/2022: Demographics, Statistics, and Predictions." Accessed May 17, 2021. https://financesonline.com/number-of-gamers-worldwide/.

9. FinancesOnline, "Number of Gamers Worldwide."

10. https://www.esportsus.org.

CHAPTER 11

1. Hosein, Anesa. "Girls' Video Gaming Behaviour and Undergraduate Degree Selection: A Secondary Data Analysis Approach." *Computers in Human Behavior* 91: 226–235 (2019). https://doi.org/10.1016/j.chb.2018.10.001.

CHAPTER 12

1. United States Census Bureau. "National STEM Day: November 8, 2020." Release number CB20-SFS.141, November 8, 2020. https://www.census.gov/newsroom/stories/stem-day.html.

2. Weststar, Johanna, Eva Kwan, and Shruti Kumar. "IGDA Develop Satisfaction Survey 2019—Summary Report." IGDA, November 20, 2019. https://s3-us-east-2.amazonaws.com/igda-website/wp-content/uploads/2020/01/29093706/IGDA-DSS-2019_Summary-Report_Nov-20-2019.pdf.

3. Games and Learning. "Survey Captures State of Higher Ed Video Game Programs." March 25, 2015. https://www.gamesandlearning.org/2015/03/25/survey-captures-state-of-higher-ed-video-game-programs/.

4. ESA. "Essential Facts: Diversity in the Video Game Industry." 2021. https://www.theesa.com/resource/essential-facts-about-diversity-in-the-video-game-industry/.

CHAPTER 13

1. YM. "Pakistan Takes the World of Global Esports by Storm." Zameen. Accessed October 17, 2020. https://www.zameen.com/blog/pakistan-secured-11th-position-global-esports-earning.html.

2. Friedman, Kareen. "These 10 Countries Are the Clear-Cut Capitals of Freelancing." *Payoneer*, December 25, 2019. https://blog.payoneer.com/freelancers/industry-tips-fl/6-countries-capitals-freelancing/.

3. Hanif, Fazeela. "Pakistan IT Exports Up by 12%." SAMAA, July 8, 2020. https://www.samaa.tv/money/2020/07/pakistan-it-exports-up-by-12/.

4. Esports Earnings. "Highest Earnings by Country." Accessed October 17, 2020. https://www.esportsearnings.com/countries.

5. The World Bank. "Population Total – Pakistan." Accessed October 17, 2020. https://data.worldbank.org/indicator/SP.POP.TOTL?locations=PK.

6. Ahmad, Shakeel. "Unleashing the Potential of a Young Pakistan." Human Development Reports, July 24, 2018. http://hdr.undp.org/en/content/unleashing-potential-young-pakistan.

7. The News. "Pakistan Produces 20,000 IT Graduates, Engineers Annually, Says Minister." November 2, 2019. https://www.thenews.com.pk/print/549580-pakistan-produces-20-000-it-graduates-engineers-annually-says-minister.

8. "Key Numbers." Newzoo. Accessed October 16, 2020. https://newzoo.com/key-numbers/.

9. "Arslan 'Ash' Siddique." Red Bull. Accessed October 17, 2020. https://www.redbull.com/pk-en/athlete/arslan-ash-siddique.

10. "Dota 2." Esports Earnings. Accessed October 17, 2020. https://www.esportsearnings.com/games/231-dota-2.

11. Haq, Riaz. "Pakistani Video Game Player Among World's Top 10 Earners." Haq's Musings, November 7, 2019. https://www.riazhaq.com/2019/11/pakistani-video-game-player-among.html.

12. "PUBG Officially Comes to Pakistan." Pakistan Cyber Gaming. Accessed October 17, 2020. https://pcgofficial.com/article/pubg-officially-comes-to-pakistan/94.

13. Mehran, Khurram Ali. "PTA Temporarily Suspends PUBG Game." Pakistan Telecommunication Authority, July 1, 2020. https://www.pta.gov.pk/en/media-center/single-media/pta-temporarily-suspends-pubg-game-010720.

14. "Court Directs PTA to Immediately Lift PUBG Ban." *The Tribune*, July 24, 2020. https://tribune.com.pk/story/2256416/court-directs-pta-to-immediately-lift-pubg-ban.

CHAPTER 14

1. United Nations. "Population Facts." UN Department of Economic and Social Affairs, Population Division, May 2015. https://www.un.org/esa/socdev/documents/youth/fact-sheets/YouthPOP.pdf.

CHAPTER 15

1. Wijman, Tom. "Global Game Revenues Up an Extra $15 Billion This Year as Engagement Skyrockets." Newzoo, November 4, 2020. https://newzoo.com/insights/articles/game-engagement-during-covid-pandemic-adds-15-billion-to-global-games-market-revenue-forecast/.

2. Entertainment Software Association. "2019 Essential Facts about the Computer and Video Game Industry." 2019. https://www.theesa.com/esa-research/2019-essential-facts-about-the-computer-and-video-game-industry/.

3. Anderson, M. & J. Jiang. "Teens, Social Media & Technology." Pew Research Center, May 31, 2018. https://www.pewresearch.org/internet/2018/05/31/teens-social-media-technology-2018/.

4. Quinn, S. & J Oldmeadow. "The Martini Effect and Social Networking Sites: Early Adolescents, Mobile Social Networking and Connectedness to Friends." *Mobile Media & Communication* 1, no. 2: 237–247 (2013).

5. Orme, S. "Playing to Win: The Global Esports Industry and Key Issues." *Video Game Debate 2: Revisiting the Physical, Social, and Psychological Effects of Digital Games*, edited by R. Kowert & T. Quandt. New York: Routledge (2020).

6. Kowert, R., & T. Quandt. (Eds.). *The Video Game Debate: Unravelling the Physical, Social, and Psychological Effects of Video Games*. New York: Routledge (2016).

7. Kowert, R., & T. Quandt. (Eds.). *The Video Game Debate 2: Revisiting the Physical, Social, and Psychological Effects of Video Games*. New York: Routledge (2020).

8. Kowert, R., M. Griffiths & J. A. Oldmeadow. "Geek or Chic? Emerging Stereotypes of Online Gamers." *Bulletin of Science, Technology, and Society* 32, no. 6: 471–479 (2012). doi: 10.1177/0270467612469078.

9. Kowert, R. & J. A. Oldmeadow. "Playing for Social Comfort: Online Video Game Play as a Social Accommodator for the Insecurely Attached." *Computers in Human Behavior, Advance online publication.* 2014. doi: 10.1016/j.chb.2014.05.004.

10. Kowert, R., R. Festl & T. Quandt. "Unpopular, Overweight, and Socially Inept: Reconsidering the Stereotype of Online Gamers." *Cyberpsychology, Behavior, & Social Networking* 17, no. 3: 141–146 (2014). doi: 10.1089/cyber.2013.0118.

11. Entertainment Software Association, "2019 Essential Facts."

12. Domahidi, E., J. Breuer, R. Kowert, R. Festl & T. Quandt. "A Longitudinal Analysis of Gaming- and Non-gaming-Related Friendships and Social Support among Social Online Game Players." *Media Psychology*, 2016.

13. Kowert & Quandt, "Unpopular, Overweight, and Socially Inept."

14. Kowert, R., J. Vogelgesang, R. Festl & T. Quandt. "Psychosocial Causes and Consequences of Online Video Game Play." *Computers in Human Behavior* 45: 51–58 (2015). doi: 10.1016/j.chb.2014.11.074.

15. Kowert & Quandt, "Unpopular, Overweight, and Socially Inept."

16. Kowert, Vogelgesang, Festl & Quandt, "Psychosocial Causes and Consequences."

17. Entertainment Software Association, "2019 Essential Facts."

18. Chen, M. "Communication, Coordination, and Camaraderie in World of Warcraft." *Games and Culture* 4, no. 1: 47–73 (2009).

19. Moore, R., N. Ducheneaut & E. Nickell. "Doing Virtually Nothing: Awareness and Accountability in Massively Multiplayer Online Worlds." *Computer Supported Cooperative Work* 16, no. 3: 265–305 (2007).

20. Pena, J. & J. T. Hancock. "An Analysis of Socioemotional and Task Communication in Online Multi-player Video Games." *Communication Research* 33, no. 1: 92–109 (2006). doi:10.1177/0093650205283103.

21. Kowert, R. *Video Games and Social Competence.* New York: Routledge, 2015.

22. Yee, N. "The Demographics, Motivations, and Derived Experiences of Users of Massively-Multi-user Online Graphical Environments." *Teleoperators and Virtual Environments* 15, no. 3: 309–329 (2006).

23. Cole, H. & M. D. Griffiths. "Social Interactions in Massively Multiplayer Online Role-Playing Games." *Cyberpsychology and Behavior* 10, no. 4: 575–583 (2007).

24. Suler, J. "The Online Disinhibition Effect." *Cyberpsychology and Behavior* 7, no. 3: 321–326 (2004).

25. Kowert, *Video Games and Social Competence.*

26. Putnam, R. D. *Bowling Alone: The Collapse and Revival of American Community.* Simon and Schuster, 2000.

27. Kowert, R. & L. Kaye. "Video Games Are Not Socially Isolating." *Video Game Influences on Aggression, Cognition, and Attention*, edited by C. J. Ferguson, 185–195. New York: Springer, 2018.

28. Wellman, B. & M. Gulia. "Net Surfers Don't Ride Alone: Virtual Communities as Communities." *Networks in the Global Village*, edited by B. Wellman, 331–366. Boulder: Westview, 1999.

29. Suler, "The Online Disinhibition Effect."

30. Morahan-Martin, J. & P. Schumacher. "Loneliness and Social Uses of the Internet." *Computers in Human Behavior* 19: 659–671 (2003).

31. Suler, "The Online Disinhibition Effect."

32. McKenna, K., & Bargh, J. "Plan 9 from cyberspace: The implications of the Internet for personality and social psychology." *Personality and Social Psychology Review*, 4(1), 57-75 (2000).

33. Kowert & Kaye, "Video Games Are Not Socially Isolating."

34. Kowert, *Video Games and Social Competence*.

35. Dye, M., C. Green & D. Bavelier. "The Development of Attention Skills in Action Video Game Players." *Neuropsychologia* 47, no. 8: 1780–89 (2009).

36. Green, C. & D. Bavelier. "Effect of Action Video Games on the Spatial Distribution of Visuospatial Attention." *Journal of Experimental Psychological Human Perception and Performance* 32, no. 6: 1465–78 (2010).

37. Dye, Green & Bavelier, "The Development of Attention Skills."

38. Madigan, J. "Forever Questing and 'Getting Gud.'" *Video Games and Well-Being: Press Start*, edited by R. Kowert, 65–76. New York: Palgrave, 2020.

39. Bowman, N. D., R. Kowert & C. J. Ferguson. "The Impact of Video Game Play on Human (and Orc) Creativity." *Video Games and Creativity*, edited by G. P. Green and J. C. Kaufman. San Diego, CA: Academic Press, 2015.

40. Fehr, Karla K. & Sandra W. Russ. "Pretend Play and Creativity in Preschool-Aged Children: Associations and Brief Intervention." *Psychology of Aesthetics, Creativity, and the Arts* 10, no. 3 (January 2016): 296–308. doi:10.1037/aca0000054.

41. Green, G. & J. Kaufman. *Video Games and Creativity*. Academic Press, 2015.

42. Johnson, D. M., P. Wyeth & P. Sweetser. "Creating Good Lives through Computer Games." *Wellbeing: A Complete Reference Guide, Volume VI, Interventions and Policies to Enhance Wellbeing*, 485–510. John Wiley & Sons Inc., 2014.

43. Kowert, R. *Video Games and Well-Being: Press Start*. New York: Palgrave, 2020

44. Suler, "The Online Disinhibition Effect."

45. Kowert, R. *Video Games and Social Competence*. New York: Routledge, 2015.

46. Sjöblom, B. "Language and Perception in Co-located Gaming." Presented at the Language, Culture, Mind III, 2008.

47. Sherry, J. L. "Flow and Media Enjoyment." *Communication Theory* 14, no. 4: 328–347 (2004).

48. Ducheneaut, N. & R. Moore. "More Than Just 'XP': Learning Social Skills in Massively Multiplayer Online Games." *Interactive Technology and Smart Education* 2, no. 2: 89–100 (2005).

49. Jang, Y. & S. Ryu. "Exploring Game Experiences and Game Leadership in Massively Multiplayer Online Role Playing Games." *British Journal of Educational Technology* 42, no. 4: 616–623 (2011).

50. Shute, V. J., M. Ventura & F. Ke. "The Power of Play: The Effects of Portal 2 and Lumosity on Cognitive and Noncognitive Skills." *Computers & Education* 80: 58–67 (2015).

51. Ferguson, C. J., N. D. Bowman & R. Kowert. "Is the Link between Games and Aggression More about the Player, Less about the Game?" *The Wiley Handbook of Violence and Aggression. Volume 1: Definition, Conception, and Development*, edited by P. Sturmey. New York: Wiley, 2017.

52. Adachi, P. J. C. & T. Willoughby. "More Than Just Fun and Games: The Longitudinal Relationships between Strategic Video Games, Self-Reported Problem Solving Skills, and Academic Grades." *J Youth Adolescence* 42: 1041–1052 (2013). https://doi.org/10.1007/s10964-013-9913-9.

CHAPTER 17

1. "2018 Global Games Market Report." Newzoo, 2019.

2. "2019 Essential Facts about the Computer and Video Game Industry." Entertainment Software Association, 2019. https://www.theesa.com/esa-research/2019-essential-facts-about-the-computer-and-video-game-industry/.

3. "Key Numbers." Newzoo. Accessed May 19, 2021. https://newzoo.com/key-numbers/.

4. Ahn, J., Collis, W. and Jenny, S. "The one billion dollar myth: Methods for sizing the massively undervalued esports revenue landscape." *International Journal of Esports* 1, 1 (2020).

5. "Social Connections." *How's Life? 2020: Measuring Well-Being*. Paris: OECD Publishing, 2020. https://doi.org/10.1787/b2090ea8-en.

6. Holt-Lunstad, J., Smith, T. B., Baker, M., Harris, T., & Stephenson, D. "Loneliness and social isolation as risk factors for mortality: a meta-analytic review." *Perspect. Psychol. Sci.* 10, 227–237 (2015). doi: 10.1177/1745691614568352.

7. Holt-Lunstad et al., "Loneliness and social isolation."

8. "Essential Facts." Entertainment Software Association.

9. Williams, D., N. Ducheneaut, L. Xiong, Y. Zhang, N. Yee & E. Nickell. "From Tree House to Barracks: The Social Life of Guilds in World of Warcraft." *Games and Culture* 1: 338–361 (2006).

10. Putnam, R. D. *Bowling Alone: The Collapse and Revival of American Community*. Simon and Schuster, 2000.

11. Steinkuehler, C. A., and Williams, D. "Where everybody knows your (screen) name: online games as 'third places'". *J. Comput. Mediat. Commun.* 11, 885–909 (2006). doi: 10.1111/j.1083-6101.2006.00300.x.

12. Huvila, I., Holmberg, K., Ek, S., and Widén-Wulff, G. "Social capital in second life." *Emerald Insight* 34, 2010. doi: 10.1108/14684521011037007.

13. Williams et al., "From Tree House to Barracks."

14. Perry, R., A. Drachen, A. Kearney, S. Kriglstein, L. E. Nacke, R. Sifa, et al. "Online-Only Friends, Real-Life Friends or Strangers? Differential Associations with Passion and Social Capital in Video Game Play." *Computers in Human Behavior* 79: 202–210 (2018).

15. Depping, A. E., C. Johanson & R. L. Mandryk. "Designing for Friendship: Modeling Properties of Play, In-Game Social Capital, and Psychological Well-Being." *CHI PLAY '18: Proceedings of the 2018 Annual Symposium on Computer-Human Interaction in Play.* New York, NY, USA: Association for Computing Machinery, 87–100 (2018). doi:10.1145/3242671.3242702.

16. Trepte, S., Reinecke, L., & Juechems, K. "The social side of gaming: How playing online computer games creates online and offline social support." *Computers in Human Behavior* 28: 832-839 (2012).

17. Freeman, G. & D. Y. Wohn. "eSports as an Emerging Research Context at CHI: Diverse Perspectives on Definitions." *Proceedings of the 2017 CHI Conference Extended Abstracts on Human Factors in Computing Systems,* 1601–8 (2017).

18. Brown et al. "Intersections of Fandom in the Age of Interactive Media: eSports Fandom as a Predictor of Traditional Sport Fandom." *Communication & Sport* 6: 418-435 (2018).

CHAPTER 18

1. "The New Face of Gamers." Lifecourse Associates, June 2014. https://www.lifecourse.com/assets/files/The%20New%20Face%20of%20Gamers_June_2014_REVISED.pdf.

CHAPTER 20

1. "Audience." Twitch Advertising. Accessed May 18, 2021. https://twitchadvertising.tv/audience/.

2. Chadha, Rishi. "Conversation Spotlight: Gaming." Twitter Marketing, April 22, 2020. https://marketing.twitter.com/en/insights/covid19-gaming-conversation-trends.

3. Takahashi, Dean. "SuperData: Games Hit $120.1 Billion in 2019, with Fortnite Topping $1.8 Billion." *VentureBeat,* January 2, 2020. https://venturebeat.com/2020/01/02/superdata-games-hit-120-1-billion-in-2019-with-fortnite-topping-1-8-billion/.

4. Chadha, Rishi. "Over 2 Billion Gaming Tweets in 2020!" Twitter Blog, January 11, 2021. https://blog.twitter.com/en_us/topics/insights/2021/over-2-billion-gaming-tweets-in-2020-.html.

5. Stream Hatchet. "Live Game Streaming Trends Q1 2021." https://insights. streamhatchet.com/q1-2021-live-game-streaming-trends.

6. "Q1 Consumer Spending on Videogames Up 30% Y-O-Y." Marketing Charts, May 25, 2021. https://www.marketingcharts.com/cross-media-and-traditional/videogames-traditional-and-cross-channel-117212.

7. Buckle, Chase & Jason Mander. "Esports Trends Report 2018." GlobalWebIndex, 2018. https://cdn2.hubspot.net/hubfs/304927/Downloads/Esports-report.pdf.

8. Buckle & Mander, "Esports Trends Report 2018."

9. Stream Hatchet, "Live Game Streaming Trends."

10. We Know Gamers Study. Momentum Worldwide.

11. Momentum Worldwide. "76% of Consumers Prefer to Spend on Experiences than on Material Items, New Study Finds." *Cision PR Newswire*, October 14, 2019. https://www.prnewswire.com/news-releases/76-of-consumers-prefer-to-spend-on-experiences-than-on-material-items-new-study-finds-300937663.html.

12. Uncovered by the research and insights team at YouGov in partnership with Riot Games LCS.

13. https://www.researchgate.net/figure/Average-Number-of-Hours-Spent-Gaming-in-a-Typical-Day-for-Female-and-Male-Gamers_fig2_283793880

14. Momentum Worldwide 2019 study on female gamers.

15. Momentum Worldwide 2019 study on female gamers.

16. "2020 Return to Live Events Survey," Enigma Research, April, 2020, http://files.ifea.com/RiskMgt/COVID19/2020ReturntoLiveEventsSurvey byEnigmaResearch.pdf.

CHAPTER 23

1. World Economic Forum.

2. World Economic Forum.

3. World Economic Forum.

4. Deloitte.

CHAPTER 24

1. Niko Partners. "Evolution of Mobile Esports for the Mass Market." Aug 2019. https://nikopartners.com/evolution-of-mobile-esports-for-the-mass-market/.

2. Taylor, T. L. *Raising the Stakes: E-Sports and the Professionalization of Computer Gaming.* MIT Press, 2012.

3. Jin, Dal Yong. *Korea's Online Gaming Empire*. MIT Press, 2010.

4. Niko Partners. "2019 Asia Games Market Report." November 2019. https://nikopartners.com/asia-games-market-report/

CHAPTER 25

1. Ilic, Jastra. "Top 5 Esports Games Hit Over $500 Million in Total Prize Money." *Golden Casino News*, February 25, 2020. https://goldencasinonews.com/blog/2020/02/25/top-5-esports-games-hit-over-%24500-million-in-total-prize-money/.

2. Carter, Shawn. "Here's How Much Money the Winners of This Year's NBA Finals Could Take Home." CNBC, June 13, 2019. https://www.cnbc.com/2019/05/30/how-much-money-the-winners-of-the-nba-finals-could-take-home.html.

3. PGA. "Masters 2019: How Much the Winner of the Masters Makes." April 15, 2019. https://www.pga.com/archive/masters-2019-how-much-winner-masters-makes.

4. "FIFA Club World Cup Prize Money 2019." Sportekz, November 11, 2019. https://www.sportekz.com/football/club-world-cup-prize-money/.

5. Jastra, "Top 5 Esports Games."

6. GSMA.

7. Hootsuite.

8. Internet World Stats.

9. Takahashi, Dean. "The U.S. Game Industry Has 2,457 Companies Supporting 220,000 Jobs." *VentureBeat*, February 14, 2017. https://venturebeat.com/2017/02/14/the-u-s-game-industry-has-2457-companies-supporting-220000-jobs/.

CHAPTER 26

1. Reyes, M. S. "Esports Ecosystem Report 2020: The Key Industry Players and Trends Growing the Esports Market, Which Is on Track to Surpass $1.5B by 2023." *Business Insider*, January 5, 2021. https://www.businessinsider.com/esports-ecosystem-market-report.

2. Brand, S. "SPACEWAR." *Rolling Stone*, December 1972.

3. "Newzoo's Global Esports & Live Streaming Market Report 2021 | Free Version." Newzoo, March 9, 2021. https://newzoo.com/insights/trend-reports/newzoos-global-esports-live-streaming-market-report-2021-free-version/.

4. "Newzoo's Global Esports & Live Streaming Market Report."

5. "Newzoo's Global Esports & Live Streaming Market Report."

6. Bradley, S. "Esports on the Rise: Evaluating Brand ROI." *The Wall Street Journal,* May 5, 2020. https://deloitte.wsj.com/cmo/2020/05/05/esports-on-the-rise-evaluating-brand-roi/.

7. Bradley, "Esports on the Rise."

8. "Justin Dellario, Twitch—'Esports and Twitch Are Synonymous.'" *The Esports Observer,* May 9, 2019. https://esportsobserver.com/justin-dellario-twitch-hive-berlin/.

9. "Justin Dellario, Twitch."

10. Carp, S. "Report: Nike to Sign US$144M Chinese League of Legends Deal." *Sports Pro Media,* November 20, 2018. https://www.sportspromedia.com/news/nike-league-of-legends-pro-league-sponsorship-deal.

11. Meola, A. "The Biggest Companies Sponsoring eSports Teams and Tournaments." *Business Insider,* January 12, 2018. https://www.businessinsider.com/top-esports-sponsors-gaming-sponsorships-2018-1.

12. Snider, M. "'Fortnite' Streaming Star Ninja Lands Partnership with Adidas." *USA Today,* August 27, 2019. https://www.usatoday.com/story/tech/talkingtech/2019/08/27/fortnite-star-ninja-signs-partnership-deal-adidas/2135304001/.

13. Liao, S. "Gaming's Biggest Names Are Ditching Twitch for $10 Million Contracts." *CNN,* January 30, 2020. https://www.cnn.com/2020/01/26/tech/video-game-streaming-wars/index.html.

14. "Ninja." *Social Blade.* Accessed May 19, 2021. https://socialblade.com/twitter/user/ninja.

15. Ninja. "Ninja—Home." YouTube. Accessed May 19, 2021. https://www.youtube.com/user/NinjasHyper.

16. "The True Value of Influencers in eSports Marketing." *Influencer Marketing Hub,* March 28, 2019. https://influencermarketinghub.com/the-true-value-of-influencers-in-esports-marketing.

17. Taylor, R. "Rise of eSports Is a Game Changer." *Huffpost,* March 4, 2015. https://www.huffpost.com/entry/rise-of-esports-is-a-game_b_6784174.

18. Spangler, T. "Fortnite World Cup Finals 2019 Draws Over 2 Million Live Viewers." *Variety,* July 29, 2019. https://variety.com/2019/digital/news/fortnite-world-cup-finals-2019-live-viewers-championship-1203282771.

19. Taylor, "Rise of eSports."

20. "Becker College Announces First-in-Nation Esports Management Degree." Becker College, June 21, 2018. https://www.becker.edu/first-in-nation-esports-management-degree.

21. Adubato, S. "Preparing Students for the Business Element in E-Sports." YouTube. Video file, 2:27 (2020). https://www.youtube.com/watch?v=nlPv7jabneo.

CHAPTER 31

1. "Canada Games Market 2018." Newzoo, July 18, 2018. https://newzoo.com/insights/infographics/canada-games-market-2018/.
2. Bradley, S. "Esports on the Rise: Evaluating Brand ROI." *The Wall Street Journal*, May 5, 2020. https://deloitte.wsj.com/cmo/2020/05/05/esports-on-the-rise-evaluating-brand-roi/.

CHAPTER 32

1. Takahashi, Dean. "John Riccitiello Q&A: How Unity CEO views Epic's Fortnite success." *VentureBeat*, September 15, 2018. https://venturebeat.com/2018/09/15/john-riccitiello-interview-how-unity-ceo-views-epics-fortnite-success/.
2. Tom Wijman. "Global Game Revenues Up an Extra $15 Billion This Year as Engagement Skyrockets." Newzoo, November 4, 2020. https://newzoo.com/insights/articles/game-engagement-during-covid-pandemic-adds-15-billion-to-global-games-market-revenue-forecast/.
3. Tom Wijman. "Global Games Market to Generate $175.8 Billion in 2021; Despite a Slight Decline, the Market Is on Track to Surpass $200 Billion in 2023." Newzoo, May 6, 2021. https://newzoo.com/insights/articles/global-games-market-to-generate-175-8-billion-in-2021-despite-a-slight-decline-the-market-is-on-track-to-surpass-200-billion-in-2023/.
4. "Emotion and Cognition in the Age of AI." *The Economist Intelligence*, 2019. https://edudownloads.azureedge.net/msdownloads/emotion_and_cognition_ai.pdf.

Index

About the Editor

Lucy is focused on the innovation space, both in terms of supporting founders and as an investor. She is the secretary general of the World Business Angels Investment Forum (WBAF) Global Women Leaders Committee and an Investment Committee Director for the WBAF Angel Investment Fund. She is also an investor with NextWave Impact Fund and The Founder Institute and is a limited partner with numerous funds globally. She has a video series targeted at entrepreneurs titled *Down to Business*.

Lucy has garnered a strong reputation as someone who has helped build the entrepreneurial ecosystem of the UAE. She was named one of #LinkedInTopVoices 2020 for MENA, was one of CEO Middle East's Influential Women in the Arab World 2020, and is *Titanium Magazine*'s Top 50 Global Inspirational Women to Look Out for in 2022. Lucy contributes regularly to entrepreneurship, corporate innovation, and investor events and forums as a speaker, moderator, and judge.

She sits on the Board of Trustees for the American School of Dubai, as well as the Solidarity Circle, UNHCR. She has been a contributing author for *Life on the Move*, an anthology of stories about expat life, and *The Possibilities Project: A Young Person's Guide to Career Success*. She is pleased to be an Ambassador for Women in Games (WIGJ) and sits on the Steering Committee of #2022FemaleAngels. She has a joint EMBA from the Kellogg Graduate School of Management at Northwestern University and the HK University of Science and Technology and a BA, International Relations, from the University of British Columbia. She is a future-focused thought leader, and *Changing the Game* is her first book.

Made in the USA
Coppell, TX
26 September 2023

22060478R00180